MARK & DIANE BUTTON

The Letter Box

A Story of Enduring Love

BEYOND
WORDS
Publishing
I   N   C

Beyond Words Publishing, Inc.
20827 N.W. Cornell Road, Suite 500
Hillsboro, Oregon 97124-9808
503-531-8700

Editor: Jenefer Angell
Managing editor: Julie Steigerwaldt
Proofreader: Marvin Moore
Design: AutHaus
Composition: William H. Brunson Typography Services

The hand lettering in the title and part openers was specially created for
The Letter Box by Clint Gorthy.

Printed in the United States of America
Distributed to the book trade by Publishers Group West

Library of Congress Cataloging-in-Publication Data
Button, Mark, 1956–
    The letter box : a story of enduring love / Mark & Diane Button.
        p.   cm.
    ISBN 1-58270-087-7
    1. Interpersonal communication—Miscellanea.   2. Intergenerational
communication—Miscellanea.   3. Letter writing—Miscellanea.
I. Button, Diane, 1959–   II. Title.
BF637.C45 B88   2002
158.2′4—dc21

                                                                2002005442

The corporate mission of Beyond Words Publishing, Inc.:
    Inspire to Integrity

The Letter Box

PART ONE

IT HAS BEEN OVER A YEAR OF CRUNCHING numbers, flying back and forth across the country, and late-night meetings with lawyers and accountants. My wife, Ronnie, and I have considered our future and how our lives will change if this deal actually happens. With my mind so focused, I have hardly taken the time to understand the emotional investment of this negotiation.

Almost everyone who my partner, Scott Stillinger, and I really care about has supported our decision to sell the business, including our upper-management team. We have all worked hard and been through so much together, yet we are ready to move on.

In terms of success and my career, I have proven myself to myself and to those who are important to me. Now I want to prove myself in other areas. I want to sit with Ronnie on our porch in Hawaii, watch the sunrise, and appreciate it completely. God only knows how many times I have sat alone in my California office and not even looked out the window for an entire day. I have been preoccupied—too busy to really be still. I wonder if I have ever truly appreciated a beautiful sunset. Success has its rewards, but I have missed out in other ways.

With the simple stroke of a pen, I knew I could win financial security for my future family and provide us the ability to live and fully enjoy our lives and each other. I don't often find myself feeling nervous or anxious, but the moment we stepped into the elevator and pushed the button to take us to the thirty-eighth floor, something hit me: All the years of my life had brought me to this one pivotal moment.

Ⓜ

The original idea for the product had come from Scott. It seemed a reasonable gamble to me: a ball that would make it easy for kids to learn how to catch. I knew from experience that success in the toy industry doesn't follow the path of adult logic. Yet there was something extra and indefinable about this. We decided on the name "Koosh Ball" and described it as "easy to catch and hard to put down." The first obstacle was that neither we, nor anyone else, knew how to manufacture it. Therefore, we didn't know how much it would cost, what it would look like, what it should sell for, or if anyone would even like it.

At the time, many of our friends and family thought we were crazy. They made comments like "I can't believe you're going to quit your jobs for a ball made out of rubber bands." We put our life savings on the line in an effort to prove them wrong. We left our secure jobs, rented an old converted barn in Silicon Valley, and started our business, OddzOn Products, Inc. Despite the odds, our first Koosh Balls were shipped only six months later—a miracle in itself. So began our decade-long obsession with colorful rubber bands. The rest became history in a quick uphill climb toward the top of the toy-industry charts.

It had been an exciting time, filled with good products, great friendships, and rapid sales growth. Like all success-ful start-ups, the company had taken on a life of its own. But after several years, I began to take a serious look at my life and priorities. The point of our business venture was to have fun and make money—with the ultimate goal of having more time and freedom. It's amazing how easy it is to become consumed by something that provides mostly money, even though money is supposed to be only the tool to reach the higher causes.

Now, with products sold all around the world, we were about to sell the company and achieve even more success than I had ever imagined. Scott and our attorney, Jeff Kramer, seemed relaxed and at ease. We were as prepared as we could possibly be. I took a deep breath and stepped into what would be the longest and most memorable meeting of my career.

Ten people were sitting along one side of a long, dark table in an air-conditioned conference room. I was thankful the gratuitous small talk was short-lived. Within minutes we were in a serious contract negotiation.

The number of people we were dealing with surprised me. They had ten—but we had Jeff, a man with more credentials following his name than any other person I have ever known. We didn't need an army to help us; we had him. We were ready to roll.

Our Thursday-morning meeting continued on into the evening. Both sides agreed to keep going. We had come too far. We weren't planning to leave until this was finished, one way or another. We went back and forth over every point. We watched the sun come up over Manhattan through the conference-room windows. The view was magnificent.

On a couple of occasions, I thought we would have to walk away from the table. It was tense. As we were going over the final details, it seemed obvious they were stalling. It was now Friday afternoon, and it seemed clear they wanted to hold up the timing until next week, which was the beginning of a new quarter. Or maybe they just wanted the interest over the weekend.

I have never seen Jeff lose his temper or even raise his voice, but I could see he was getting frustrated. He was cautious because he had our future at stake, but he was firm.

Jeff had asked the lawyers several times to insert a small but critical clause into our contract. They had agreed, but each time it came back for us to review, it was incorrect.

Finally I leaned over to a senior lawyer, handed him a piece of paper, and said, "The language has to be just like this, exactly like this, and not any different. If it doesn't come back exactly like this, we won't close this deal. If we don't close this deal by the end of the day, we're not doing it on Monday. Got it?"

I sat back and held my breath.

The corrections were made; we signed the contract and waited at the office until we received confirmation that the wire transfer had come through. OddzOn Products, Inc., and all its Koosh-brand products were now the property of someone else. We finally left the office and, I must say, the elevator ride down was a lot more fun than going up had been.

When I returned to California, Ronnie was waiting for me at the airport. We hugged tightly, looked at each other, and smiled that magical, deep smile of common amazement. We wanted to celebrate, but more importantly, we realized that our lives had just changed in ways we couldn't yet begin to understand.

SPRING

To some of my friends and casual acquaintances, I may appear unsentimental, but this is not the case at all. I savor traditions and I love deeply. No one knows this more than my wife of almost eight years, Ronnie Lew.

True, I don't often lavish her with expensive gifts, but I have not yet missed an opportunity to celebrate our life and our love. Wedding anniversaries and birthdays do not slip by unnoticed in our house. Maybe the entire festivity entails only a simple card and a kiss, but she knows that my heart belongs to her alone.

We both love to sail, and we have discovered that a compass, a rudder, a mast, or almost anything that has to do with sailing in the open sea can be a reflection of the wonder of life, a mirror into our very soul. Last Valentine's Day my card was a metaphor of sorts:

Ronnie Lew,

You are the wind,
and the stars,
my compass and
my helm.

Unfurl my sails.
Guide my way.
Help me
to be the best
I can be.

Fill my life with
your fullness . . . and
let our love spill
over for others to
see.

Forever, Mark

The day I proposed to Ronnie, I promised her that we would someday build our own house and fill it with as many children as she wanted. We also hoped to travel and see some other places in the world. Many of these dreams have already come true. On our first vacation after our honeymoon, we stumbled upon a magical spot on the North Shore of Oahu. One breezy afternoon we were relaxing in Adirondack chairs underneath a palm tree listening to the ocean. I had just come in from surfing, and I was feeling completely at peace with our surroundings.

I looked around the quiet beachfront community and said to Ronnie, "This is good. I mean really good. We could live here."

"And it's a neighborhood," added Ronnie. "This could be a perfect place to raise our kids."

A year later we put in offers up and down the street. Nothing had sold in years, but eventually we were able to buy a small lot and build our dream home. All we needed to do was move to our house on the beach and fill it up with children.

(M)

We've already been trying to get pregnant for over four years, with no success. We've seen specialists at Stanford. We've tried fertility drugs. At the recommendation of an expert in San Francisco, we attempted in-vitro fertilization. It's been years filled with countless injections, disappointments, and tears.

Ronnie wants children more than anything else in life, and for that reason alone I think it may be time to consider adoption. I know it hurts her to hear me say that. She simply isn't ready to give up trying yet. It's not that we wouldn't immediately fall in love with any newborn baby. I don't want to push her, but the adoption attorneys say it could take up to a year. Ronnie wants to give in-vitro one more try, so I have agreed to that, but I've suggested that we move forward with the adoption paperwork as well.

Once again, seeing Ronnie's eggs fertilized in a dish was anything but romantic, but for us they mean hope. And despite the clinical trappings, this hope may in fact be our first emotional bond with our potential family.

We know from past experience that the insemination process causes slight discomfort. The doctors suggest listening to calming music during the procedure, but Ronnie wanted me to read to her from the book she's just started, *A Severe Mercy*, written by Sheldon Vanauken. Although it is a tragic story of a man who loses his beloved wife, it's so eloquently written that I felt like I was reading her a passionate love story. Even the doctor commented on how soothing it was.

Waiting for two long weeks after the insemination to go in for a pregnancy test has been tough. But it was worth the wait, because the news is good: positive—finally!

It's so exciting! Ronnie and I talk about boys versus girls, how our life together will change, and how happy we are.

This baby is an answered prayer. We've decided not to tell anyone yet. It's still early. Maybe after the next appointment, when the doctor confirms the news with an ultrasound, we can make the announcement to our family and friends.

When Ronnie's doctor did the ultrasound, we saw the baby's heart beating strongly—but as we looked closer at the image on the screen, we saw another heart beating too.

The doctor smiled at us and said, "Congratulations, you're having twins."

Our thrill at having twins is only exceeded by our relief at seeing those two heartbeats. We'd gotten to this stage before only to find that the little heart was not beating. This time, our dream is really coming true. A new generation is on the way.

I had a dream the other night that we already had three children, but I knew it was a dream because Ronnie and I didn't recognize them. It was an odd feeling because we seemed distant somehow, like we hadn't yet connected as a family. Besides, they all had blond hair, which is very unlikely, given Ronnie's dark hair and brown eyes. I can't help myself; now I keep teasing her that we are actually having three.

She always wants me to rub her tummy in this certain way. Sometimes I pretend to count the babies when I rub her stomach, and after I get to two, I pause to look at the smile on her face. She looks like an angel to me now. But then I can't resist, and after counting to two, I feel around a little bit more and finally say, "Three." She always laughs. It's so easy to make her laugh. I've always loved that about her.

During our routine checkup yesterday, the doctor said that some of our "numbers" were a bit higher than normal. He told us not to be alarmed, but he wanted to do another ultrasound just to be sure everything was progressing normally. After all we've been through, it was impossible not to worry.

He stared at the monitor, squinted his eyes, and wrinkled his forehead for a long time without speaking.

"Is everything all right?" Ronnie asked him, a bit nervously.

"I'm just taking a closer look. Don't worry, everything looks fine," he reassured us. Then he showed us what he was seeing.

Not only were both babies growing normally, but a third—an identical twin—was there as well.

"Oh my, triplets!" Ronnie beamed.

We couldn't believe it. This was by far the happiest moment of our life together. Here was the large family we had been dreaming about for so many years.

The doctor and nurses stepped out to give us a minute alone. I didn't really even think of needing a minute alone until they left. I looked at Ronnie, and her smile just grew and grew. She looked at me so sweetly and just said, "Three." We hugged, and I felt myself welling up with tears. Finally these were the good kind of tears. We were going to be the proud parents of triplets!

We left the clinic overjoyed. On our way home, as we drove across the Golden Gate Bridge, I looked over and saw that Ronnie had the giggles.

"What's so funny?" I asked her.

Between the laughter she looked over at me and said, "I think God has an incredible sense of humor."

Later that day, I was standing in the front yard when my best friend, Dave, drove up and parked in my driveway. I must have looked like a child on a pogo stick, jumping up and down with excitement.

"What's up with you?" he asked.

"There's three!" I cheered.

"Three what? Three—no way. Don't tell me." Dave looked stunned.

"Yep. We're having triplets!" I smiled proudly.

"You have no idea what you're in store for. Just wait, you have no idea." Dave was smiling, but he was obviously not as wildly ecstatic to hear the news as I was to tell it. He knows from experience how much energy it takes to raise three children, not to mention three in diapers.

Dave laughed and went on, "Well, congratulations. Your life is going to change more than you could ever imagine."

He is such a realist.

(M)

I've never seen Ronnie enjoy being the center of attention, but she definitely enjoyed every minute of it this past week in Phoenix. She was the talk of the town. Our friends at the Toy Manufacturers of America meeting were spreading the news that we were expecting triplets, and Ronnie was just glowing. Friends were there from around the country, and it was so special for us to get to share the news with everyone in person.

Though officially out of the toy business, I still found myself in meetings most of the day. While I was busy, Ronnie took advantage of her free time by going to the health spa. She also relaxed with her friends and took some leisurely desert trail hikes.

The doctors have told her to take it easy during the first trimester, so she joked that she would forego horseback riding for now. She got a bit of a headache on Tuesday—probably from all the excitement. She just rested quietly that afternoon, and we flew home this morning.

In terms of both business and pleasure, it was a fabulous trip. Who says you can't have it all? I can't imagine life could get much better than this.

On the ninth of May, just a few days from Mother's Day, Ronnie rolled over and snuggled into my arms. She nudged me softly and whispered, "Do you realize that next year on Mother's Day three bouncing babies will be climbing into our bed?"

I have never seen her so happy.

Ronnie left for a doctor's appointment around ten o'clock. I hadn't been feeling well, so I stayed home. I was resting in bed and reading when the phone rang. The doctor was on the line and said that my wife was in the office and that she was complaining of a severe headache.

I spoke briefly to Ronnie and she asked if I could come and get her. I grabbed my keys and drove to the doctor's office to pick her up.

As I pulled up to the clinic, I saw an ambulance in front and lots of activity. Two paramedics were rushing into the building with a stretcher. I went down the street and parked to stay away from the commotion, but as I entered the building I realized the paramedics were there for Ronnie. I ran to her side and told her not to worry, that I loved her, and that we would take care of this. Still, I had no idea what was going on, but she looked as if her head was throbbing, and she seemed to be dizzy.

I jumped in my car and followed the ambulance, speeding behind it all the way to the hospital. The drive seemed to take forever, like a slow-motion movie. I wondered if the triplets were in jeopardy. Ronnie had already had two miscarriages, and I knew that losing these babies would devastate her.

I prayed.

When we finally made it to the hospital, I ran to the ambulance to see Ronnie. I could tell immediately that her condition had worsened. She seemed to be only partially aware of her surroundings, and I was beginning to get frightened. I tried to calm her by telling her that everything would be fine, but I'm afraid that my own fear was impossible to hide.

I called Dave, and within half an hour he was there. It was about that time the doctor came out to talk to me. I sat stunned as he told me the news. Ronnie had a brain aneurysm and needed to get to surgery as soon as possible. It had nothing to do with the triplets or a miscarriage. It was much more serious than I had ever imagined.

The wait was an eternity. The doctor assured me that Ronnie was in the best possible hands and that everything would be done to care for her and to protect the lives of the triplets. That made me feel better for a while.

By the time the surgery was completed it was late evening and I was surrounded by several of my friends and family. The doctor said the surgery went well, but we would need to wait until morning to be certain there was no permanent damage. They gave me five minutes to go in and see her. Her head was wrapped in bandages, so I couldn't kiss her face. I sat and held her hand instead. She was breathing with the help of a machine and appeared to be sound asleep. I wasn't allowed to stay with her too long; she needed rest and quiet. The doctor and nurses encouraged me to go home and get some sleep, and they promised to call if there were any changes in her condition. I reluctantly went home to try to get some sleep.

Before dawn I was on my way back to the hospital, feeling positive because I didn't get a call during the night. I expected to walk into Ronnie's room and be greeted with a groggy smile, but I soon found out that wasn't the situation at all. The doctor looked solemnly at me. He was noticeably uneasy as he told me that Ronnie had never regained consciousness. He said he was sorry to have to tell me that she was brain-dead and that soon they should take her off life support. There was nothing more they could do for her.

My world was slowly coming to a stop. I saw people talking all around me, but I could not make sense of what they were saying. A woman with the doctor was reminding me that Ronnie had signed an organ-donor card years before. My eyes blurred, yet I could see them going about their business in a practiced way. Ronnie's liver would fail soon and time was of the essence. I was told that she was gone and that I was going to lose the triplets, too.

I couldn't accept those words. I wouldn't allow them to take Ronnie off life support. I needed time. With the help of my closest and most resourceful friends, we called every place we possibly could to find out if anything could be done to save them.

It was soon clear that Ronnie was not coming back. At times it seemed there might be hope for the triplets, but in the end we learned that they were too young. It had never been done before. It was impossible.

My friends and family went in to say their good-byes to Ronnie. Dozens of people were gathered in the waiting room. I went in last and sat by her side. I held her hand, told her I loved her, and recited our wedding vows. There were no other words. I left the room, and the life-support system was removed. Ronnie and the babies died at 3:05 P.M. on Sunday afternoon. It was May 12. Mother's Day.

I can't recall how I made it home from the hospital, although I am certain I didn't drive. All I can remember is the unbearable sadness I felt climbing into bed alone that first night.

Days have been a blur. Dave and many other close friends have virtually taken over my life, including making plans for the funeral and all of the details that seem so surreal yet so final. It's all too much for me to believe. Life has rendered me empty and vulnerable.

There are no words that can possibly console me, though everybody has tried. My close friend Jamie, who flew out to be with me as soon as he heard the news, did tell me one story that gave me some small comfort. It's from *A Man Called Peter*, a movie about Peter Marshall, a former chaplain for the United States Senate. In the movie, Peter Marshall gives a sermon about a young boy who is dying of a terminal illness. One night the boy asks his mother, "Mommy, what happens when you die?"

Jamie explained that the mother wants to be truthful but also wants her son to be comforted as much as possible. She tells the little boy that it is like when he falls asleep on the couch at night and his daddy picks him up in his big, strong arms and carries him upstairs. He gets tucked into bed, kissed goodnight, and later he wakes up in his own room.

I knew he was right. I knew that the same thing had happened to Ronnie. She had fallen asleep in a soft, cozy bed, and God had picked her up in His strong arms and carried her home. When Ronnie was alive, we had almost everything one could desire on earth. Now I believe she has much more—but I have lost everything.

I want her back. No, I want to go with her and the children. What could possibly be left for me here without them?

My body aches. My lungs fill with unwanted air and my heart beats against its own will. I feel lost. No amount of sleep will wake me from this nightmare. The doctors say I'm healthy. They poke and prod the shell of a man. The real me is not here. The real me has gone.

I've had a wonderful life. I was blessed with a beautiful wife. I've made more money than I am likely to spend. Of course, the money is meaningless now; it can't turn back the clock. It doesn't ease the pain in my heart or help me to sleep. I guess I'm just waiting now—waiting for an end to my suffering.

When Ronnie had gotten on the phone that morning at the doctor's office, her voice was so soft and apologetic: "Sweetheart, can you come pick me up? I really need you." I had no way of knowing it would be one of the "snapshot memories" the psychiatrists warned me about. I had no way of knowing she was already leaving me behind. I had no time to tell her, "No! Don't leave me. It is I who really needs you."

All that I feel now is the pain.

There is no silver lining here. Right now it's all just too real. Dave called me this morning asking what I wanted Ronnie's headstone to say.

"How about 'Ronnie Lew Button, loving wife'?" I paused a moment to consider the option of using her legal and more formal name, Veronica.

"That's perfect, Mark, and so true. Do you want to include the dates of her birth and death?" This was Dave's way of making sure the final decision was indeed mine.

What I really wanted it to say was "Ronnie Lew Button, the most amazing loving wife of eight years, thoughtful and sincere friend who was always there for anyone, excellent and creative photographer of bizarre objects, avid reader, and lover of flowers of all kinds who dreamed of lots of happy children running around her house."

"Yes, Ronnie Lew Button, a loving wife, December 9, 1957, to May 12, 1996." I still couldn't believe I was saying those words.

I hung up the phone and thought to myself, "Mother's Day. What an unbelievable twist of fate that Ronnie should die on the very holiday she most dreamed of celebrating."

I called Dave back. "I've changed my mind about the headstone. What I want it to say is 'Ronnie Lew Button, a loving wife, mother, and friend' and then the dates underneath."

Maybe she didn't have the gift of time with her children, but she had the love for them in her heart. That was a blessing and an answer to her final prayer. In my heart and hers, she was a mother.

(M)

My parents are hurting just looking at me; I can see it in their eyes. Their pain is different. They did not lose a child, though they loved Ronnie dearly. They are suffering, watching their son in pain. They are frustrated and feeling helpless, like everyone else, knowing that there is nothing they can do.

Mom hugged me tightly this morning and said, "I wish I could trade places with her."

I understood her words because I would have done the same thing in a second.

(M)

Calling Ronnie's memorial a "celebration of life" made it sound like a joyful event—which was perhaps fitting because hers was indeed a joyful life. So many people loved her and so many will miss her; it was a happy kind of sad.

More than three thousand red roses, Ronnie's favorite flower, lined the altar, and their scent permeated every corner of the church. They created a warm and familiar feeling, as if we were at home, in her garden.

In Ronnie's eulogy, I made a public and very personal commitment to life, to family, and to love. I think God has a plan for each and every one of us. Ronnie was a teacher not only to me but to all whose lives she touched.

One thing I've already learned is this: Life is fragile. Not just mine but the lives of those all around me. Every breath we take is a precious gift. We need to remember to love, and to cherish, and to help others *now*—not at some vague time in the future.

Cards and letters keep pouring in from friends and family all over the world. I open them all, and day after day I read them and cry. Ronnie was greatly loved, and although I knew this when she was alive, the steady flood of love coming in every day comforts me.

I recently received a long letter from a close friend who had been with me when I fell in love with Ronnie on a trip to the Grand Canyon. Barry and Ronnie had the same sense of humor, and they knew each other quite well. Like the rest of us, he was struggling to understand.

He began, "It took one of the most special people we have ever met to penetrate the armor of our daily clutter in which we've cocooned ourselves. Work, money, cars, houses, shopping for dinner, laundry, bills. Why does it take a tragedy to lift the shades and illuminate the important things in life?

"I do not pretend to understand why this happened, but my gut tells me that the good will uncover itself in time. This is the only good reason I can think of and perhaps this is Ronnie's legacy. Her life and death will permanently alter many lives for the better.

"If the death of someone can fan away the fog and improve even one person's life, then maybe that's a gift. I believe Ronnie is delivering presents even now to many, many people."

I stopped reading for a moment and looked out to her garden. Red roses were blooming everywhere, more gorgeous and perfect presents from Ronnie. Barry's next words surprised me.

"Mark, right now you are the unluckiest person in the world. You are also one of the luckiest. Most people go through life with one, two, or maybe a small handful of people that get invited across the bridge into the 'good friends' camp. People who truly care about you, think often about you, never question you, share your complete honesty, listen to you, and will be there to support and help you when tragedy hits. Some campsites are barren wastelands with one sad person sitting by a smoldering fire.

"You may not see it yet, but you are incredibly blessed. The outpouring of love and support has been for Ronnie, but it is for you, too. I have rediscovered through this that the distinction between good friends and family is blurred. I believe with absolute certainty that you will be happy again one day.

"Your campsite is a crowded bonfire with lots of good friends. I like to think it's on the Grand Canyon where we all became friends, and Ronnie is out there, somewhere, with us.

"Somehow, inconceivably, the world is a little better place today. And I feel a little bit wiser. My gift from Ronnie Lew."

That was a beautiful message of hope for me, but the future seems like such a faraway place. I hope his insight proves to be right.

It seems a lifetime since she was near me. Alone at night, I stare at her picture. I find myself clutching her favorite pillow and I've drifted over to her side of the bed. Each night is lonelier than the last, yet the mornings are the most difficult. It's hard to face another day without her.

I still can't believe she's gone. I can close my eyes and still feel the warmth of her breath, the parting of her lips, the weight of her chest resting on mine. Her every curve and scent and pleasure seemed to be made just for me. And they were—just as she was—made just for me.

But I wonder now: Was my life and love equally well-suited and designed for her? Would she close her eternal eyes and remember us as we once were? Or would she recall me as cold and distant from all the work and ambition that at times had dominated my waking moments?

It's not just the long hours I spent working into the night. It was the ease with which I left her behind. Yet she seemed so proud to be my wife. If only there had been more time. We were supposed to grow old together.

(M)

They say that you can't take it with you, but they were wrong. All that I had is gone. Ronnie has taken it all with her. It's ironic that I am content in knowing she will never have to feel this pain. She will never be left behind.

I have this disturbing vision that keeps me awake at night. A little boy sits strapped in an empty shopping cart in the middle of a busy grocery store. He cannot find his mother and becomes frightened. People are busy all around him. They don't really notice him. He is lost and alone, waiting for her to return. That is how I feel.

I keep seeing women who remind me of Ronnie. Maybe it's someone with a similar hairstyle or who walks like she did. For a second I will have this impulse to run up to that person. I know it isn't really her, but I still have to fight the urge to hope for the impossible. And then she turns to look at me or I hear her speak, and I know it is someone else's wife or lover or friend.

（M）

Sometimes I must stop and wonder why. It seems so unfair and senseless. Why did God allow this? Why must I lose the only thing of any real value in my life?

These are good questions with no good answers. I feel such deep sadness. I often wish I could have been there to make her feel unafraid and to welcome her into heaven with open arms—though I'm sure God was there instead.

Time is not the healer, but clearly, healing takes time. At the moment, I feel like half a man living half a life. So many of the best parts of me came from her. Was it really that wonderful or am I just remembering it that way? I know life wasn't perfect, but it seemed so close.

I'm beginning to see two lives going on inside of me. One life is trying to remember the past, trying to keep everything just the way it was. At first I couldn't even move a chair without thinking about the change it created. The other life knows that my memories of Ronnie will always keep her alive in my spirit. She would want me to move on and to start a new life.

At times God reminds me how fortunate I am to have had so much to lose. My heart continues to ache, yet hope fills my empty future.

SELF-PITY IS QUITE IMMOBILIZING, NOT to mention extremely unattractive. It's clear I need a wake-up call, a reason to stop feeling sorry for myself. My plans have taken a dramatic turn toward the unknown, and I'm facing an uncertain future as a single, pregnant, first-time mother-to-be. But what is the big deal? I've handled stress and instability before. I'm independent and have never really needed anyone to rescue me. Maybe my life hasn't been easy, but I've always managed to make it on my own.

So, why am I sitting all alone at the kitchen counter with my weary head in my hands, feeling sorry for myself? How long can I waste energy questioning myself, wondering, "What was I thinking? How could I have let this happen?"

It's amazing how perspective can change in one moment. Yesterday, in the midst of my wallowing, my friend Dave called me. I hadn't heard from him in months, and I imagined that he was calling to sympathize with my unfortunate situation, but that wasn't to be the case at all.

"Have you heard about Mark's wife?" he asked.

I remembered Dave bringing Mark and his wife, Ronnie, to my restaurant a few times. They were always lovingly holding hands, while I was hustling and bustling through my days. Once I saw them in a shopping mall; they were strolling along together, again holding hands. I was in a rush to buy panty hose or something equally ridiculous, and I passed by them. I barely stopped to say hello, but that was how I was, always on a mission. That was the last time I had seen them, but I had heard she was finally pregnant.

"No, why?" I wondered.

There was pain in his voice. "She died on Mother's Day. The triplets died, too."

I was stunned. "That's unbelievable," I said, before all the obvious questions about the specifics. I wondered to myself why details are so often a prerequisite for grasping a situation, especially a tragedy.

Dave went on, "Mark is absolutely devastated. All he does is walk around the house and the garden looking for pieces of what he calls his past life. He doesn't even want anyone to do the laundry. He asks everyone not to touch or move anything. Nothing can change. I think he needs to get out of the house."

It turned out that Dave was calling not just to tell me what had happened to Ronnie but to encourage me to have lunch with him and Mark sometime the following week. I wondered why he had called me. What could I possibly have to say to a man whose wife had just died? I nervously and reluctantly said yes. What else could I say to Dave? He's such a close friend, and I knew he wouldn't have asked unless it was important to him.

I hung up the phone. My problems instantly became insignificant compared with Mark's.

A moment before Dave's call I had been thinking my life was somehow a failure, but in truth I was fortunate and suddenly also thankful. There was a precious treasure growing inside me, a child to hold and love. My life was moving forward while Mark's had come to a screeching halt.

It's only lunch, so why do I feel compelled to call my girlfriends to help me decide what to wear? We all agree that the real issue is my protruding belly. It needs to be hidden; that's my priority. My pregnancy is not a secret to Mark or anyone else, but I don't want my bulging waistline to be a reminder of his loss.

Ⓓ

Coping with tragedy is not my strength. Add to that a dose of initial shyness and there I was, at a local café with Mark and Dave, feeling out of place and speechless.

It was hard not to talk about Ronnie; it was so soon after her death, and Mark was visibly sad. I really didn't know what to say. A mention of travel would provoke a memory of a past vacation. Talk of the future was uncomfortable. There was an awkward understanding that Mark's future was no longer the beautiful dream he held in his heart with his wife and three children.

At first, I couldn't wait for lunch to be over so my tension could dissolve and I could go home, but by the time we were drinking coffee and relaxing a bit, something had changed. I realized that Mark was comfortable being sad. How could he be any other way? It made sense; his heart was hurting. Once Dave and I became comfortable with Mark's sadness, we enjoyed our time together. Soon I was feeling like I was in the presence of two good friends.

After lunch, Dave and I went back to his office. "Thanks for taking the time to get together with us. I hope it wasn't too uncomfortable for you," he said.

"No, not at all. It was my pleasure, but I don't think I was very helpful. He seems like he's going to be sad for a long, long time," I answered.

"Yeah, he's in a lot of pain. He says he feels like he's been ripped in half," Dave explained.

"He looks like it," I said. "You can see it in his distant eyes and even in his lonely hands. He was fidgeting constantly, like he was looking for something to hold."

Dave looked right at me. "Personally, I think Mark is one of those people who may never get married again. It's going to be hard for him to move on. He loved Ronnie so much I doubt he will ever find someone else to love as much."

I stared back at him, and the words seemed to come not from my mouth but from my heart. I said, "You know what, Dave? I think he will marry again for that very reason. A man with the capacity to love a woman that deeply will surely fall in love again."

D

The three of us had dinner together last Friday in an Italian restaurant with bright fluorescent lights and no ambiance. The atmosphere was fitting, almost as if the mood was determined for us before we arrived. The sterile walls were shouting at us, telling us loud and clear that intimacy was not an option.

After dinner Mark and I exchanged e-mail addresses and agreed to keep in touch. I let Mark know that I was still a bit of a dinosaur in the area of technology, but I promised to send him e-mail. I arrived home after dinner and turned on my computer. I seemed to have no trouble navigating my way to the right place, though I wasn't absolutely sure how to send a letter.

I typed, "Did I find you?" and sent it away.

Within two minutes I got a simple reply: "Yes, you found me."

I couldn't help myself. I went to bed that night with Mark on my mind.

SUMMER (D)

Dave doesn't chaperone us anymore. Walks along the beach and long coastal drives have become regular activities for us. We talk for hours at a time. From the very first time we met for lunch alone, we've been comfortable with each other. Somehow it's easy for Mark to cry with me. I'm not there to fix him, change him, or heal him. I know I'm not capable of any of that, so I'm simply there.

He's told me about the rafting trip on the Grand Canyon when he met Ronnie. He's told stories about all their travel adventures to Greece, Tonga, Sumatra, Italy, Austria, and the last winter they spent together in Lake Tahoe. I've learned all about creating Koosh toys from rubber bands and the ingenious contraption his brother-in-law invented to make them.

Every day at 3:05 P.M., Mark's wristwatch alarm sounds as a reminder of the time of day when Ronnie died.

Our friends have been cautioning us constantly not to spend so much time together, and we understand why.

They are worried about us. Is Mark on the rebound? Are we each looking for an easy replacement for the love and family we long for? We've talked rationally about everyone's valid concerns and have decided that, even if this time together is just for healing and friendship, we are a gift in each other's lives. We're aware that we are both at the most vulnerable point in our lives, but we just can't stop.

And as my belly grows, so does our attraction to each other.

Mark surprised me after dinner the other evening by leaning over and kissing me. It wasn't a long or particularly passionate kiss, but it was a tender moment. I had been secretly hoping for that kiss for a while.

I've learned a lot about Ronnie—that she was nearly flawless, in fact, perfect, at least as memorialized in Mark's mind. Their life together was like a beautiful waltz until the day the music stopped playing. Mark loved her, and everyone else did, too. That's a tough act to follow, especially for me.

In my entire life I have never known anyone who was perfect. In fact, I have gravitated toward the imperfect among us. Most of my close friends have had difficulties in life and have struggled many years to discover themselves. There is a certain camaraderie among "us." The people we have become today are each like the phoenix rising from the ashes, emerging strong and confident.

So, here we are, Mark and I together, and I am not Ronnie. I'm beginning to see how that is often difficult for Mark to accept. Sometimes I frustrate him, and I can see why. Everything between us happened so suddenly. He wants his old life back, and that is the one thing that I can never give him.

I am not living under the illusion that our relationship, or any relationship, should or even could ever be perfect. I take these roadblocks as opportunities for growth and deeper understanding. Usually, in the beginning of a relationship the problems are clouded by the bliss. But I haven't gotten that with Mark. We skipped the bliss and dove right into each other's problems. There's the normal stuff and a whole lot more.

We've both been wondering if our friends who say we are moving too fast are actually right. We are falling in love with each other. We want to know everything about each other and we're impatient. We justify our haste by acknowledging that neither of us is often prone to poor judgment in regard to people. Still I have to question, is this really right or do we just want it to be? I know some serious bumps are still lying in the road ahead.

Some of my friends are taking a quick trip to Mexico in a couple of weeks. I'm more in the mood to stay home and nest, but maybe a week away is a good idea right now.

I was right. It was good to have some time to think. The dry, desert heat made sleeping difficult, and so in the middle of the first night I found myself on a lounge chair near the pool, looking up at the sky. The moon was full and never more beautiful than it was that night. It was so peaceful. I rubbed my pregnant belly and felt a deep love for the baby girl growing inside me.

One of my dearest and funniest friends—known by her nickname, Smedgie—came out and joined me. We both had insomnia, but for different reasons. Mine was due to pregnancy, hers due to menopause. Beginnings and endings, we were at different places in the cycle of life.

At about three o'clock in the morning we decided to take a swim in the pool. The water was warm and calming. We talked until the sun came up about our lives, our fears and self-doubts. We talked about Mark and the concerns I was having.

"Sometimes I feel like I'm just not good enough for him," I explained. "I feel like he judges me, or compares me, which makes me insecure. Then I wonder, how can I compete with his perfect family, perfect wife, perfect life?"

"Don't worry, Diane. He just doesn't know you like we do yet." Smedgie gave me a big hug.

"I know. It's just that I've spent a lot of years getting to a point where I feel good about myself and now I'm with a guy who wants me to be someone else."

"Are you in love with him?" Smedgie asked me.

"I think so, but I'm just not sure I know him," I answered.

She looked puzzled, so I went on, "Maybe under less complicated circumstances it would be obvious. I know he cares about me, but he is still so in love with someone else. And he is often so sad and distant. I understand completely, but I don't know if his distance is really who he is or just a temporary result of his circumstances."

I was scared and she knew it.

D

The next day we swam for hours in the Sea of Cortez. I was weightless in the water, which was so relaxing. That night we had a fabulous Mexican fiesta at the Trailer Park Café, and though we laughed and enjoyed ourselves, at times I silently wished Mark was with us. Later, Smedgie and I found ourselves swimming in the pool again in the middle of the night.

I knew I was in for a lecture. Smedgie began, "You know, Diane, you need to take care of yourself and your baby right now. Maybe the timing just isn't right with Mark and you'd be better off alone."

"So I'm supposed to just stop caring for him? Just like that?" I became defensive.

"He's a great guy, Diane, but he's got so much baggage. A dead perfect wife is a lot of baggage."

I couldn't control myself even though I knew she was right, "Baggage? You want to talk about baggage? Look at me. I'm the one with the baggage. I'm emotional, opinionated, stubborn, and to top it off, I'm unemployed and pregnant."

"You're right, Diane. You're a project, too."

After thinking about it for several minutes, she added, "I've spent my entire life looking for someone over the age of five with no baggage and I haven't found one person yet. At least with Mark you know he doesn't have commitment problems."

"So what do I do?" I asked her.

"Embrace the baggage," she said, smiling.

IT'S BEEN A SCORCHING CALIFORNIA summer. Since Diane came back from Mexico, we've spent a lot of time by the pool at her condo. One day last week, Diane was in the pool floating, which she now calls her favorite sport. I had some magazines to read, and she had brought a book filled with over ten thousand baby names. I picked it up and flipped through.

Diane swam over to the edge, and I asked her, "Have you thought of any new names for the baby yet?"

"No," she replied, "If it were a boy, it would be easy. I'd name him Charlie, after my grandfather. I suppose she could be Rosemary, after my mom and grandmother, but that just sounds so old-fashioned."

As she swam away she called out to me, "Why don't you take a look? Maybe you can find a name."

Always up for a challenge, I opened the book and started reading.

Diane's grandfather had been a kind and generous doctor, but what Diane admired most about him was his humility and his sense of humor. His humor apparently saved them from many tears. He had loved mint jelly. He would eat it with anything. During the last week of his life, at a rather solemn moment he said to his family, "You know, I'm really going to miss mint jelly."

When he died, Diane was holding him in her arms. She said that the windows were open and there was a cool breeze blowing in his bedroom. His eyes closed and there was a big smile on his face. He knew he was going to heaven. At the same moment the church bells rang and echoed a sweet melody in the room. He had lived in peace and died in peace. I prayed it had been like that for Ronnie.

I knew it would mean a lot to Diane if she could honor him, so I looked up the name Charles, which led me through a list of boy's names and eventually to a section of girl's names. I looked over the list until I read one that sounded just right. The name was Carly.

I looked up the name Rosemary. Directly following it was the abbreviated version, Rose.

"I got it," I said to Diane after only about five minutes.

"Already?"

"Carly Rose," I said.

She smiled at me and said, "I love it. Carly Rose. It's perfect."

I am learning to accept that my life will never return to the life I left behind the day Ronnie died. Even the simple things have changed forever. My clothes will never be folded the same way and my routines will probably never be the way I remember they used to be each and every morning. Everything is different.

Though sometimes I seem to regress and take a step back in time, it has become obvious that I am looking and hoping for a heart that no longer beats. Ronnie and I will not grow old together. I know I cannot go back. There is nothing there but loneliness. So where do I go from here? It's time to move forward.

I must be healing, at least a little, because lately my days have been filled with anticipation rather than wishful uncertainty. I may even be getting excited about the future, but it's still so confusing. I'm becoming more accustomed to my loss, more resigned to my "fate." Certainty is a thing of the past. I am beginning to have a glimmer of hope and curiosity about the future.

I can't quite explain the feeling I had last night. Diane and I went out for dinner. It was so strange sitting across the table from another woman and looking into her eyes. Somehow, as if I had an epiphany, it occurred to me that they weren't Ronnie's dark eyes I was gazing into. They were blue. They were beautiful yet so unfamiliar.

The restaurant was familiar, but in so many ways the woman was still a stranger to me. And I was even a bit of a stranger to myself, editing my words and concerned with my table manners as if I was going to leave with a report card. Etiquette has never been a concern of mine, and I am not used to being so self-conscious. It's been a long time since I worried about what someone else thought about me. Not that I didn't have a good time. Diane was pleasant, funny, and also seemed to enjoy herself.

And so did I. She is so understanding, but I can see that getting used to someone new will be a slow process for me. My habits are just so ingrained. I hope she can be patient with me; I hope her grandfather taught her that, too.

◉

Circumstances change, life changes, and of that we can be certain. We often hear that nothing good lasts forever— that is the bad news. But we also need to remember the inverse: nothing bad lasts forever, either.

Diane is beginning to feel comfortable around my house. When she is here, it feels like a home again. She enjoys her quiet days with me and seems content with simplicity. I want to feel that contentment again myself. Today I watched Diane outside the back window. She was leaning over in Ronnie's garden, smelling each rose, as if each one had its own unique scent.

She has been supportive and a source of great comfort for me, yet I fear I hurt her often with my distance and poorly chosen words. Words are powerful tools, but they can also be potent weapons. I must learn to choose more wisely. A heart is a tender thing, and I should know that better than most.

I have so much to learn. Maybe the formative years never really end.

I'm also beginning to believe that maybe one thing does last forever—love.

I've changed. My confidence is shaken and I no longer trust my intuition. It is difficult to recognize my old self sometimes because I still choose to live in fear. It may, understandably, be the fear of loving again, but on a deeper level it may really be the fear of losing again. No one would ever want to endure such heartache twice in one lifetime. Nevertheless, I finally get it: I am responsible for my own happiness, and this fear is a ball and chain around my ankles.

It is time to let go of the past, embrace the present moment, and peacefully look forward to tomorrow. Diane fills my heart and brings me joy again. She deserves to have all of me. I must cease the relentless excuses and make a choice to live a full life right now. Simply existing is not an option. I cannot give up on life or life will surely give up on me. There are still dreams left to fill, and I know Ronnie would want that for me.

It is time.

Earlier today, I was sitting at the dining-room table and looking out to the garden. Diane's back was toward me and she was kneeling down. She was wearing a soft green floral dress with a plain white T-shirt underneath. For a moment I saw Ronnie. My thoughts flashed back to the way she looked in her favorite dress, the one I later buried her in.

I felt sad, but as Diane stood and turned toward me, I was filled with something deeper. I realized at that moment that time was indeed healing. At first, perhaps, Diane was filling a gap in my life. But over time, our love has grown into much more than a replacement for the love I lost. She is special and different. Together we are different. And even though my love for Ronnie is still here, I feel free to love again.

New seeds have been planted and new flowers are ready to bloom.

THE MOVEMENT IN MY STOMACH HAS

been an unusual source of entertainment for us lately. We could charge admission because it's been quite a show. Mark sings songs and plays the guitar, usually either James Taylor or the Beatles. I sit close to him, and within less than a minute Carly will start dancing in my stomach—arms and legs flying around. Every once in a while we are convinced she knows the Macarena.

With the exception of the usual complaints, my pregnancy was pure joy. Up until the day before Carly was born I went to the gym. I took the trip to Mexico with my friends and spent lots of time with Mark. All that freedom and fun was intertwined with lots of emotions and difficulty, but I generally stayed healthy and happy in spite of the unusual circumstances. Life has certainly changed in these past few months.

To my surprise, birth was also pure joy. Seeing Carly's little body and holding her in my arms for the first time was absolutely the most beautiful and present moment of my life. I know that Mark loved her the moment he saw her, too.

It was difficult knowing that Ronnie had died right down the hall from where I had just experienced the incomparable miracle of birth. Life and death were separated only by a cold corridor of unopened doors. And if it bothered me, I know it must have been so much harder for Mark, the bittersweet blending of old memories and new. I am reminded of life's unpredictability, and that spontaneity is not a positive word where death is concerned.

Within hours after Carly was born, I was inspired to write a letter for her to read someday. Memories may fade, but they are also the building blocks of history. Experiences are the bricks, but our feelings are the mortar that holds a relationship together forever. Carly will hear the story of her birth a dozen times, but I also want her to know my feelings.

Mark cradled Carly in his arms and sang to her as I began to write. I have since addressed this letter, sealed it, and mailed it to Carly. On the back I printed, "To open when your first child is born."

D

TO OPEN WHEN YOUR FIRST CHILD IS BORN

Dear Carly,

Can you believe it? No one could ever imagine what birth is like until they've experienced it firsthand. Never has anything taken over my life with such power. I felt so scared and so confident at the same time. Most of all, I just wanted to see you, know that you were healthy, and hold you in my arms. The doctors said to rest up so I would have plenty of energy for delivery, but I couldn't sleep. I stayed awake all night wondering what you would look like and praying you would be healthy.

I went to the hospital and began what turned out to be the most unbelievably painful experience of my life. As my contractions became more severe, I remember thinking, "This is probably as bad as pain can get. I can take it." And then the pain would intensify, and I couldn't believe that something this beautiful could hurt this much.

What a miracle! You were born at 9:27 P.M. on October 18, 1996. You weighed eight pounds and three ounces. You are a beautiful girl. I will never forget this day and the moment I first held you in my arms.

The sweetest, most beautiful bundle of love is sleeping soundly in the crib next to me. God is amazing. I can't stop crying, just looking at you. Sometimes I feel like I don't know what to do, but Mother Nature is an incredible guide.

I have heard that, as the years go by, of all the experiences in life, birth and child-raising will keep you in the present moment more than anything else. This is a gift in itself. I can feel that already. My perspective on life has changed in an instant.

Just the idea of you hurting in your lifetime for any reason saddens me so. Everyone knows that life includes a certain amount of sorrow and pain. But I look at you now, so innocent and pure. If I could wrap you in my arms and protect you for a lifetime I would, but that is not life. What I can do is give you guidance, showing you how to weather life's challenges with grace and how to be grateful for God's abundant love. Remember I will always be here for you.

> *You are deeply loved,*
> *Mom*

To Mark, this baby is the earthly equivalent of an angel. We are all so fortunate. Months ago we were worried about the day Carly would arrive and how that would change us. We were so excited, yet we wondered if this would be the time that our paths would separate, that our needs would collide, and if the magnitude of our circumstances would cause us to walk away from each other. To my relief and happiness, we grew even closer.

I'm convinced that Mark is made of Velcro. Carly is always stuck somewhere on him. Her first naps were spent snuggled into Mark's chest.

Healing is a long process, maybe even a lifelong one. I understand that there are actually two lives going on inside of Mark's heart. He is holding on to an old love while falling in love with Carly and me. It is so simple yet so complex. It is one of those times when absolute acceptance is critical. I have to let him go through it, all of it. I have been told repeatedly about the "one-year grief cycle"—and have recently been accused of interrupting the "process." Maybe it's true, but love is not like a waterspout that I can just turn off.

One cold and dreary day we were driving in the pouring rain to a doctor's appointment. Along the roadside there were giant puddles, and it sounded like thousands of tiny needles were dropping on the roof of our car.

At the stoplight, Mark looked over at me and said, "People are worried because I'm starting to live again. Are you?"

His question took me by surprise. I answered him cautiously, "If anything, I'm concerned that sometimes I get in the way of your sadness. People say you need time to heal. The doctors told you that most people need a year, and if you feel that way too, I want you to have that time."

He pulled over to the side of the road and parked. "Diane, I have cried with you almost every day for months now. I am grieving, I am sad, but what are my options? Do I help others to grieve as well by sitting alone in my house waiting for visitors to stop by to share their tears with me? Or do I take the lesson we all learned from Ronnie's death, to live each moment as the special gift that it is?"

"I know, it must be confusing for you," I reassured him. It was confusing for me, too.

Mark continued, "They don't realize that I will continue to grieve, maybe forever. Even the doctor tells me I should be angry, but there is no one to blame. Who would I get angry at? God? Why should I blame God for giving me so much, for filling me so full?"

I nodded in understanding and wondered silently where he was going with his thoughts. It was a common feeling I had. One thing I learned about Mark was that he appreciated someone who could sit with him and just listen. He is the type who can be comforted by silence.

Staring out at Marin General Hospital, Mark said, "Not long ago I followed a screeching ambulance carrying my wife and three unborn children to the front door of that building. It was dark and rainy, just like today. That is where they died, the final destination in their journey on earth."

His eyes were watering as he continued, "A few weeks ago I arrived back at that same building. It was a crisp and bright fall day. I hugged you, put Carly safely in her car seat, and drove the two of you home. That is where she was born, the first destination in her journey here on earth."

"A lot has changed so quickly, hasn't it?" I started to understand.

Mark continued, "And how can I possibly make sense of this? Both events were life-changing. Both remind me that life is precious. But we each grieve differently and in our own time, and to spend my days wondering why these things happen is like placing a limit on God's love for me. God's ways are not our ways, and I may never know why Ronnie died."

Not knowing what to say, I offered him my hand.

"Well, we can either move forward cautiously or wait for social convention to give us permission. A lot has happened, but we're here together now and I love you."

He started the car and we drove away.

I recently realized that the letter I wrote to Carly in the hospital was only one of many times I would want to preserve memories for her. Mark was inspired by my idea; now he plans to write her letters as well. In our desire to communicate our love to Carly throughout her life, our plans have become more elaborate. We have bought a journal of sorts and made it into what we call the "Letter Box." Although I couldn't resist decorating it, the exterior is not the point. It's simple, but as the years go by we intend to fill it to overflowing with love, memories, and dreams.

I've written a letter to explain the gift to Carly. It will remain sealed until the day she receives it, which will likely be her high school graduation day.

All the other letters we will write for the different seasons she will experience in her lifetime will be sealed and mailed to our home. The cancelled postage on the outside will make each envelope a mini–time capsule, with a stamp and date that freezes the letter in a moment of history. We will keep them in the Letter Box. The letters will be for good times and bad, but each and every one will contain the pure essence of our love for her. What a joy it will be to share this with her throughout the experiences in our lives!

Dear Carly,

Today you are so young and curious. I want to remember everything from the first time I heard you cry till the day you leave for college, but I know that I will not remember it all, so I am attempting to preserve some history for you now, while the memories are still fresh in my mind.

This Letter Box is a lifelong gift to you. I wrote you the first letter a few hours after you were born. That one, and all the others, have been written for you to open on a special milestone in your life. Please open each letter on that day.

I am inspired to create this gift because I often wonder where the years will take us. What adventures and hardships will we share? How will you live your life? My hope is that you are filled with confidence and love that you find peace and take joy in the simplest pleasures. I pray that you laugh often and ride with dignity and grace down life's sometimes bumpy roads.

Maybe when you open some of these letters, I will be sitting by your side so I can tell you stories and laugh with you. Perhaps you will live far away and we will talk on the telephone. But if God has taken me from this earth, let this book be a living legacy of my love and pride for you.

You are the greatest joy I have ever known, and I don't want to miss a single reason to celebrate your life, even if only in spirit.

> I will love you through all the years,
> Mom

PILES OF BOOKS HAVE STACKED UP IN the corner of the room, all unopened, all thoughtful gifts received over these past months from well-meaning friends and relatives. I started off in a deep, dark place with very little interest in crawling out. Few knew what to say, but everyone wanted to help. My world had been turned upside down and shaken, and various continents had fallen off. God's spirit was with me, but my spirit, I felt, had left.

And then along came Diane. She was somehow easy—a comforting, accepting place to rest. She took my mind off starting over and allowed me to be sad and uncertain. I never felt pressure.

Out of chaos and turmoil she has gradually found my remaining pieces and polished them until they shine. She found enough of me to make a new person again, although I can only imagine that it was quite a large project to undertake. I know with certainty that she didn't take this project on by chance but by providence.

Now I realize that Diane and Carly have been placed in my life for much more than just putting me back together again. There is joy, and hope, and a life to plan and care for.

As I contemplate a life with Diane, a friend of mine has said to me, "Are you crazy? You could be one of the most eligible bachelors in town."

I responded without hesitation, "I'd prefer to be one of the most happily married men instead."

M

Earlier today, Diane created another memory for Carly's letter box. It is a true story, written for Carly, but a very special memory for Diane. I'm beginning to understand the power of the letter box. It will someday be a priceless treasure for Carly, but it is also a key that opens the door to Diane's heart. Those letters hold her deepest thoughts and say so much about how she feels.

When she finished writing the letter she came upstairs, handed it to me, and said, "I wrote this for Carly's letter box, but it is also for you."

Inside the envelope were two pieces of light blue stationery trimmed with colorful fish and a photo of an old man I had never seen before.

Dear Carly,

It was 4:30 A.M. on a crisp, foggy San Francisco morning. The salmon-fishing boat had left the pier in Sausalito. We were headed out for a day trip out of the bay and under the Golden Gate Bridge. I was the only woman, surrounded by eighteen salty old men of the sea. I never would have guessed that this would be the day I learned what true love really means, but it was.

As the sun rose and the boat pounded through the waves, I spotted an old man with a sweet face sitting on a bench. He was looking at some photographs. Nausea was setting in and I needed to sit down, so I asked if I could join him.

Henry was from Los Angeles. He was 96 and had just driven himself up to Sausalito the night before to go on this fishing trip. He showed me the photos of himself and his wife. The photo was old, but it looked like they were on the exact same boat we were on that day. They were fishing together.

Apparently they would drive up to Sausalito once every year for a day of fishing. Then they would put the catch in a cooler, head back to Los Angeles, and have a huge party and salmon barbecue with all of their friends.

He said his wife loved to fish more than he did, and I wondered why he had come alone. Soon he told me that his wife had died earlier that year and one of the last things she told him was to keep on fishing. And so he did.

He cried as he talked of their love and the memories of their life together. This was before I had met your dad, so I had never experienced such love or such loss. I couldn't even imagine the pain he was experiencing. I must confess I selfishly wondered about myself as he spoke. Would I ever know a love like that? Would a man ever miss me so much that he would feel as if his body had been ripped in half when I was gone?

I made a commitment to myself that day on that dirty, smelly boat to make love a priority in my life. No longer would I wait for Mr. Perfect. After all, I certainly wasn't Ms. Perfect. No longer would I be too busy for love.

During the same time I was taking a photography class at the Academy of Art College in San Francisco, and my assignment was to take some pictures in the fog. I had my camera and snapped two full rolls of the old man reeling in what would most likely be the last salmon of his life-time. He was smiling, and he began to relax and enjoy the day. We talked, and I cried with him, and then we fished some more. Thank God the fish were biting.

After the final exam in my photography class, I packed up the photos of Henry and sent them to him in Los Angeles. I knew he would love them. His spirit was shining in every shot; clearly, he believed his wife was there with him.

Several weeks later I received a letter in the mail. It was from his daughter. She was writing to thank me for the photos. He had told her all about his trip and his day of fishing on the bay, but he never got to see the photos. She said that her father had passed away and these were the last photos ever taken of him. She was so pleased he was smiling. The pictures had confirmed what she had always known about her parents: Love was the foundation of their world.

That day taught me what really matters in life. When you find true love, the pieces of the puzzle will fit together and you will feel safe and secure. True love lives on and on for-

*ever. I know that now. I have that love in my heart, and I
pray for a love like that for you. Keep your heart wide open.*

> *Love,*
> *Mom*

Ⓜ

Diane has added so much to my life. In fact, she has given
a life back to me, the very life I thought I had lost forever.
She is so generous with her heart, and I imagine that is
exactly how she'll still be fifty years from now.

Maybe that's why, when I looked in the mirror this morning, I saw the face of a man who may be ready for marriage. It startled me at first because I hadn't welcomed that
thought before, but I am fortunate to have found a gentle
woman who honors my past and the other woman I loved
so dearly. God has blessed me with a loving companion
and also with a beautiful child.

Ⓜ

We headed off to Hawaii for a vacation on the North
Shore, with Carly asleep in my arms. The airline celebrated

its anniversary that day, complete with games and prizes and an overall mood of relaxation and fun.

The flight attendant came by with a large dessert tray. Though Diane declined, after the attendant had served me my dessert, she put a small box on a dessert plate on Diane's tray. "And this one is for you," she said to Diane, smiling. "Enjoy your dessert."

Diane leaned over to me and said, "Why is everyone always giving me chocolate?"

She kept talking with me about Hawaii, asking me so many questions because she knew I wanted to live there. Finally, I looked over at her tray and said, "Open the box. Let's see what's in it."

Diane handed me the box and said, "You can open it. The last thing I need is more chocolate. You're the skinny one."

I gave her what she describes as "the look," and she reluctantly said, "OK, I'll open it, but don't let me eat any."

She opened the box. Inside was a small black velvet box. "Maybe it's earplugs," I joked.

"Or really good chocolate," she said. She smiled and looked at me. She opened the velvet box, and tears filled her eyes as she pulled out a plain and simple platinum wedding band, the one she once said she had always wanted.

I proposed to her on the plane, and by the time we landed on Oahu we had decided to get married in California as soon as we could plan our wedding. There was every reason to wait, but we didn't want to.

OUR GRAND WEDDING PLANS SOON became complicated and increasingly difficult to coordinate. Our goal was to keep our life as simple as possible—just like the wedding band—and this was no way to get started.

One morning last week, as we were having coffee on the porch watching the waves, I said to Mark, "Who are those people with the patience and enthusiasm to plan a year in advance for a wedding? Not me, that's for sure. I know my mom wishes I wanted to plan an elaborate and formal wedding, but I just don't want to take the time."

"Well, then how do you feel?" he asked.

"I just don't want to become frustrated and stressed planning the most special day of our life together," I explained.

"Hmmm," he muttered under his breath, and I looked at him wondering what exactly that meant.

We sat quietly for a minute. I could tell Mark was thinking. His eyes were gazing far away, beyond the horizon. This particular look usually means that something profound or at least thought-provoking was about to come out of his mouth.

He turned to me and asked, "Can your mom get here in the next three days?"

"I think so. Why?" I wondered.

"Let's get married here. I mean right here on this beach," he said.

"In three days?"

"I'd marry you in three minutes if I could. Let's do it in three days." Mark's enthusiasm and determination is very convincing. I listened, trying to weigh his points against the fact that I'd waited so many years for the day I'd be joining my life with a man I knew I would love forever. Sensing my openness to the idea, he continued, "Why wait? We've got plenty of experiences and challenges ahead of us, and I'd like to start facing all of them as a family."

Mark's choice of the words "as a family" proved more convincing than any comments that followed.

We changed our grand plans and opted instead for a small but intimate ceremony on the beach in the back-yard. Within a couple of hours, we arranged for our mothers and my aunt to fly over, and we invited a couple of neighborhood friends. We ordered leis and a cake and even arranged for a photographer to come.

That same morning, I ventured out alone to the next town, Haleiwa, and went to Silver Moon, a fashionable women's clothing store. I knew what I wanted. A white dress, not a wedding gown, just a simple white dress I could wear without shoes on the beach.

Within twenty minutes I had picked out my wedding dress. I surprised Mark when I returned home before noon.

We found a bright floral dress for Carly and a Hawaiian aloha shirt for Mark. Before we knew it, the wedding was planned and we were on our way to the airport to pick up our guests.

Three days after Mark suggested the idea, the wedding took place. Our local Hawaiian minister performed much of it in Hawaiian. Even though we definitely did say "I do," I still wonder sometimes if we are officially married. I have no idea what I agreed to. I just said yes to everything. Mark claims that was to his advantage.

D

Who needs a honeymoon when you get married in Hawaii? I was so happy to wake up the next morning with Mark and watch the sun come up and listen to the waves crashing along the shore.

Later that morning, Carly was sleeping soundly by my side and Mark was out surfing. I could see him in the distance. There were several surfers out at the surf break that day, but I could tell which one was Mark. They all begin to have a signature style that sets them apart from the others. I recognize Mark by his wobbly arms. He may not like that, but it's true.

It was a peaceful time, so I decided to add to Carly's letter box while the memories of our wedding day were still dancing in my mind.

Dear Carly,

Yesterday was a day that you will never remember but I will never forget. Today I am sitting here looking at you, a tiny angel, and imagining the day many years from now when you will walk down the aisle and into the arms of your husband.

I wonder what music you will dance to on your wedding day. I wonder if you are young or a late bloomer like your mom. I could never make up my mind because I always wanted to wait for Mr. Perfect. So I waited and waited and waited. And then finally I met your dad.

It's clear I have married someone very different from me. He knew what he wanted early in life. He was always such a committed man. I respected that about him from the moment I met him.

On our wedding day I woke up grinning from ear to ear. It was before dawn and even the birds were still sleeping. I just sat on the porch and waited patiently for the sun to rise.

For a long time I pondered my future. I imagined how my family would grow, becoming part of his family. I imagined how our friendships would grow and merge and change over the years. I wondered how many children we would have.

And then suddenly, I became overwhelmed by the enormity of the decision we made. Not frightened or alarmed, but simply awestruck.

Somehow God gives us certain parents, certain relatives, and certain siblings, and these people become our family. We did not choose them. But a husband is different. He's a man that you actually choose out of a cast of millions. What an awesome feat! I actually picked this man out of all the men walking on the planet. He will become the most significant part of my family—my husband, the man I will share my hopes and dreams with until death do we part. In all my crazy life I had never made such an important decision. Yet I wonder, did I really pick Mark, or did God pick him for me?

As the minister was reading our vows, I looked into your dad's eyes and I knew I had picked the right man. He is perfect for me. Not perfect, mind you, just perfect for me. Certainly he has his faults, as I have mine. Just like everyone else, we will have to work at our marriage to make it stronger as the years go by.

And all of that hard work to come was condensed into a brief second as the Hawaiian minister gently nudged me back to reality. Apparently it was my turn to say "I do."

The next day those words "I do" kept ringing in my ears. Yes, I do love him, and I do commit myself to him, and I do honor him. But more than just that, I do respect him, I do trust him, and I do admire his integrity and his kind heart. And lucky me, because now he is my husband! Sure there are hard times, and there are problems. We are alive, therefore we struggle—but we do it together.

I am hopeful that your wedding day may be one of the most precious days of your life! Lord knows that every day is precious, but my prayer for you is that on this day you can look into your husband's eyes and feel the same love, respect, and trust that I felt for your dad on the day we were married.

Enjoy your new life together, Carly. I wish you and your husband all the happiness and love in the world.

> *Love,*
> *Mom*

I enclosed a photo from our wedding, sealed the letter, and wrote "To open on your wedding day" on the back. I put it out in our mailbox and lifted the flag so it would be postmarked that day. It was mailed to our home address and said "Mom" in the corner.

The next day it was delivered back to me with the postal seal and date on it. I put it away with the other letters in Carly's letter box.

D

I heard the other day that the postal carrier wondered if I had realized what I was doing. Why on earth would anyone mail a letter to someone at their own house? She was convinced it was a mistake. I thought nothing would surprise them.

FALL D

We flew back to California after the wedding, but the dream house on the North Shore of Oahu is calling our name. Mark has long intended for Hawaii to be his home. On Carly's first birthday we packed our belongings and moved.

Although I had visited the house before, when we opened the door and stepped inside, it felt different. It is no longer a place to go for vacations, it is home.

The first night we put Carly to bed earlier than usual. The time change was in our favor, so Mark and I sat on the deck in the backyard and watched the pounding surf.

"How does it feel to be here?" asked Mark. He held my hand.

"This moment it feels great. I'm already relaxed. This has been a crazy year. I feel like a washing machine that's been on a constant spin cycle."

"Well, you should be nice and dizzy," joked Mark.

"Yeah, but I just want to soak for a while." Mark then reassured me that I was in the right place for "soaking" and maybe even some "floating," even though this was a big change for me. He had certainly gone out of his way to prepare the house for our arrival, including everything from a house full of tropical flowers to fences and all the safety precautions necessary for a small child living on the beach.

D

I am thankful I arrived before my boxes; it has given me time to adjust.

It's an odd feeling, moving into another woman's life. I cook with her pots and pans and season our food with her spices. I sleep on her side of the bed and use her shampoo and bath towels. It feels like I have given up my own familiar life and now I am intruding on someone else's. This is by no means apparent to Mark, but it's a bigger adjustment than I expected.

The most challenging moment came last week. We had kept ourselves busy for days getting Carly's room ready and filling the house with groceries and other essentials. We returned home one day and there they were, a large box for Carly and three others for me. I had been living out of a suitcase until that day, eagerly awaiting the arrival of my clothes.

It didn't fully sink in until I saw those boxes. Then it hit me: all of Ronnie's things were still hanging in the closet.

Last year, Mark and a couple of Ronnie's best friends had packed up all of her clothes and toiletries in their California house. It took an entire day, and it had been terribly difficult for Mark.

So there we were, in a different closet in a different place and time. Mark and I walked upstairs and looked inside. There were years of life and experiences neatly folded in those drawers and hanging brightly from the wooden racks.

Mark apologized. "Sorry I haven't gotten to this yet."

"That's OK. I know this is a tough one for you."

"Yeah, it's just so final. Last time it took forever, and I had friends to help me."

"I'll help you. I can even do it myself if you don't want to go through it all again."

Mark hugged me tight.

We agreed that I would get started with the obvious stuff and that when Mark returned we would finish the task together.

As I always assume I can handle anything, I dove right in. I decided to begin with the drawers. Mark would return to no major changes, and I would be making progress. Quietly and alone, I stepped into the closet. Instantly Ronnie came to life for me. It's been a year and a half since her passing, but at that moment I felt so strongly the presence of the woman who walked in those dresses.

Eventually, I opened the top dresser drawer. Underwear. "Can I do this?" I asked myself. This was a job that required assistance from my best friend.

Debrah answered the phone and I immediately started talking.

"OK. I'm standing in Ronnie's closet, which is apparently now my closet. I need to move my things in, which also involves moving her things out. I'm not sure if I'm up for this."

Deb always calls me Dee. She likes solutions, just like Mark. "OK, this is what you need to do." I knew directions would follow. "Start with the T-shirts. Then go to socks and accessories. Work your way to underwear and call me later."

"Thanks, Deb." I hung up with a plan, which made venturing into this uncomfortable and personal territory easier to face.

T-shirts and socks were easy. From there, I went through drawers of accessories and trinkets that I knew her sister would love to have. I set her earrings aside for Mark to look at. I packed up purses, belts, shoes, and shirts. Suddenly I found myself back at the underwear drawer.

Going through it wasn't too difficult at all until the moment I discovered that her underwear was tiny and her bras were way bigger than I thought they'd be. "Can this get any harder?" I asked myself.

I called Deb back. "I am such a girl," I said as soon as she answered.

"What do you mean? How's it going?"

"Well, let's just say I thought I was doing a pretty decent job of not feeling jealous of Mark's perfect first wife until right now."

"Why, what happened? Is it the closet thing?" Deb asked.

"It's the underwear thing," I admitted with a slight moan in my voice. "It's just much, much harder going through someone else's life than I thought it would be."

Deb clearly wasn't used to hearing me sound so insecure. "Just keep it up, Dee. You're almost done, and then you can get settled. What a year you guys have had, but just think about it, now you have each other and your life together is really about to begin." She is always so encouraging.

"I know, Deb, you're right. I just want to soak for a while."

"You'll get there soon," she reassured me, as if she had heard my analogy the night before.

Ⓓ

Carly's adjustment to her new surroundings is a task she takes seriously. She's determined to explore every item in every box, drawer, and cabinet in the house, and her exploits prepare us all for a nice long nap each day. The other day, when she was sleeping soundly in her crib, Mark and I poked our heads into her room. We watched her sleep for a minute, her little chest raising up and down with every peaceful breath. Mark whispered in my ear, "She is just the sweetest angel."

The next day, when Carly was in an exaggerated moment of pure frustration, I looked over at Mark and asked, "How can someone who's only two-foot-four possibly be so demanding?"

He laughed and said, "Just wait. Someday she'll be five-foot-four."

Some of my most priceless memories are the quiet times that Mark and I spent together just staring at her smiling face.

There's something about Hawaii. It's a fertile place. Some say it's the weather; others say it's the water. Personally, I think it's the relaxed atmosphere, especially where we live on the North Shore. There are children everywhere, lots of them. It's old-fashioned family-style living, like I would imagine our grandparents used to live.

We've been here only five weeks, and we have just discovered a new baby is already on the way. Maybe it's the water. Mark is so excited I think he walked around with tears in his eyes for two full days.

This is a wonderful neighborhood, but settling into a small town has its disadvantages as well. People are curious about almost everything. We've been doing some gardening, and there was a pile of dirt near the front of our house. This afternoon three different people stopped to ask us what the pile of dirt was for.

We started making up different answers.

"It's an escape tunnel."

"It's a burial ground for ex-boyfriends."

"It's a neighborhood ant farm."

Actually, it's a pile of dirt.

Ⓓ

Twila, my neighbor down the street, has told me about the stir Mark and I created the first time I visited here while I was still very pregnant.

I can understand the curiosity. The people in Hawaii reacted differently. Ronnie died in California, we had lots of friends in common there, and people had seen us together for months. But Mark's friends and neighbors on the North Shore hadn't seen him much since Ronnie died, and then he shows up one day with me, and I was eight months pregnant.

Every morning, I would go swimming and snorkeling in the ocean for exercise. I would swim in one direction and then return home on the beach. Apparently the neighbors were anxious to get a glimpse of me and my huge stomach, and according to Twila, the coconut telegraph was burning up the wires when I passed from house to house.

"Mark's new pregnant girlfriend is walking down the beach, check her out." Thank goodness I had no idea.

At least I can laugh with Twila over that one now.

Ⓓ

Our son, Jackson, had a rough time entering this world. During delivery his heart rate dropped dramatically. Four doctors and a nurse were in the delivery room, and for a few silent moments they were all standing still watching the equipment that monitored his heart rate.

I was frightened. Our son was in danger and timing was critical. The doctors were unsure why he would not come out, but they said I should give it all I had. We needed to hurry.

Jack was born, but he was blue and the umbilical cord was wrapped around his neck two times. Our doctor said it was a miracle that he made it out naturally, without a C-section, since the cord was wrapped so tight. Quickly his color changed to a healthy pink and he began to cry. We all cried too.

I thanked God that Jack had made it, and I also thanked God for sparing Mark the pain and agony of losing another unborn child. That would have been too much.

We returned home from the hospital with our car loaded with flowers and our new son.

The next morning he was sleeping in his daddy's arms. The look of love in Mark's eyes was simply beautiful. It's amazing how you fall so immediately in love with a new baby. Every finger and toe is a miracle. I counted them all twice and then stared at each little part of his face for a very long time.

I went to my desk drawer and picked out some stationery with a border of tiny blue footprints. I grabbed my favorite pen, sat down, and wrote a letter to Jack, the beginning of his letter box.

By now we've settled into our new routine. Carly loves Jack, who she assumes is a new toy, some amazing reward for good behavior. She enjoys tugging on his ears and poking him all over his tiny body. She was the first one to make him smile, so he must like it.

Early this morning, the whole family went down to the beach for a breakfast picnic. For me, this is always the calmest and most peaceful time of day to go to the beach. I was holding Jack while Carly was digging for sand crabs right next to us.

I looked at Mark, and by the faraway look on his face, I couldn't tell if he was happy or sad.

"Are you OK?" I asked.

"Yeah, I'm good," he said as he put his arm around me. "This may sound strange, but I was just wishing Ronnie could be here to meet the kids."

With a proud smile he looked over at Carly digging in the sand. Then he looked at Jack and said, "She would have loved them."

The way I live my own life has greatly improved because of Ronnie. It's odd, because I didn't know her well, but the lessons from her life and death have had a profound impact on my everyday life. Her gift to me is a deeper understanding of how to love and be loved. Since the phone call when I first heard about Ronnie's death, I have rarely looked back with regret for my life and the unexpected changes I have encountered along the way. I have learned to be content without trying to predict the ending to my story. In the case of life and death, the ending writes itself.

There are others who have also touched my life as Ronnie did. Most of them are still alive today, and it occurred to me recently that I have not always taken the time to tell them. I am thankful to those who have raised me, educated me, loved me, listened to me, mentored me, been patient with me, and showed me the way. Some of them don't even know the difference they have made. Ronnie has motivated me to share my heart with others while I still can, which I have learned to do with just a simple letter from my heart.

I also have seen the pain that remains in the hearts of those left behind after a loved one dies, but now I have found a special way to share my love forever, whether I am alive or not. Inside my letter box is a legacy of love, and I see clearly now that even the letter box is a gift from Ronnie.

Today, I was inspired to write what may appear to be a sad letter. The reason for this letter is also part of the gift that Ronnie left. We will all leave a legacy when we die, of this we may be certain. I imagine that our everyday experiences will be memorable to those who knew us, the obvious results of the seeds we have planted on our walk along the road toward heaven.

But who will know our heart if we don't take the time to share it? Our feelings are left to the interpretation of those around us, even in life, but especially in death. I don't want the message in my heart to be left for those I love to only imagine. I want them to know that if I could, I would proclaim my love for them for today, for tomorrow, and for eternity.

Today I am writing for a time in the future. I am writing about death, but I am certainly not sick. I am alive and healthy, and I stand in awe of the capacity for one heart to love so greatly.

To open upon my death

My dearest children,

As you can imagine, this is the most difficult letter for me to write. Right now, as I contemplate death, it is not fear of dying that causes me pain but rather the thought of leaving my family behind.

When I was younger, I was always so grateful for living, but I was also so curious about why we are here and where we were going after this part of our journey ends. I spent hours thinking about the meaning of life and, in particular, what was I doing here. Of course, I never had any answers to these age-old questions, so I would end my internal philosophy lesson with the feeling that there must be something more besides this existence on earth. Part of me could not wait to find out what that was.

I suppose I can dig deep down and still find that feeling, but something drastically changed in me after I married your dad and started our family.

For the first time I planted roots. I mean emotional roots. The kind of roots that attach you to another human being and are so strong that they stretch to the far corners of the earth.

I can remember being afraid to love your dad as much as I did. I thought love was like this mathematical equation. The amount that a heart loves is in direct proportion to the amount that a heart can feel pain. As I grew more deeply in love, I was acutely aware of how painful it would be to lose him.

And then you children came along. That bond is so different. It was solid from the second you were born. Life began to make more sense to me, and I could not imagine life without my family.

Every year, every day, every moment is a gift. I have been blessed with many wonderful memories that bring a smile to my face or tears of happiness to my eyes. I have also struggled and suffered, and I remember those times as well with a smile on my face, because in the end, so far, every struggle has helped form the person that I am.

As I think about my own death—and my own life— I keep coming back to that mathematical equation about love. The pleasure of knowing and giving love is what really matters on earth. And I feel content. I have felt love and I continue to feel love every moment of every day.

I may not be the richest, most beautiful, or healthiest person. Considering the size of this planet, I may not know very many people intimately and deeply. And God knows I have not suffered or felt the deep pain that many others have in this lifetime. So, was my life worth it? Did I make a difference? Did I laugh and cry through the years? And most importantly, did I know love?

Yes, yes, yes. And I pray that in your lifetime, you, too, will experience all the pleasure and pain that life brings you with open arms. This way, you will also leave this earth with a full heart.

I can only imagine this to be a difficult time for you as well. Find strength in your faith. Let our fond memories comfort you now. We have had so much. You have given me so much. Now your outgoing spirit and your generous heart will fill you with the desire to go on to live a wonderful life and to share your gifts with others.

I will close with this, my dears. As you get older, I pray that your life will be filled with people and love. Make loving one another your priority, for as I have heard many times before, when that final day comes, you will not be concerned with how much money is in your bank account or how successful you were in business. You will only care about the people you love and the wonderful memories of times spent with them. So, please take the time to cultivate those memories and you will reap the harvest of life's sweetest fruit.

I have enjoyed each and every moment of this life with you. I can still remember the first moment I saw your face and held you in my arms. My memories are filled with your sweet smiles and your chunky tears and everything in between. I will remember you and everything about you.

Although I will miss you greatly, I believe that someday we will be together again. On that day I will look into

*those sweet eyes to thank you once again for bringing
more joy to my life than I could have ever imagined.*

So until that day, good-bye.

> *I love you,*
> *Mom*

(D)

Wednesdays are date night, complete with adult conversation and dinner. We recently decided to make them more interesting by trying some different activities together. Last week we went fishing for little Hawaiian bait-fish, and Mark thought that was the perfect date. This week, it was my turn.

After three trips from the car to unload our things, we set up our cooler and other essentials on the warm sand at Waimea Bay, about twenty minutes from our home.

"Is this really date night or is this some weeklong adventure you have planned?" Mark asked with a sarcastic grin.

"Honey, I promise someday you will come to appreciate my planning skills—maybe not tonight, but someday." He didn't look convinced.

"You got any hula dancers in there?" He couldn't control himself.

We went swimming and snorkeling until sunset. We saw many colorful fish and eels, and Mark even saw a small shark. I'm sure at that moment he was thankful I had packed his fins.

Later, we poured glasses of wine and watched the sun set into the ocean. We had a wonderful picnic, and as the night air became cool we cuddled close into each other's arms.

"Let's have another baby." His words came from nowhere.

"Now," I responded, for lack of anything better to say.

"Well, soon. Let's have another baby soon. Then they'll all be close in age and we can do more together when they are young. And then they'll be close when they grow up. And besides, you make such beautiful babies. What do you think?"

When Mark owned his company, they often used a hand gesture that constituted absolute agreement with no turning back. It meant a final decision had been made and everyone had taken ownership of it. You simply take your clenched fist and "bonk" yourself on the forehead. Everyone has to agree, or it isn't valid.

We talked for the rest of the evening about the idea of having a third child. Before we packed up our things to head home, we bonked on it.

The following week we found out I was already pregnant.

This pregnancy has not been fun. The nausea is indeed nauseating. The mood swings have been epic. But it is the insomnia that has been most unbearable. There have been very few nights, especially as we get near the end, that I sleep more than three or four hours. And then a couple of fully-charged, die-hard batteries wake up promptly at 5 A.M., run down the hall, and grace Mark and me with their presence.

On one occasion, after being up all night, I decided to take a bath at about 3 A.M. I added half of a jar of my favorite aromatherapy bath milk and managed to relax so much I woke up two hours later in an ice-cold tub with my head part way in the water.

I must say, I am grateful the kids woke up or I might have drowned, and that would have been just too much for Mark to deal with. I can see the headlines now: "Pregnant woman drowns in bathtub from aromatherapy overdose."

The week before Hannah was born, I was getting desperate. My doctor said she was ready, but she just wouldn't come out. I called my next-door neighbor, "Della, can you come down to Twila's with me? We can walk down with the kids."

"Sure," said Della. She's always ready to go.

On the way to Twila's, I revealed my mission. I had a plan. If anything would help me go into labor it would be this.

"No way," said Della. "This, I've got to see."

We made it to Twila's front yard with me waddling the entire way. The kids followed behind, imitating me like a flock of baby ducks. Today, the kids would have to wait to get on the trampoline. It was my idea and I was first. The kids ran for cover. Passing cars honked, waved, and drove by slowly to get a good glimpse of me bouncing up and down.

My doctor has a picture of this undignified event hanging on the wall in her office with a joke underneath that says, "If this won't induce labor, nothing will!" It's true, it didn't help me at all, but a week later Hannah Lee Button was born. This birth was actually fun and easy, and every difficult moment from the months before vanished the second I saw her face.

I love our first family photo. Mark is beaming with his arm around all of us. Time alone doesn't heal wounds—it takes love, too.

Having kids has brought out a refreshing piece of our hearts that we rarely saw in each other before. In some ways, we hadn't even seen them in ourselves for many years. I think they were lying dormant somewhere between the responsibility gene and the career gene. It's the easy-going playful gene that knows deep down that we never really have to grow up.

One recent sunny afternoon the Hawaiian sky decided to bless us with a beautiful tropical downpour. We were just leaving the house and Mark asked me to grab an umbrella.

"Umbrella?" I questioned him, as if he were an alien. "You want me to bring an umbrella?"

"Yeah, it's pouring," he informed me, as if I had no idea.

"Well, sorry, but I don't own an umbrella. I don't like them. To me, they are a sign of aging, and not the good kind.

"Besides," I continued, "don't you love to play in the rain? Come on. Let's go." I tucked my arm into his and pulled him outside.

"I think our friends were right. Maybe we got married too soon," Mark joked.

"Isn't there anything you like to do that reminds you of being a kid?" I asked him. "Like jumping in puddles?"

We walked down the street in the rain to our neighbor's house. Mark and I spent half an hour looking at all the rainbow colors and reflections and then jumping in the puddles along the road.

"I'm a fun guy, you know. You just haven't had the opportunity to see that part of me yet," Mark tried to convince me.

"That's because we're just finally getting a chance to play," I assured him.

We returned home looking like we had just come in from an afternoon swim with our clothes on. We made hot chocolate, a rare event in Hawaii, and then rolled on the floor and tickled each other until we cried.

I knew right then and there that Mark had indeed remembered how to laugh. It must have pleased Ronnie, as it certainly did me, to see that Mark's spirit had found its way back.

SIX YEARS HAVE PASSED SINCE THAT unforgettable spring day that I lost my first wife. I have learned since then that we are indeed given second chances in life, but we must dig deep within to find the strength and courage to seek them out. It doesn't always make sense, and that is where faith and trust become important. I may never truly understand why Ronnie had to die when she was so very young and alive. But God knows, and in this I have found peace.

What I believe to be true is that there is a beloved and loving dark-haired angel with three bouncing babies watching over me every moment from above.

What I see right now is that there is a beautiful woman with three sweet children playing out in the backyard. I hear them calling me now: "Daddy, come play with us."

Your Own Letter Box

PART · TWO

MARK & DIANE

Dear Friends,

Now you know the story of how we first created our letter boxes and how we have made them part of our lives as future gifts to our children. When we first started telling people about the idea, everyone was immediately intrigued, and many began to create boxes for their own loved ones. We have included this section of the book to help those of you who may wish to do the same.

We feel that one of the strengths of the "Letter Box" idea lies in its simplicity: It's for anyone who has loved deeply and who wants to preserve that tie for generations to come. Whether directed to a friend, mentor, or family member, the acts of expressing and sharing that love are inherently enriching for all involved. Letter boxes are for all parents who have felt the incomparable bond between themselves and their children and who dream about watching them grow from bouncing babies through adulthood, cherishing every memory in between.

As the years have passed, we have continued writing to our children, and now Carly, Jack, and Hannah each have a letter box. Over time we have gathered together a collection of letters expressing our deepest feelings, thoughts, and hopes for the future to encourage them through life. Each letter has been mailed, postmarked, and safely stored away, to be opened at a certain significant moment in their respective lives. Besides the loving support we provide our children each day, we believe that these letters are one of the most valuable gifts they will receive from us. Their letter boxes are our lifelong connection to them, time taken to ensure that important words have not been left unspoken.

In our own lives, loved ones have already left us, taking with them thoughts and feelings we will never know. Maybe you, too, have lost a parent, grandparent, aunt, friend, or other loved one. Wouldn't opening a letter written years ago by the hand of that person be an incomparable gift? Wouldn't you cherish forever their words of love, wisdom, and faith? Such a letter might bring back beautiful memories or perhaps reveal something important about that person which you never knew before. Perhaps just a simple expression of love before the signature would be a treasure in itself.

The Letter Box is our invitation for you to cast your own legacy into the hearts of those you treasure. Don't worry about grammar or punctuation, and don't wait to get started. Our time on earth is precious and uncertain, consisting of lessons, sacrifices, challenges, successes, failures, highs, lows, and a whole lot more. Tell your story. Share your heart. It will be a testament to both your mortality and immortality—a legacy that endures for generations.

We believe you are a special and important link in a very long chain.

> *With love,*
> *Mark & Diane Button*

GETTING STARTED ON YOUR LETTER BOX

1 Write a letter for a particular occasion, to be opened now or in the future. On some occasions, you may wish to ask another special person to write a letter or note to include with yours.

2 Add photos or other special memorabilia such as newspaper clippings, world statistics, grocery receipts, magazine articles, quotes, cartoons, or any other interesting memorabilia. You may choose to personalize your stationery with stickers, stamps, calligraphy, art, or drawings.

3 Seal the letter, specify the occasion it should be opened on the envelope, and (if possible) mail it, "care of" yourself at your own address. Remember, for those letters that will be opened in the future, the postmark and stamp mark their places in history.

4 Finally, look for a box or album to keep your letters in, such as an old cigar box. You may want to try your hand at making one yourself, turning an ordinary box into a special one.

5 Have fun!

TIPS TO MAKE YOUR
LETTERS LAST A LIFETIME

1 Since these letters may be sealed for decades, it is important to choose permanent markers and pens. Plain ink may dull over time, so we recommend fade-resistant, waterproof ink. Craft stores carry a variety of these in different colors and tip styles. Be creative.

2 Paper should be acid-free so it will withstand the test of time. Higher pH paper may crack or deteriorate over the years; it may also damage your photographs.

3 Glue should be permanent as well. Ask a craft-store retailer for the kinds that are used by library archivists.

4 You may wish to archive your letters in your computer or make copies to store in a separate place. As your collection grows, this testament of your love for your friends and family will likely become one of your most cherished possessions.

TIPS FOR LETTER WRITING

We all want to know that we are loved. Each letter box is a golden opportunity to create a legacy of love and to guarantee that a piece of your heart lives on. Whichever way you choose to convey your deepest feelings to those you care about, the most important thing is to get them down on paper. Don't be afraid to show the real you. Those who are dear to you will love you and accept you, flaws and all. Share your memories of your own past as well as memories that include the person for whom the letter is intended. Children will want to know about things they did and family adventures they may not remember. Parents, friends, or mentors will be touched to learn how special they are to you. Be lavish with praise, generous with your heart, but above all, write from a place of love.

THOUGHTFUL QUESTIONS FOR YOUR LETTER BOX LETTERS

The questions on the following pages are provided as a springboard from which to start your letter writing. We hope they remind you of meaningful experiences you may have forgotten or of sides of yourself you may not often think about but would enjoy sharing in your letters.

Keep in mind that not every question is intended for any one person who reads this book. The questions about giving marital advice won't necessarily help an unmarried reader; the questions about reflecting back on old age won't help a young one. Ignore the questions that don't apply to you; there are plenty of thought-provoking questions for everyone.

FOR A GRADUATION, OR ANY SUCCESSFULLY COMPLETED PROGRAM OF STUDY

• Where did you go to school and why? If you didn't go to college, what do you consider the most educational experience you've ever had?

• How did your education, formal or otherwise, change your personality or the way you view the world?

• If you have experienced a formal learning environment, what was the best part? What was your favorite subject or course?

• What was the most difficult part? What was your least favorite subject or course?

• Where did you live during your "learning years"? What did you eat?

• What did you do for fun during this time? What sports and activities were you involved in? What music did you listen to?

• Were there any teachers or friends who became a mentor or role model to you? Who taught you the most? Did you like or respect that person? Did you ever receive help from someone you didn't fully appreciate until later?

• What advice would you give your letter's recipient as he or she enters the work force and adjusts to a new life?

• How has your education or training contributed to your success in life?

• What did you "always want to be when you grew up"? Did that dream change? Are you glad about it? Regretful?

For difficult times

• What was the most difficult situation you have ever encountered?

• How did you handle it? How did you feel?

• What emotions do you show easily? Which ones do you hide? Do you wish you could share more or less than you do?

• What is your philosophy about pain and suffering? Why do you believe humans suffer so much?

• Has any person or group of people helped you through a particularly tough time? Who?

• Have any of your beliefs helped you heal? Explain how.

• What saying or thought has given you comfort and strength that you would like to pass on to the person who receives this letter?

• Are your feelings easily hurt? Do you place importance on what others think of you?

• Have you learned any valuable life lessons through the trials in your life? What?

• What regrets do you have? What do you do in your present life to cope with these feelings? What do you do now to avoid making similar mistakes?

• What have you learned about yourself from the mistakes you have made? Have you changed? What are you still working to change?

• When was the first time you fell in love? How old were you? Was this the person you married?

• Where did you go on your first date with this person? When and where was your first kiss?

• What did falling in love feel like the first time?

• Who do you know who has a "love" relationship you admire?

• What does love mean to you?

• Who is your love now? Do you feel better about yourself with this person in your life?

• Did you fall in love immediately or did it grow over time? Were you "best friends" first?

• How did you know you were falling in love? Were you always staring at each other or could you see your unborn children in your partner's eyes?

• What was the most fun thing you ever did with this person? Did you laugh often? Do you still laugh often?

• What do you feel is the secret to keeping the spark alive in a relationship? Have you ever fallen out of love? Could it have been avoided?

• How did you meet your spouse? What were your first impressions? Did you have a lot in common?

• How long did you date? Why did you fall in love? What qualities did your spouse have that you admired? Are these the same things you admire now?

• What did you believe marriage would be like? What were your concerns? How has it been different than you expected?

• What do you remember most about your wedding day?

• Where did you go on your honeymoon?

• How did you feel about the family you were marrying into?

• What advice would you give the recipient of this letter as he or she takes this important step? About love? About commitment? About the struggles? About making the bond last?

• What was the first year of your marriage like? Do you remember a special day or weekend you spent together during the first year? What do you do for fun together now?

• What is the most difficult part about being married? How do you handle the conflict?

• What is the best part about being married? What do you love most about your spouse now?

FOR THE BIRTH OF A CHILD

• Describe the months you (or your partner) were pregnant. How did you feel emotionally and physically?

• Who attended the birth? Were they helpful?

• How was the delivery? Was it in a hospital, at home, or elsewhere?

• How did you feel the first time you saw your baby?

• Who was there to help in the beginning? Family? Friends and neighbors?

• Who chose your child's name? How was the decision made? What were the other possibilities?

• What were you like as a new parent? Were you surprised by your attitudes or parenting styles? Did you and your partner have conflicting thoughts about how to raise children?

• What was the biggest challenge as a new parent? What was your favorite part?

• How has your life changed from this experience?

• What would you like the recipient of this letter to keep in mind as a new parent?

FOR ANY WINTER HOLIDAY CELEBRATION

• How did you spend your most memorable holiday? Where were you? Who were you with?

• What are your family traditions? What were the holidays like when you were a child? Who do you associate with the holidays who is now gone but who you would like the person who gets this letter to know about?

• Do you have a favorite holiday song, story, or play?

• What does the holiday season mean to you? What would you like the recipient of this letter to remember about these gatherings right now or in the future?

• What was the best holiday gift you have ever received? Who gave it to you and why did it mean so much? What was the best holiday gift you have ever given?

• Do you go to any religious services during the holidays? Where?

• How do you decorate your home?

• Have you ever been away from loved ones during the holiday season? What was the cause? Where were you? How did it feel?

• What was the coldest winter you can ever remember? Or the warmest? What did you do? Where were you?

• What do you and your family usually eat during the holidays? Do you cook? What is your favorite dish?

FOR ANY VALENTINE'S DAY

• How did you spend your most memorable Valentine's Day? Who were you with?

- What does Valentine's Day mean to you?

- Do you have any Valentine's Day traditions?

- What is your idea of a "perfect" Valentine's Day?

- How do you make the one you love feel special?

- Is romance an important part of your life?

- What is the most romantic thing someone could do for you on Valentine's Day?

- Do you remember your first Valentine? Who was it? What did this person do to make you feel special?

- Was Valentine's Day a special day in your family when you were a child? What did you do?

- How would you define the word *love* to someone?

FOR A WEDDING ANNIVERSARY

- If you are married, how do you spend your wedding anniversaries? Do you have any traditions?

- Do you always remember your anniversary? Does your spouse? Have either of you ever forgotten?

• How many years have you been married? How did you celebrate your first anniversary?

• How has your love grown or changed over the years? Are you closer now or when you were first married?

• Do you enjoy spending time together? What hobbies, interests, and activities do you have in common?

• What is the best advice you could give the person who gets this letter to learn and understand about marriage as the years go by?

• What do you love, appreciate, and respect most about your spouse?

• Looking back over your family history, did couples stay married for life or were there many divorces? What do you do to make your marriage work?

• Who else have you known with a loving and inspirational marriage? Why? What seems to make it work?

• When you remember marrying your spouse, what was the reason you chose this particular person? Do you still love the same things about your spouse that you did in the beginning? Why?

FOR A LOVED ONE AFTER YOUR DEATH

• Who have you loved deeply in your life?

• What are your spiritual beliefs? How do they affect your thoughts about death?

• What do you look forward to or fear about death?

• From your own perspective, has your life been a success?

• Have you ever left anything unsaid that you now regret? What would you like to say to the recipient of this letter that you've never been able to say before?

• What have you cherished most in life?

• What has been the greatest lesson you have ever learned?

• What motto or philosophy has helped get you through life's challenges?

• What was your happiest, saddest, or most special memory?

• How do you want to be remembered?

• How did this person first come into your life?

• What qualities, talents, or gifts does this person have that you admire most?

• Why is this person special to you?

• What specific thing did this person say or do that changed your life? Did it happen over time or in one sudden epiphany?

• What have you learned from your experience with this person?

• How have you applied what he or she taught you to your life?

• Have you, in turn, been able to pass this wisdom on to others?

• How are you different because of the effect this person had on your life? How often do you reflect on what this person taught you?

• Is there anything specific that always reminds you of your teacher or mentor?

• What would you like the world to know about this person? What would you like this person to know about how much he or she has meant to you?

FOR SOMEONE YOU WANT TO THANK

• Why are you grateful to this person?

• What did this gesture mean to you? How did you feel when you received it?

• How has your life changed because of this person?

• How different might your life be if not for this person and the impact they had on you?

• Have you gone on to help others as a result of this person's generosity? What have you done? Who have you helped?

• How would you describe this person to others?

• When did you first meet this person? What was your first impression of him or her?

• What qualities make this person stand out?

• What are your thoughts about giving?

• How will this person's gift affect your life in the future? How did it affect the future of others?

For healing broken relationships

• What are some special qualities you admire about this person? What do you miss about your relationship? Can you remember any good times?

• How has your life been different without this person? How have you changed? How would your relationship be different today?

• Why did you choose this point in time to write this letter?

• Are you ready to make amends and begin healing?

• Would you like this person to be a part of your life again? Why? If not, what would you desire the outcome to be?

• If you could say only one thing, one sentence, to this person, what would you say?

• If you could go back in time and change the situation, what would you do differently?

• Can you take responsibility for any mistakes you may have made? If appropriate, can you apologize and ask for forgiveness? Can you forgive yourself?

• Have you forgiven past mistakes this person may have made that hurt you? Are you willing to let go of the past and begin anew?

• With peace and love as your goals, what do you want to say?

For a dear friend

• When did you first become friends? How did your friendship grow?

• Why is this person your friend? When did your relationship turn the corner from acquaintances to friends and then to close friends?

• What qualities does he or she have that are special for you?

• What was the best advice your friend has ever given you? Did you take it to heart? Did you benefit from it?

• How has your friend changed your life? How would your life be different if that person wasn't there?

• What challenges has your friendship withstood? Have you ever had a falling out and patched things up again?

• Does this friend know things about you that no one else does? What? Is there any secret you have never shared with this friend that you would like to? Can you share it now? Why haven't you mentioned it before?

• When have you been the most appreciative of this person's friendship?

• Was there a time when this friend supported you that you have never forgotten?

• What do you value most about your friendship? Is there anything you would change if you could? How do you anticipate your friendship to be in the future? What are you looking forward to?

• What is your fondest memory of this friend?

• What were your dreams and goals at this time in your own life? What did you most look forward to?

• Were you confident? Optimistic? Pessimistic?

• Were you close to your parents and family? How has your relationship with them changed since then?

• Who were your best friends?

• Where did you live? Did you enjoy this place?

• What was the best part of life during your twenties? What was the most difficult? What would you encourage the person who receives this letter to think about as he or she enters adulthood?

• What were your spiritual beliefs? Have they changed? Did you go to church or temple?

• Did you have any special talents or "gifts"? What were they?

• What kind of music did you listen to? Who were your favorite artists? Did you dance? Did you play any musical instruments? Which ones?

• What did you do for fun on the weekends? Did you exercise or participate in any other activities or groups? What were they?

• What was the most exhilarating or vivid moment of your thirties?

• How would you have described yourself then? If you are old enough to look back at this age, what would you now say about yourself at thirty?

• What are your best qualities? What about the not-so-great ones?

• What style of clothing do you wear? Do you consider yourself to be fashionable?

• What are your three favorite foods? What items do you always have in your refrigerator?

• Do you enjoy sports and exercise? Which ones do you participate in regularly?

• How have you changed as a person since you were young? How has the world changed?

• Who or what do you appreciate most in life? What would you encourage the person who will receive this letter to savor most in his or her life at this age?

• What are your plans for the next decade? What excites you most in your life?

• What is the best advice you have ever received?

FOR A FORTIETH BIRTHDAY

• How did you feel about hitting the big four-oh? How did you feel physically? Emotionally? If you haven't turned forty yet, what do you expect life to be like at this time?

• If you are there already, what surprised you about being in your forties?

• Is a sense of community important to you? Politics? What do you believe about giving back and charity in general?

• Are you in a career that you enjoy? What is your philosophy about work?

• What is your philosophy about money? How do you feel about your own financial situation?

• Who are the most special people in your life? Why?

• What goals and dreams have you accomplished in your life? What have been your biggest disappointments?

• What have you come to feel is the most important thing in life? How can the person to whom you are writing this letter learn from your knowledge and experience?

• What has changed the most in your life or in society over the past decade?

• What are you looking forward to doing with the rest of your life?

FOR A FIFTIETH BIRTHDAY

• Did turning fifty feel like a special milestone to you? What did it mean?

• What is the greatest success of your life so far? What is the greatest failure? What obstacles have you overcome in your lifetime?

• What was the best vacation you ever took? Who was with you? Where do you still want to go?

• Who are the most important people in your life? Who do you call when you need support?

• What was the funniest moment you can remember in your life? What happened? Who were you with? Do you have a favorite joke?

• What regret do you have that could have been avoided? What advice can you give your letter's recipient about living life in the most rewarding and satisfying way possible?

• What is the greatest book you have ever read? Who is your favorite author? Do you have a favorite song or movie?

• What was your most embarrassing moment?

• What is your favorite season of the year? Why?

• If you hadn't chosen the career or path in life you did, what career would you have wanted to choose?

AS TIME GOES ON—

FOR ANY TIME AFTER AGE FIFTY

• What possessions and personal belongings are important to you now? What no longer seems important that once did?

• What is the best idea you have ever had?

• What does "security" mean to you?

• What were the biggest fears in your life? What are your fears now? What would you advise the recipient of this letter to not worry about?

• Do you remember yourself as a child? What are some of your first memories? Do you still have any of those "childlike" qualities? What are they?

• In retrospect, what was the happiest time of your life? What was the saddest?

• What is the most challenging thing you have ever had to do?

• What was the last unexpected or spontaneous thing you have done? Would you do it again?

• What are the most significant changes you have seen in your lifetime? In society? In technology? In our environment? In you?

• What have you been most passionate about in your life? What are you passionate about today? What are you looking forward to in the future?

• Is there any "secret" you have never shared but wanted to? Can you do it now?

SOME THOUGHTS TO PONDER FOR A VARIETY OF OCCASIONS

• Who would you choose to be if you could be any person in the history of the world?

• Who would you describe as the most influential person in history?

• What do you think is the most powerful emotion a human being can express?

• Using your own definition of the term, who is the most "beautiful" person you know?

• Who would you like to be with you when you die? What do you want to say?

• What is the closest thing to a miracle you have ever experienced or witnessed?

• What is your idea of a perfect day? What about a perfect life?

• If you could do one thing to change the world for the better, what would you do?

• Who has been the greatest role model in your life?

• What does "God" mean to you? What makes a "spiritual" person?

• If you could pray for only one thing in life, what would it be?

Acknowledgments

With boundless gratitude we thank those who have walked along the path with us to make this dream come true.

First and foremost, to God, our creator and the one true author of our lives.

To our parents and our families, for your constant and loving support and guidance over the years. We love you and we thank you.

To our children, for your sweet smiles. You make it all worthwhile.

To Cindy Black, Richard Cohn, and the entire staff at Beyond Words Publishing, for seeing the heart and soul of this project and indeed inspiring us to integrity. We could not have asked for a more collaborative, resourceful, and creative team. Thank you all.

A special thanks to Jenefer Angell, our editor. You are a kind, insightful, and uncompromising word wizard.

To everyone at the Maui Writers Conference and Retreat, for creating opportunities and friendships.

To Scott Stillinger, the "real" Koosh Ball inventor, and everyone at OddzOn. You are an exceptional group of talented people.

To Ronnie's family, for wonderful and precious memories.

To Holly Perreira and Pania Robinson, for going the extra mile to keep order in our lives and food in our refrigerator.

To our cheerleaders—our many friends and mentors who have helped us through challenging times and encouraged us to share this story. That list is long and wide. It includes John Barbour, Mauna Berkov, Elizabeth Boorstein, Paul and Karen Burrous, Dave and Cathy Capper, Peter Carter, Reggie Casadei, Shelton and Nalani Choy, Diane Cirincione, Terry Codington, Kawika Dowsett, Bill and Denise Duke, Debrah Farentino, Kathryn Friedman, Barry and Mary Golombik, Jan Hansen-Zakin, Bro. Al Henson, Jerry Jampolsky, D'Arcy Kerrigan, Jeff and Cindy Lee, Rich Marik, Ken and Kendra Martyn, Tom Mitchell, Jamie O'Rourke, Everett and Della Peacock, David and Twila Richvalsky, George and Courtney Tidmarsh, and so many others.

To the many people who have enriched our lives and shown us that love knows no limitations and recognizes no obstacles.

If you would like to contact the authors, you can e-mail them at *theletterbox@hawaii.rr.com*. Or write them at

The Letter Box
P.O. Box 150497
San Rafael, CA 94915-0497

OTHER BOOKS FROM
BEYOND WORDS PUBLISHING, INC.

The Art of Thank You
Crafting Notes of Gratitude
Author: Connie Leas
$14.95, hardcover

Part inspirational, part how-to, *The Art of Thank You* will rekindle the gratitude in all of us and inspire readers to pick up a pen and take the time to show thanks. It stresses the healing power that comes from both giving and receiving thanks and provides practical, concrete, and inspirational examples of when to write a thank-you note and what that note should include. With its appealing and approachable style, charming examples, and real-life anecdotes, *The Art of Thank You* has the power to galvanize readers' resolve to start writing their all-important thank-you notes.

Hindsights
The Wisdom and Breakthroughs of Remarkable People
Author: Guy Kawasaki
$22.95, hardcover

What have you learned from your life that you would like to share with the next generation? Get a fresh appreciation of the human experience in this inspirational collection of interviews with thirty-three people who have overcome unique challenges. They are candid about their failures and disappointments, and insightful about turning adversity into opportunity. Guy Kawasaki spent over two years researching and interviewing such people as Apple Computer co-founder Steve Wozniak, management guru Tom Peters, and entrepreneur Mary Kay. But not everyone in the book is a celebrity. They share their revelations and life experiences, motivating the reader for both personal and professional growth.

Create Your Own Love Story
The Art of Lasting Relationships
Author: David W. McMillan, Ph.D.
Foreword: John Gray, Ph.D.
$21.95, hardcover; $14.95, softcover

Create Your Own Love Story breaks new ground in the crowded and popular field of relationship self-help guides. *Create Your Own Love Story* is based on a four-part model—Spirit, Trust, Trade, and Art—derived from McMillan's twenty years' work in community theory and clinical psychology. Each of these four elements is divided into short, highly readable chapters that include both touching and hilarious examples from real marriages, brief exercises based on visualization and journal writing that are effective whether used by one or both partners, and dialogues readers can have with themselves and/or their partners. This book shows readers how they can use their own energy and initiative, with McMillan's help, to make their marriage stronger, more enduring, and more soul-satisfying.

Nurture Your Child's Gift
Inspired Parenting
Author: Caron Goode, Ed.D.
$14.95, softcover

Nurture Your Child's Gift helps parents create space and support for their children to recognize their personal vision and make their unique contribution in life. This book answers parents' questions, such as "How can I help my children find a direction for their lives? How can I motivate them? How can I help them be happy?" Goode explains the three building blocks for children to successfully achieve their life vision—esteem, empowerment, and expression—and shows parents how to help bring these forth.

Raising Children Who Think for Themselves
Author: Elisa Medhus, M.D.
$14.95, softcover

Raising Children Who Think for Themselves offers a new approach to parenting that has the power to reverse the trend of external direction in children—that tendency to make decisions based on outside influences—and to help parents bring up empathetic, self-confident, moral, independent thinkers. Filled with real-life examples, humorous anecdotes, and countless interviews with parents, children, and teachers, this book identifies the five essential qualities of self-directed children, outlines the seven strategies necessary for parents to develop these qualities in their children, and offers solutions to nearly one hundred child-raising challenges.

To order or to request a catalog, contact
Beyond Words Publishing, Inc.
20827 N.W. Cornell Road, Suite 500
Hillsboro, OR 97124-9808
503-531-8700

You can also visit our Web site at *www.beyondword.com* or e-mail us at *info@beyondword.com*.

Beyond Words Publishing, Inc.

OUR CORPORATE MISSION

Inspire to Integrity

OUR DECLARED VALUES

We give to all of life as life has given us.
We honor all relationships.
Trust and stewardship are integral to fulfilling dreams.
Collaboration is essential to create miracles.
Creativity and aesthetics nourish the soul.
Unlimited thinking is fundamental.
Living your passion is vital.
Joy and humor open our hearts to growth.
It is important to remind ourselves of love.

BIG SUR

Written some time after Kerouac's best-known works, *Big Sur* follows his comedown from a carefree youth and unwanted fame. After staying for several weeks in a cabin in the northern California town of Big Sur, Kerouac undertook a mature confrontation with some of his most troubling emotional issues, including struggles with alcoholism, addiction, and insecurity. In prose that reaches sublime heights, he records his changing states of consciousness and powerful moments of epiphany. Praised by the *New York Times* as "his grittiest book," *Big Sur* is a masterpiece of wrenching personal expression, a challenging and poignant book by one of America's most beloved and influential authors.

"A humane, precise account of the extraordinary ravages of alcohol delirium tremens on Kerouac, a superior novelist who had strength to complete his poetic narrative. . . . With prose set in the middle of his mind, he reveals consciousness in all its syntactic elaboration, detailing the luminous emptiness of his own paranoiac confusion. Such rich writing is nonpareil in later half XX century."
—*Allen Ginsberg*

JACK KEROUAC was born in Lowell, Massachusetts, in 1922, the youngest of three children in a Franco-American family. He attended local Catholic and public schools and won a football scholarship to Columbia University in New York City, where he first met Neal Cassady, Allen Ginsberg, and William S. Burroughs. He quit school in his sophomore year after a dispute with his football coach and joined the Merchant Marine, beginning the restless wanderings that were to continue for the greater part of his life. His first novel, *The Town and the City*, appeared in 1950, but it was *On the Road*, published in 1957 and memorializing his adventures with Neal Cassady, that epitomized to the world what became known as the "Beat generation" and made Kerouac one of the most controversial writers of his time. Publication of many other books followed, among them *The Dharma Bums*, *The Subterraneans*, and *Big Sur*. Kerouac considered all of his fiction to be a part of *The Duluoz Legend*. "In my old age," he wrote, "I intend to collect all my work and reinsert my pantheon of uniform names, leave the long shelf full of books there, and die happy." He died in St. Petersburg, Florida, in 1969, at the age of forty-seven.

ROB ADMIRAAL was born in Holland in 1960. He has worked as an illustrator, typographer, and portraitist. He began tattooing in 1993, and currently runs Admiraal Tattoo Studio in Amsterdam.

JACK KEROUAC

BIG SUR

PENGUIN BOOKS

PENGUIN BOOKS
Published by the Penguin Group
Penguin Group (USA) Inc., 375 Hudson Street, New York, New York 10014, U.S.A.
Penguin Group (Canada), 90 Eglinton Avenue East, Suite 700,
Toronto, Ontario, Canada M4P 2Y3 (a division of Pearson Penguin Canada Inc.)
Penguin Books Ltd, 80 Strand, London WC2R 0RL, England
Penguin Ireland, 25 St Stephen's Green, Dublin 2, Ireland
(a division of Penguin Books Ltd)
Penguin Group (Australia), 250 Camberwell Road,
Camberwell, Victoria 3124, Australia (a division of Pearson Australia Group Pty Ltd)
Penguin Books India Pvt Ltd, 11 Community Centre, Panchsheel Park,
New Delhi – 110 017, India
Penguin Group (NZ), 67 Apollo Drive, Rosedale,
North Shore 0632, New Zealand (a division of Pearson New Zealand Ltd)
Penguin Books (South Africa) (Pty) Ltd, 24 Sturdee Avenue, Rosebank,
Johannesburg 2196, South Africa

Penguin Books Ltd, Registered Offices:
80 Strand, London WC2R 0RL, England

First published in the United States of America by Farrar Straus & Giroux 1962
Published in Penguin Books 1992
This edition published in Penguin Books 2011

9   10   8

PUBLISHER'S NOTE
This is a work of fiction. Names, characters, places, and incidents are either the product of
the author's imagination or are used fictitiously, and any resemblance to actual persons,
living or dead, business establishments, events, or locales is entirely coincidental.

THE LIBRARY OF CONGRESS HAS CATALOGED THE HARDCOVER EDITION AS FOLLOWS:
Kerouac, Jack, 1922–1969.
Big Sur.
I. Title.
PS3521.E735B5 1981
813'.54   81–8279
ISBN 978-0-14-016812-9 (pbk.)
ISBN 978-0-14-311923-4 (Penguin Ink pbk.)

Printed in the United States of America

My work comprises one vast book like Proust's except that my remembrances are written on the run instead of afterwards in a sick bed. Because of the objections of my early publishers I was not allowed to use the same personae names in each work. On the Road, The Subterraneans, The Dharma Bums, Doctor Sax, Maggie Cassidy, Tristessa, Desolation Angels, Visions of Cody *and the others including this book* Big Sur *are just chapters in the whole work which I call* The Duluoz Legend. *In my old age I intend to collect all my work and re-insert my pantheon of uniform names, leave the long shelf full of books there, and die happy. The whole thing forms one enormous comedy, seen through the eyes of poor Ti Jean (me), otherwise known as Jack Duluoz, the world of raging action and folly and also of gentle sweetness seen through the keyhole of his eye.*

JACK KEROUAC

Foreword

Jack Kerouac was the handsome high school football star of Lowell, Massachusetts, who scored a winning touchdown and caught the attention of Lou Little, Columbia's famous football coach, who offered him a college scholarship.

Kerouac came from a working-class French Canadian family—his father was a printer—and the trip from Lowell to Morningside Heights was epochal. Suddenly the all-American boy, who quickly had fallen out of favor with Little, was sitting in the West End Bar opposite fellow Columbian Allen Ginsberg, not long out of New Jersey, and the two, joined by William Burroughs, a little older and out of St. Louis via Harvard, posed in the same photograph—"acting," as Ginsberg put it, "as if we were International Debauchés as in Gide."

Enter Neal Cassady, the legendary driver, Ginsberg's fabled "cocksman and Adonis of Denver," who blew into New York with his girlfriend Luanne and a fired-up determination to learn all about writing from Allen, Jack, and Bill, in return for which he'd tell them all about his life in the West, and the Beat Generation was ready to roll. In fact, Kerouac wrote *On the Road* about the first years after Neal showed up, but it took seven more years to get it published, and those were the years that saw the writer, with a thickening knapsack of manuscripts, as the true literary nomad of his day. Then, when *On the Road* came out in 1957 and made him famous, the knapsack was unloaded and all the books published helter-skelter.

Tristessa, maybe Kerouac's sly homage to *Bonjour Tristesse* (which had made Françoise Sagan a star overnight in 1955), is about his love affair with a Mexico City prostitute, and came out as an Avon paperback original. *Visions of Cody* is a second take on the hero of *On the Road*, this time incorporating tape-recorded conversations between Jack and Neal (a decade or more in advance of the technique à la Warhol and "oral biography").

In *Big Sur* we have the plaintive but magnificent aftermath: the "King of the Beatniks" going across the country in a Pullman sleeper for one more round with the boys and girls before retirement to his study, bottle, and typewriter, and then, in 1969, of a massive abdominal hemorrhage brought on by drink, death. He was forty-seven.

Jack Kerouac was the American hero in looks and deeds who dared to have a series of long, tender nervous breakdowns in the prose of his dozen or so books. His work at its best brought something of the luminous pleasures of the French Impressionists into American writing, and something too of the brooding syntactic circuitry of Proust. Above all, he was a tender writer. It would be hard to find a mean-spirited word about anybody in all his writing.

ARAM SAROYAN

BIG SUR

1

The church is blowing a sad windblown "Kathleen" on the bells in the skid row slums as I wake up all woebegone and goopy, groaning from another drinking bout and groaning most of all because I'd ruined my "secret return" to San Francisco by getting silly drunk while hiding in the alleys with bums and then marching forth into North Beach to see everybody altho Lorenz Monsanto and I'd exchanged huge letters outlining how I would sneak in quietly, call him on the phone using a code name like Adam Yulch or Lalagy Pulvertaft (also writers) and then he would secretly drive me to his cabin in the Big Sur woods where I would be alone and undisturbed for six weeks just chopping wood, drawing water, writing, sleeping, hiking, etc. etc.——But instead I've bounced drunk into his City Lights bookshop at the height of Saturday night business, everyone recognized me (even tho I was wearing my disguise-like fisherman's hat and fishermen coat and pants waterproof) and 't'all ends up a roaring drunk in all the famous bars the bloody "King of the Beatniks" is back in town buying drinks for everyone—— Two days of that, including Sunday the day Lorenzo is supposed to pick me up at my "secret" skid row hotel (the Mars on 4th and Howard) but when he calls for me there's no answer, he has the clerk open the door and what does he see but me out on the floor among bottles, Ben Fagan stretched out partly beneath the bed, and Robert Browning the beatnik painter out on the bed, snoring——So says to himself "I'll pick him up next weekend,

I guess he wants to drink for a week in the city (like he always does, I guess)" so off he drives to his Big Sur cabin without me thinking he's doing the right thing but my God when I wake up, and Ben and Browning are gone, they've somehow dumped me on the bed, and I hear "I'll Take You Home Again Kathleen" being bellroped so sad in the fog winds out there that blow across the rooftops of eerie old hangover Frisco, wow, I've hit the end of the trail and cant even drag my body any more even to a refuge in the woods let alone stay upright in the city a minute——It's the first trip I've taken away from home (my mother's house) since the publication of "Road" the book that "made me famous" and in fact so much so I've been driven mad for three years by endless telegrams, phonecalls, requests, mail, visitors, report- ers, snoopers (a big voice saying in my basement window as I prepare to write a story:—ARE YOU BUSY?) or the time the reporter ran upstairs to my bedroom as I sat there in my pajamas trying to write down a dream——Teenagers jumping the six-foot fence I'd had built around my yard for privacy—— Parties with bottles yelling at my study window "Come on out and get drunk, all work and no play makes Jack a dull boy!"——A woman coming to my door and saying "I'm not going to ask you if you're Jack Duluoz because I know he wears a beard, can you tell me where I can find him, I want a real beatnik at my annual Shindig party"——Drunken visitors puking in my study, stealing books and even pencils——Uninvited acquaintances staying for days because of the clean beds and good food my mother provided——Me drunk practically all the time to put on a jovial cap to keep up with all this but finally realizing I was surrounded and outnumbered and had to get away to solitude again or die——So Lorenzo Monsanto wrote and said "Come to my cabin, no one'll know," etc. so I had sneaked into San Francisco as I say, coming 3000 miles from my home in Long Island (Northport) in a pleasant roomette on the California Zephyr train watching America roll by outside my private picture window, really happy for the first time in three years, staying in the roomette all three days and three nights with my instant coffee and sandwiches——Up the Hudson Valley and over across New York State to Chicago and then the Plains, the mountains, the desert, the final mountains of California, all so easy and dreamlike compared to my old harsh hitch hikings before I made enough money to take transcontinental trains (all over America highschool and college kids thinking "Jack Duluoz is 26 years old and on the road all the time hitch hiking" while there I am almost 40 years old, bored and jaded in a roomette bunk crashin across that Salt Flat)——But in any case a wonderful start towards my retreat so generously offered by sweet old Monsanto and instead of going thru smooth and easy I wake up drunk, sick, disgusted, frightened, in fact terrified by that sad song across the roofs mingling with the lachrymose cries of a Salvation Army meeting on the corner below "*Satan* is the cause of your alcoholism, *Satan* is the cause of your immorality, Satan is *everywhere* workin to destroy you unless you repent *now*" and worse than that the sound of old drunks throwing up in rooms next to mine, the creak of hall steps, the moans everywhere——Including the moan that had awakened me, my own moan in the lumpy bed, a moan caused by a big roaring Whoo Whoo in my head that had shot me out of my pillow like a ghost.

2

And I look around the dismal cell, there's my hopeful rucksack all neatly packed with everything necessary to live in the woods, even unto the minutest first aid kit and diet details and even a neat little sewing kit cleverly reinforced by my good mother (like extra safety pins, buttons, special sewing needles, little aluminum scissors)——The hopeful medal of St. Christopher even which she'd sewn on the flap——The survival kit all in there down to the last little survival sweater and handkerchief and tennis sneakers (for hiking)——But the rucksack sits hopefully in a strewn mess of bottles all empty, empty poorboys of white port, butts, junk, horror. . . . . "One fast move or I'm gone," I realize, gone the way of the last three years of drunken hopelessness which is a physical and spiritual and metaphysical hopelessness you cant learn in school no matter how many books on existentialism or pessimism you read, or how many jugs of vision-producing Ayahuasca you drink, or Mescaline take, or Peyote goop up with——That feeling when you wake up with the delirium tremens with the *fear* of eerie death dripping from your ears like those special heavy cobwebs spiders weave in the hot countries, the feeling of being a bentback mudman monster groaning underground in hot steaming mud pulling a long hot burden nowhere, the feeling of standing ankledeep in hot boiled pork blood, ugh, of being up to your waist in a giant pan of greasy brown dishwater not a trace of suds left in it——The face of yourself you see in the mirror with its expression of unbearable anguish so hagged and awful with sorrow you cant even cry for a thing so ugly, so lost, no connection whatever with early perfection and therefore nothing to connect with tears or anything: it's like William Seward Burroughs' "Stranger" suddenly appearing in your place in the mirror——Enough! "One fast move or I'm gone" so I jump up, do my headstand first to pump blood back into the hairy brain, take a shower in the hall, new T-shirt and socks and underwear, pack vigorously, hoist the rucksack and run out throwing the key on the desk and hit the cold street and walk fast to the nearest little grocery store to buy two days of food, stick it in the rucksack, hike thru lost alleys of Russian sorrow where bums sit head on knees in foggy doorways in the goopy eerie city night I've got to escape or die, and into the bus station——In a half hour into a bus seat, the bus says "Monterey" and off we go down the clean neon hiway and I sleep all the way, waking up amazed and well again smelling sea air the bus driver shaking me "End of the line, Monterey."—— And by God it *is* Monterey, I stand sleepy in the 2 A.M. seeing vague little fishing masts across the street from the bus driveway. Now all I've got to do to complete my escape is get 14 miles down the coast to the Raton Canyon bridge and hike in.

3

"One fast move or I'm gone" so I blow $8 on a cab to drive me down that coast, it's a foggy night tho sometimes you can see stars in the sky to the right where the sea is, tho you cant see the sea you can only hear about it from the cabdriver——"What kinda country is it around here? I've never seen it."

"Well, you cant see it tonight—Raton Canyon you say, you better be careful walkin around there in the dark."

"Why?"

"Well, just use your lamp like you say——"

And sure enough when he lets me off at the Raton Canyon bridge and counts the money I sense something wrong somehow, there's an awful roar of surf but it isnt coming from the right place, like you'd expect it to come from "over there" but it's coming from "under there"——I can see the bridge but I can see nothing below it——The bridge continues the coast highway from one bluff to another, it's a nice white bridge with white rails and there's a white line runnin down the middle familiar and highwaylike but something's wrong——Besides the headlights of the cab just shoot out over a few bushes into empty space in the direction where the canyon's supposed to be, it feels like being up in the air somewhere tho I can see the dirt road at our feet and the dirt overhang on the side——"What in the hell is this?"——I've got the directions all memorized from a little map Monsanto's mailed me but in my imagination dreaming about this big retreat back home there'd been something larkish, bucolic, all homely woods and gladness instead of all this aerial roaring mystery in the dark——When the cab leaves I therefore turn on my railroad lantern for a timid peek but its beam gets lost just like the car lights in a void and in fact the battery is fairly weak and I can hardly see the bluff at my left——As for the bridge I cant see it anymore except for graduating series of luminous shoulder buttons going off further into the low sea roar——The sea roar is bad enough except it keeps bashing and barking at me like a dog in the fog down there, sometimes it booms the earth but my God where is the earth and how can the sea be underground!——"The only thing to do," I gulp, "is to put this lantern shinin right in front of your feet, *kid*do, and follow that lantern and make sure it's shinin on the road rut and hope and pray it's shinin on ground that's gonna be there when it's shining," in other words I actually fear that even my lamp will carry me astray if I dare to raise it for a minute from the ruts in the dirt road——The only satisfaction I can glean from this roaring high horror of darkness is that the lamp wobbles huge dark shadows of its little rim stays on the overhanging bluff at the left of the road, because to the right (where the bushes are wiggling in the wind from the sea) there aint no shadows because there aint no light can take hold——So I start my trudge, pack aback, just head down following my lamp spot, head down but eyes suspiciously peering a little up, like a man in the presence of a dangerous idiot he doesnt want to annoy—— The dirt road starts up a little, curves to the right, starts down a little, then suddenly up again, and up——By now the sea roar is further back and at one point I even stop and look back to see nothing——"I'm gonna put out my light and see what I can see" I say rooted to my feet where they're rooted to that road——Fat lotta good, when I put out the light I see nothing but the dim sand at my feet.

Trudging up and getting further away from the sea roar I get to feel more confident but suddenly I come to a frightening thing in the road, I stop and hold out my hand, edge forward, it's only a cattle crossing (iron bars imbedded across the road) but at the same time a big blast of wind comes from the left where the bluff should be and I spot that way and see nothing. "What the hell's going on!" "Follow the road," says the other voice trying to be calm so I do but the next instant I hear a rattling to my right, throw my light there, see nothing but bushes wiggling dry and mean and just the proper high canyonwall kind of bushes fit for rattlesnakes too——(which it was, a rattlesnake doesnt like to be awakened in the middle of the night by a trudging hump-backed monster with a lamp.)

But now the road's going down again, the reassuring bluff reappears on my left, and pretty soon according to my memory of Lorry's map there she is, the creek, I can hear her lappling and gabbing down there at the bottom of the dark where at least I'll be on level ground and done with booming airs somewhere above——But the closer I get to the creek as the road dips steeply, suddenly, almost making me trot forward, the louder it roars, I begin to think I'll fall right into it before I can notice it——It's screaming like a raging flooded river right below me——Besides it's even *darker* down there than anywhere! There are glades down there, ferns of horror and slippery logs, mosses, dangerous plashings, humid mists rise coldly like the breath of death, big dangerous trees are beginning to bend over my head and brush my pack——There's a noise I know can only grow louder as I sink down and for fear how loud it can grow I stop and listen, it rises up crashing mysteriously at me from a raging battle among dark things, wood or rock or something cracked, all smashed, all wet black sunken earth danger—— I'm *afraid* to go down there——I am *affrayed* in the old Edmund Spenser sense of being *frayed* by a whip, and a wet one at that——A slimy green dragon racket in the bush——An angry war that doesnt want me pokin around——It's been there a million years and it doesnt want me clashing darkness with it——It comes snarling from a thousand crevasses and monster redwood roots all over the map of creation——It is a dark

clangoror in the rain forest and doesnt want no skid row bum to
carry to the sea which is bad enough and waitin back there———I
can almost feel the sea pulling at that racket in the trees but
there's my spotlamp so all I gotta do is follow the lovely sand
road which dips and dips in rising carnage and suddenly a flat-
tening, a sight of bridge logs, there's the bridge rail, there's the
creek just four feet below, cross the bridge you woken bum and
see what's on the other shore.

Take one quick peek at the water as you cross, just water over
rocks, a small creek at that.

And now before me is a dreamy meadowland with a good old
corral gate and a barbed wire fence the road running right on left
but this where I get off at last. Then I crawl thru the barbed wire
and find myself trudging a sweet little sand road winding right
thru fragrant dry heathers as tho I'd just popped thru from hell
into familiar old Heaven on Earth, yair and Thank God (tho a
minute later my heart's in my mouth again because I see black
things in the white sand ahead but it's only piles of good old
mule dung in Heaven).

4

And in the morning (after sleeping by the creek in the white sand) I do see what was so scary about my canyon road walk——The road's up there on the wall a thousand feet with a sheer drop sometimes, especially at the cattle crossing, way up highest, where a break in the bluff shows fog pouring through from another bend of the sea beyond, scary enough in itself anyway as tho one hole wasnt enough to open into the sea—— And worst of all is the bridge! I go ambling seaward along the path by the creek and see this awful thin white line of bridge a thousand unbridgeable sighs of height above the little woods I'm walking in, you just cant believe it, and to make things heart-thumpingly horrible you come to a little bend in what is now just a trail and there's the booming surf coming at you whitecapped crashing down on sand as tho it was higher than where you stand, like a sudden tidal wave world enough to make you step back or run back to the hills——And not only that, the blue sea behind the crashing high waves is full of huge black rocks rising like old ogresome castles dripping wet slime, a billion years of woe right there, the moogrus big clunk of it right there with its slaverous lips of foam at the base——So that you emerge from pleasant little wood paths with a stem of grass in your teeth and drop it to see doom——And you look up at that unbelievably high bridge and feel death and for a good reason: because underneath the bridge, in the sand right beside the sea cliff, *hump*, your heart sinks to see it: the automobile that crashed thru the bridge rail a decade ago and fell 1000 feet straight down and landed upsidedown, is still there now, an upsidedown chassis of rust in a strewn skitter of sea-eaten tires, old spokes, old car seats sprung with straw, one sad fuel pump and no more people——

Big elbows of Rock rising everywhere, sea caves within them, seas plollocking all around inside them crashing out foams, the boom and pound on the sand, the sand dipping quick (no Malibu Beach here)——Yet you turn and see the pleasant woods winding upcreek like a picture in Vermont——But you look up into the sky, bend way back, my God you're standing directly under that aerial bridge with its thin white line running from rock to rock and witless cars racing across it like dreams! From rock to rock! All the way down the raging coast! So that when later I heard people say "Oh Big Sur must be beautiful!" I gulp to wonder why it has the reputation of being beautiful above and beyond its *fearfulness*, its Blakean groaning rough-rock Creation throes, those vistas when you drive the coast highway on a sunny day opening up the eye for miles of horrible washing sawing.

5

It was even frightening at the other peaceful end of Raton Canyon, the east end, where Alf the pet mule of local settlers slept at night such sleepfull sleeps under a few weird trees and then got up in the morning to graze in the grass then negotiated the whole distance slowly to the sea shore where you saw him standing by the waves like an ancient sacred myth character motionless in the sand——Alf the Sacred Burro I later called him——The thing that was frightening was the mountain that rose up at the east end, a strange Burmese like mountain with levels and moody terraces and a strange ricepaddy hat on top that I kept staring at with a sinking heart even at first when I was healthy and feeling good (and I would be going mad in this canyon in six weeks on the fullmoon night of September 3rd)——The mountain reminded me of my recent recurrent nightmares in New York about the "Mountain of Mien Mo" with the swarms of moony flying horses lyrically sweeping capes over their shoulders as they circled the peak a "thousand miles high" (in the dream it said) and on top of the mountain in one haunted nightmare I'd seen the giant empty stone benches so silent in the topworld moonlight as tho once inhabited by Gods or giants of some kind but long ago vacated so that they were all dusty and cobwebby now and the evil lurked somewhere inside the pyramid nearby where there was a monster with a big thumping heart but also, even more sinister, just ordinary seedy but muddy janitors cooking over small woodfires——Narrow

dusty holes through which I'd tried to crawl with a bunch of
tomato plants tied around my neck——Dreams——Drinking
nightmares——A recurrent series of them all swirling around
that mountain, seen the very first time as a beautiful but
somehow horribly green verdant mist enshrouded jungle peak
rising out of green tropical country in "Mexico" so called but
beyond which were pyramids, dry rivers, other countries full of
infantry enemy and yet the biggest danger being just hoodlums
out throwing rocks on Sundays——So that the sight of that
simple sad mountain, together with the bridge and that car that
had flipped over twice or so and landed flump in the sand with
no more sign of human elbows or shred neckties (like a terrify-
ing poem about America you could write), agh, HOO HOO
of Owls living in old evil hollow trees in that misty tangled
further part of the canyon where I was always afraid to go
anyhow——That unclimbably tangled steep cliff at the base of
Mien Mo rising to gawky dead trees among bushes so dense and
up to heathers God knows how deep with hidden caves no one
not even I spose the Indians of the 10th Century had ever
explored——And those big gooky rainforest ferns among light-
ningstruck conifers right beside sudden black vine cliff faces
rising right at your side as you walk the peaceful path——And
as I say that ocean coming at you higher than you are like the
harbors of old woodcuts always higher than the towns (as
Rimbaud pointed out shuddering)——So many evil combina-
tions even unto the bat who would come at me later while I slept
on the outdoor cot on the porch of Lorenzo's cabin, come circle
my head coming real low sometimes filling me with the tradi-
tional fear it'll get tangled in my hair, and such silent wings, how
would you like to wake up in the middle of the night and see
silent wings beating over you and you ask yourself "Do I really
believe in Vampires?"——In fact, flying silently around my
lamplit cabin at 3 o'clock in the morning as I'm reading (of all
things) (shudder) *Doctor Jekyll and Mister Hyde*——Small
wonder maybe that I myself turned from serene Jekyll to hys-

terical Hyde in the short space of six weeks, losing absolute control of the peace mechanisms of my mind for the first time in my life.

But Ah, at first there were fine days and nights, right after Monsanto drove me to Monterey and back with two boxes of a full grub list and left me there alone for three weeks of solitude, as we'd agreed——So fearless and happy I even spotted his powerful flashlight up at the bridge the first night, right thru the fog the eerie finger reaching the pale bottom of that high monstrosity, and even spotted it out over the farmless sea as I sat by caves in the crashing dark in my fisherman's outfit writing down what the sea was saying——Worst of all spotting it up at those tangled mad cliffsides where owls hooted ooraloo——Becoming acquainted and swallowing fears and settling down to life in the little cabin with its warm glow of woodstove and kerosene lamp and let the ghosts fly their asses off——The Bhikku's home in his woods, he only wants peace, peace he will get——Tho why after three weeks of perfect happy peace and adjustment in these strange woods my soul so went down the drain when I came back with Dave Wain and Romana and my girl Billie and her kid, I'll never know——Worth the telling only if I dig deep into everything.

Because it was so beautiful at first, even the circumstance of my sleepingbag suddenly erupting feathers in the middle of the night as I turned over to sleep on, so I curse and have to get up and sew it by lamplight or in the morning it might be empty of feathers——And as I bend poor mother head over my needle and thread in the cabin, by the fresh fire and in the light of the kerosene lamp, here come those damned silent black wings flapping and throwing shadows all over my little home, the bloody bat's come in my house——Trying to sew a poor patch on my old crumbly sleepingbag (mostly ruined by my having to sweat out a fever inside of it in a hotel room in Mexico City in 1957 right after the gigantic earthquake there), the nylon all rotten almost from all that old sweat, but still soft, tho so soft I have to

cut out a piece of old shirt flap and patch over the rip——I
remember looking up from my middle of the night chore and
saying bleakly "They, yes, have bats in Mien Mo valley"——
But the fire crackles, the patch gets sewn, the creek gurgles and
thumps outside——A creek having so many voices it's amazing,
from the kettledrum basin deep bumpbumps to the little gurgly
feminine crickles over shallow rocks, sudden choruses of other
singers and voices from the log dam, dibble dabble all night long
and all day long the voices of the creek amusing me so much at
first but in the later horror of that madness night becoming the
babble and rave of evil angels in my head——So not minding
the bat or the rip finally, ending up cant sleep because too awake
now and it's 3 A.M. so the fire I stoke and I settle down and read
the entire *Doctor Jekyll and Mister Hyde* novel in the wonderful
little handsized leather book left there by smart Monsanto who
also must've read it with wide eyes on a night like that——
Ending the last elegant sentences at dawn, time to get up and
fetch water from gurgly creek and start breakfast of pancakes
and syrup——And saying to myself "So why fret when something goes wrong like your sleepingbag breaking in the night,
use self reliance"——"Screw the bats" I add.

Marvelous opening moment in fact of the first afternoon I'm
left alone in the cabin and I make my first meal, wash my first
dishes, nap, and wake up to hear the rapturous ring of silence or
Heaven even within and throughout the gurgle of the creek——
When you say AM ALONE and the cabin is suddenly home
only because you made one meal and washed your firstmeal
dishes——Then nightfall, the religious vestal lighting of the
beautiful kerosene lamp after careful washing of the mantle in
the creek and careful drying with toilet paper, which spoils it by
specking it so you again wash it in the creek and this time just let
the mantle drip dry in the sun, the late afternoon sun that
disappears so quickly behind those giant high steep canyon
walls——Nightfall, the kerosene lamp casts a glow in the cabin,

I go out and pick some ferns like the ferns of the Lankavatara Scripture, those hairnet ferns, "Look sirs, a beautiful
hairnet!"——Late afternoon fog pours in over the canyon walls,
sweep, cover the sun, it gets cold, even the flies on the porch are
as so sad as the fog on the peaks——As daylight retreats the
flies retreat like polite Emily Dickinson flies and when it's dark
they're all asleep in trees or someplace——At high noon they're
in the cabin with you but edging further towards the open door-
sill as the afternoon lengthens, how strangely gracious——
There's the hum of the bee drone two blocks away the racket of it
you'd think it was right over the roof, when the bee drone swirls
nearer and nearer (gulp again) you retreat into the cabin and
wait, maybe they got a message to come and see you all two
thousand of em——But getting used to the bee drone finally
which seems to happen like a big party once a week——And so
everything eventually marvelous.

Even the first frightening night on the beach in the fog with
my notebook and pencil, sitting there crosslegged in the sand
facing all the Pacific fury flashing on rocks that rise like gloomy
sea shroud towers out of the cove, the bingbang cove with its
seas booming inside caves and slapping out, the cities of seaweed
floating up and down you can even see their dark leer in the
phosphorescent seabeach nightlight——That first night I sit
there and all I know, as I look up, is the kitchen light is on, on the
cliff, to the right, where somebody's just built a cabin overlook-
ing all the horrible Sur, somebody up there's having a mild and
tender supper that's all I know——The lights from the cabin
kitchen up there go out like a little weak lighthouse beacon and
ends suspended a thousand feet over the crashing shore——
Who would build a cabin up there but some bored but hoary old
adventurous architect maybe got sick of running for congress
and one of these days a big Orson Welles tragedy with screaming ghosts a woman in a white nightgown'll go flying down that
sheer cliff——But actually in my mind what I really see is the

kitchen lights of that mild and tender maybe even romantic supper up there, in all that howling fog, and here I am way below in the Vulcan's Forge itself looking up with sad eyes——Blanking my little Camel cigarette on a billion year old rock that rises behind my head to a height unbelievable——The little kitchen light on the cliff is only on the end of it, behind it the shoulders of the great sea hound cliff go rising up and back and sweeping inland higher and higher till I gasp to think "Looks like a reclining dog, big friggin shoulders on that sonofabitch"——Riseth and sweepeth and scareth men to death but what is death anyway in all this water and rock.

I fix up my sleepingbag on the porch of the cabin but at 2 A.M. the fog starts dripping all wet so I have to go indoors with wet sleepingbag and make new arrangements but who cant sleep like a log in a solitary cabin in the woods, you wake up in the late morning so refreshed and realizing the universe namelessly: the universe is an Angel——But easy enough to say when you've had your escape from the gooky city turn into a success—— And it's finally only in the woods you get that nostalgia for "cities" at last, you dream of long gray journeys to cities where soft evenings'll unfold like Paris but never seeing how sickening it will be because of the primordial innocence of health and stillness in the wilds——So I tell myself "Be Wise."

6

Though there are faults to Monsanto's cabin like no screened windows to keep the flies out in the daytime just big board windows, so that also on foggy days when it's damp if you leave them open it's too cold, if you leave them closed you cant see anything and have to light the lamp at noon——And but for that no other faults——It's all marvelous——And at first it's so amazing to be able to enjoy dreamy afternoon meadows of heather up the other end of the canyon and just by walking less than a halfmile you can suddenly also enjoy wild gloomy sea coast, or if you're sick of either of these just sit by the creek in a gladey spot and dream over snags——So easy in the woods to daydream and pray to the local spirits and say "Allow me to stay here, I only want peace" and those foggy peaks answer back mutely Yes——And to say to yourself (if you're like me with theological preoccupations) (at least at that time, before I went mad I still had such preoccupations) "God who is everything possesses the eye of awakening, like dreaming a long dream of an impossible task and you wake up in a flash, oops, No Task, it's done and gone"——And in the flush of the first few days of joy I confidently tell myself (not expecting what I'll do in three weeks only) "no more dissipation, it's time for me to quietly watch the world and even enjoy it, first in woods like these, then just calmly walk and talk among people of the world, no booze, no drugs, no binges, no bouts with beatniks and drunks and junkies and everybody, no more I ask myself the question *O why*

is God torturing me, that's it, be a loner, travel, talk to waiters
only, in fact, in Milan, Paris, just talk to waiters, walk around,
no more self imposed agony . . . it's time to think and watch and
keep concentrated on the fact that after all this whole surface of
the world as we know it now will be covered with the silt of a
billion years in time . . . Yay, for this, more aloneness"——"Go
back to childhood, just eat apples and read your Cathechism—
sit on curbstones, the hell with the hot lights of Hollywood"
(remembering that awful time only a year earlier when I had to
rehearse my reading of prose a third time under the hot lights of
the Steve Allen Show in the Burbank studio, one hundred tech-
nicians waiting for me to start reading, Steve Allen watching me
expectant as he plunks the piano, I sit there on the dunce's stool
and refuse to read a word or open my mouth, "I dont have to
REHEARSE for God's sake Steve!"——"But go ahead, we just
wanta get the tone of your voice, just this last time, I'll let you off
the dress rehearsal" and I sit there sweating not saying a word
for a whole minute as everybody watches, finally I say "No I
cant do it" and I go across the street to get drunk) (but surprising everybody the night of the show by doing my job of reading
just fine, which surprises the producers and so they take me out
with a Hollywood starlet who turns out to be a big bore trying to
read me her poetry and wont talk love because in Hollywood
man love is for sale)——So even that marvelous, long remembrances of life all the time in the world to just sit there or lie there
or walk about slowly remembering all the details of life which
now because a million lightyears away have taken on the aspect
(as they must've for Proust in his sealed room) of pleasant mental
movies brought up at will and projected for further study——
And pleasure——As I imagine God to be doing this very
minute, watching his own movie, which is us.

Even when one night I'm so happy sighin to turn over to
resume my sleep but a rat suddenly runs over my head, it's marvelous because I then take the folding cot and put a big wide
board on it that covers both sides, so I wont sink into the canvas

confines there, and place two old sleepingbags over the board, then my own on top, I have the most marvelous and rat free and in fact healthy-for-the-back bed in the world.

I also take long curious hikes to see what's what in the other direction inland, going up a few miles along the dirt road that leads to isolated ranches and logging camps——I come to giant sad quiet valleys where you see 150 foot tall redwood trees with sometimes one little bird right on the topmost peaktwig sticking straight up——The bird balances up there surveying the fog and the great trees——You see one single flower nodding on a cliff side far across the canyon, or a huge knot in a redwood tree looking like Zeus' face, or some of God's little crazy creations goofing around in creek pools (zigzag bugs), or a sign on a lonely fence saying "M.P.Passey, No Trespassing," or terraces of fern in the dripping redwood shade, and you think "A long way from the beat generation, in this rain forest"——So I angle back down to the home canyon and down the path past the cabin and out to the sea where the mule is on the sea shore, nibbling under that one thousand foot bridge or sometimes just standing staring at me with big brown Garden of Eden eyes——The mule being a pet of one of the families who have a cabin in the canyon and it, as I say Alf by name, just wanders from one end of the canyon where the corral fence stops him, to the wild seashore where the sea stops him but a strange Gauguinesque mule when you first see him, leaving his black dung on the perfect white sand, an immortal and primordial mule owning a whole valley——I even finally later find out where Alf sleeps which is like a sacred grove of trees in that dreaming meadow of heather——So I feed Alf the last of my apples which he receives with big faroff teeth inside his soft hairy muzzle, never biting, just muffing up my apple from my outstretched palm, and chomping away sadly, turning to scratch his behind against a tree with a big erotic motion that gets worse and worse till finally he's standing there with erectile dong that would scare the Whore of Babylon let alone me.

All kinds of strange and marvelous things like the weird Ripley situation of a huge tree that's fallen across a creek maybe 500 years ago and's made a bridge thereby, the other end of its trunk is now buried in ten feet of silt and foliage, strange enough but out of the middle trunk over the water rises straight another redwood tree looking like it's been planted in the treetrunk, or stuck down into it by a God hand, I cant figure it out and stare at this chewing furiously on big choking handfulls of peanuts like a college boy——(and only weeks before falling on my head in the Bowery)—— Even when a rancher car goes by I daydream mad ideas like, here comes Farmer Jones and his two daughters and here I am with a 60-foot redwood tree under my arm walking slowly pulling it along, they are amazed and scared, "Are we dreaming? can anybody be that strong?" they even ask me and my big Zen answer is "You only think I'm strong" and I go on down the road carrying my tree——This has me laughing in clover fields for hours——I pass a cow which turns to look at me as it takes a big dreamy crap——Back in the cabin I light the fire and sit sighing and there are leaves skittering on the tin roof, it's August in Big Sur——I fall asleep in the chair and when I wake up I'm facing the thick little tangled woods outside the door and I suddenly remember them from long ago, even to the particular clumpness of the thickets, stem by stem, the twist of them, like an old home place, but just as I'm wondering what all this mess is, bang, the wind closes the cabin door on my sight of it!——So I conclude "I see as much as doors'll allow, open or shut"——Adding, as I get up, in a loud English Lord voice nobody can hear anyway, "An issue broached is an issue smote, Sire," pronouncing "issue" like "iss-yew"—— And this has me laughing all through supper——Which is pota- toes wrapped in foil and thrown on the fire, and coffee, and hunks of Spam roasted on a spit, and applesauce and cheese——And when I light the lamp of aftersupper reading, here comes the nightly moth to his nightly death at my lamp——After I put out the lamp temporarily, there's the moth sleeping on the wall not realizing I've put it on again.

Meanwhile by the way and however, every day is cold and cloudy, or damp, not cold in the eastern sense, and every night is absolutely fog: no stars whatever to be seen——But this too turns out to be a marvelous circumstance as I find out later, it's the "damp season" and the other dwellers (weekenders) of the canyon dont come out on weekends, I'm absolutely alone for weeks on end (because later in August when the sun conquered the fog suddenly I was amazed to hear laughing and scratching all up and down the valley which had been mine only mine, and when I tried to go to the beach to squat and write there were whole families having outings, some of them younger people who'd simply parked their cars up on the high bridge bluff and climbed down) (some of them in fact gangs of yelling hoodlums)——So the rainforest summer fog was grand and besides when the sun prevailed in August a horrible develop-ment took place, huge blasts of frightening gale like wind came pouring into the canyon making all the trees roar with a really frightening intensity that sometimes built up to a booming war of trees that shook the cabin and woke you up——And was in fact one of the things that contributed to my mad fit.

But the most marvelous day of all when I completely forgot who I was where I was or the time a day just with my pants rolled up above my knees wading in the creek rearranging the rocks and some of the snags so that the water where I stooped (near the sandy shore) to get jugfuls would, instead of just sluggishly passing by shallow over mud, with bugs in it, now come rushing in a pure gurgly clear stream and deep too——I dug into the white sand and arranged underground rocks so now I could stick a jug in there and tilt the opening to the stream and it would fill up instantly with clear rushing unstagnated bugless drinking water——Making a mill race, is what it's called——And because now the water rushed so fast and deep right by the sandy stooping place I had to build a kind of seawall of rocks against that rush so that the shore would not be silted away by the race——Doing that, fortifying the outside of the seawall

with smaller rocks and finally at sundown with bent head over
my sniffling endeavors (the way a kid sniffles when he's been
playing all day) I start inserting tiny pebbles in the spaces
between the stones so that no water can sneak over to wash away
the shore, even down to the tiniest sand, a perfect sea wall, which
I top with a wood plank for everybody to kneel on when they
come there to fetch their holy water——Looking up from this
work of an entire day, from noon till sundown, amazed to
see where I was, who I was, what I'd done——The absolute
innocence like of Indian fashioning a canoe all alone in the
woods——And as I say only weeks earlier I'd fallen flat on my
head in the Bowery and everybody thought I'd hurt myself——
So I make supper with a happy song and go out in the foggy
moonlight (the moon sent its white luminescence through) and
marveled to watch the new swift gurgling clear water run with
its pretty flashes of light——"And when the fog's over and the
stars and the moon come out at night it'll be a beautiful sight."

And such things——A whole mess of little joys like that
amazing me when I came back in the horror of later to see how
they'd all changed and become sinister, even my poor little wood
platform and mill race when my eyes and my stomach nauseous
and my soul screaming a thousand babbling words, oh——It's
hard to explain and best thing to do is not be false.

7

Because on the fourth day I began to get bored and noted it in my diary with amazement, "Already bored?"——Even tho the handsome words of Emerson would shake me out of that where he says (in one of those little redleather books, in the essay on "Self Reliance" a man "is relieved and gay when he has put his heart into his work and done his best") (applicable both to building simple silly little millraces and writing big stupid stories like this)——Words from that trumpet of the morning in America, Emerson, he who announced Whitman and also said "Infancy conforms to nobody"——The infancy of the simplicity of just being happy in the woods, conforming to nobody's idea about what to do, what should be done——"Life is not an apology"——And when a vain and malicious philanthropic abolitionist accused him of being blind to the issues of slavery he said "Thy love afar is spite at home" (maybe the philanthropist had Negro help anyway)——So once I again I'm Ti Jean the Child, playing, sewing patches, cooking suppers, washing dishes (always kept the kettle boiling on the fire and anytime dishes need to be washed I just pour hot hot water into pan with Tide soap and soak them good and then wipe them clean after scouring with little 5-&-10 wire scourer)——Long nights simply thinking about the usefulness of that little wire scourer, those little yellow copper things you buy in supermarkets for 10 cents, all to me infinitely more interesting than the stupid and senseless "Steppenwolf" novel in the shack which I read with a shrug, this old fart reflecting the "conformity" of today and all the while he thought he was a big Nietzsche, old imitator of Dostoevsky 50 years too late (he feels tormented in a "personal hell" he calls it because he doesnt like what other people like!)——Better at noon to watch the orange and black Princeton colors on the wings of a butterfly——Best to go hear the sound of the sea at night on the shore.

Maybe I shouldna gone out and scared or bored or belabored myself so much, tho, on that beach at night which would scare any ordinary mortal——Every night around eight after supper I'd put on my big fisherman coat and take the notebook, pencil and lamp and start down the trail (sometimes passing ghostly Alf on the way) and go under that frightful high bridge and see through the dark fog ahead the white mouths of ocean coming high at me——But knowing the terrain I'd walk right on, jump the beach creek, and go to my corner by the cliff not far from one of the caves and sit there like an idiot in the dark writing down the sound of the waves in the notebook page (secretarial notebook) which I could see white in the darkness and therefore without benefit of lamp scrawl on——I was afraid to light my lamp for fear I'd scare the people way up there on the cliff eating their nightly tender supper——(later found out there was nobody up there eating tender suppers, they were overtime carpenters finishing the place in bright lights)——And I'd get scared of the rising tide with its 15 foot waves yet sit there hoping in faith that Hawaii warnt sending no tidal wave I might miss seeing in the dark coming from miles away high as Groomus——One night I got scared anyway so sat on top of 10 foot cliff at the foot of the big cliff and the waves are going "Rare, he rammed the gate rare"——"Raw roo roar"——"Crowsh"——the way waves sound especially at night——The sea not speaking in sentences so much as in short lines: "Which one? . . . the one ploshed? . . . the same, ah Boom". . . Writing down these fantastic inanities actually but yet I felt I had to do it because James

Joyce wasnt about to do it now he was dead (and figuring "Next year I'll write the different sound of the Atlantic crashing say on the night shores of Cornwall, or the soft sound of the Indian Ocean crashing at the mouth of the Ganges maybe")——And I just sit there listening to the waves talk all up and down the sand in different tones of voice "Ka bloom, kerplosh, ah ropey otter barnacled be, crowsh, are rope the angels in all the sea?" and such*——Looking up occasionally to see rare cars crossing the high bridge and wondering what they'd see on this drear foggy night if they knew a madman was down there a thousand feet below in all that windy fury sitting in the dark writing in the dark——Some sort of sea beatnik, tho anybody wants to call me a beatnik for THIS better try it if they dare——The huge black rocks seem to move——The bleak awful roaring isolateness, no ordinary man could do it I'm telling you——*I am a Breton!* I cry and the blackness speaks back *"Les poissons de la mer parlent Breton"* (the fishes of the sea speak Breton)——Nevertheless I go there every night even tho I dont feel like it, it's my duty (and probably drove me mad), and write these sea sounds, and all the whole insane poem "Sea."

Always so wonderful in fact to get away from that and back to the more human woods and come to the cabin where the fire's still red and you can see the Bodhisattva's lamp, the glass of ferns on the table, the box of Jasmine tea nearby, all so gentle and human after that rocky deluge out there——So I make an excellent pan of muffins and tell myself "Blessed is the man can make his own bread"——Like that, the whole three weeks, happiness——And I'm rolling my own cigarettes, too——And as I say sometimes I meditate how wonderful the fantastic use I've gotten out of cheap little articles like the scourer, but in this instance I think of the marvelous belongings in my rucksack like my 25 cent plastic

---

* The complete poems written by the sea are to be found at the end of this book, in the appendix, entitled "SEA": Sounds of the Pacific Ocean at Big Sur. JK.

shaker with which I've just made the muffin batter but also I've
used it in the past to drink hot tea, wine, coffee, whisky and even
stored clean handkerchiefs in it when I traveled——The top part
of the shaker, my holy cup, and had it for five years now——And
other belongings so valuable compared to the worthlessness of
expensive things I'd bought and never used——Like my black
soft sleeping sweater also five years which I was now wearing in
the damp Sur summer night and day, over a flannel shirt in the
cold, and just the sweater for the night's sleep in the bag——
Endless use and virtue of it!——And because the expensive things
were of ill use, like the fancy pants I'd bought for recent recording
dates in New York and other television appearances and never
even wore again, useless things like a $40 raincoat I never wore
because it didnt even have slits in the side pockets (you pay for the
label and the so called "tailoring")——Also an expensive tweed
jacket bought for TV and never worn again——Two silly sports
shirts bought for Hollywood never worn again and were 9 bucks
each!——And it's almost tearful to realize and remember the old
green T-shirt I'd found, mind you, eight years ago, mind you, on
the DUMP in Watsonville California mind you, and got fantastic
use and comfort from it——Like working to fix that new stream
in the creek to flow through the convenient deep new waterhole
near the wood platform on the bank, and losing myself in this like
a kid playing, it's the little things that count (clichés are truisms
and all truisms are true)——On my deathbed I could be remembering that creek day and forgetting the day MGM bought my
book, I could be remembering the old lost green dump T-shirt and
forgetting the sapphired robes——Mebbe the best way to get into
Heaven.

I go back to the beach in the daytime to write my "Sea," I
stand there barefoot by the sea stopping to scratch one ankle
with one toe, I hear the rhythm of those waves, and they're
saying suddenly "Is Virgin you trying to fathom me"——I go
back to make a pot of tea.

Summer afternoon——
Impatiently chewing
The Jasmine leaf

At high noon the sun always coming out at last, strong, beating down on my nice high porch where I sit with books and coffee and the noon I thought about the ancient Indians who must have inhabited this canyon for thousands of years, how even as far back at the 10th Century this valley must have looked the same, just different trees: these ancient Indians simply the ancestors of the Indians of only recently say 1860——How they've all died and quietly buried their grievances and excitements——How the creek may have been an inch deeper since logging operations of the last 60 years have removed some of the watershed in the hills back there——How the women pounded the local acorns, acorns or shmacorns, I finally found the natural nuts of the valley and they were sweet tasting—— And men hunted deer——In fact God knows what they did because I wasnt here——But the same valley, a thousand years of dust more or less over their footsteps of 960 A.D.——And as far as I can see the world is too old for us to talk about it with our new words——We will pass just as quietly through life (passing through, passing through) as the 10th century people of this valley only with a little more noise and a few bridges and dams and bombs that wont even last a million years——The world being just what it is, moving and passing through, actually alright in the long view and nothing to complain about—— Even the rocks of the valley had earlier rock ancestors, a billion billion years ago, have left no howl of complaint——Neither the bee, or the first sea urchins, or the clam, or the severed paw—— All sad So-Is sight of the world, right there in front of my nose as I look,——And looking at that valley in fact I also realize I have to make lunch and it wont be any different than the lunch of those olden men and besides it'll taste good——Everything is the same, the fog says "We are fog and we fly by dissolving like ephemera," and the leaves say "We are leaves and we jiggle in the wind, that's all, we come and go, grow and fall"——Even the paper bags in my garbage pit say "We are man-transformed paper bags made out of wood pulp, we are kinda proud of being paper bags as long as that will be possible, but we'll be mush again with our sisters the leaves come rainy season"——The tree stumps say "We are tree stumps torn out of the ground by men, sometimes by wind, we have big tendrils full of earth that drink out of the earth"——Men say "We are men, we pull out tree stumps, we make paper bags, we think wise thoughts, we make lunch, we look around, we make a great effort to realize everything is the same"——While the sand says "We are sand, we already know," and the sea says "We are always come and go, fall and plosh"——The empty blue sky of space says "All this comes back to me, then goes again, and comes back again, then goes again, and I dont care, it still belongs to me"——The blue sky adds "Dont call me eternity, call me God if you like, all of you talkers are in paradise: the leaf is paradise, the tree stump is paradise, the paper bag is paradise, the man is paradise, the sand is paradise, the sea is paradise, the man is paradise, the fog is paradise"——Can you imagine a man with marvelous insights like these can go mad within a month? (because you must admit all those talking paper bags and sands were telling the truth)—— But I remember seeing a mess of leaves suddenly go skittering in the wind and into the creek, then floating rapidly down the creek towards the sea, making me feel a nameless horror even then of "Oh my God, we're all being swept away to sea no matter what we know or say or do"——And a bird who was on a crooked branch is suddenly gone without my even hearing him.

8

But there's moonlit fognight, the blossoms of the fire flames in the stove——There's giving an apple to the mule, the big lips taking hold——There's the bluejay drinking my canned milk by throwing his head back with a miffle of milk on his beak——There's the scratching of the raccoon or of the rat out there, at night——There's the poor little mouse eating her nightly supper in the humble corner where I've put out a little delight-plate full of cheese and chocolate candy (for my days of killing mice are over)——There's the raccoon in his fog, there the man to his fireside, and both are lonesome for God—— There's me coming back from seaside nightsittings like a muttering old Bhikku stumbling down the path——There's me throwing my spotlight on a sudden raccoon who clambers up a tree his little heart beating with fear but I yell in French "Hello there little man" (*allo ti bonhomme*)——There's the bottle of olives, 49¢, imported, pimentos, I eat them one by one wondering about the late afternoon hillsides of Greece——And there's my spaghetti with tomato sauce and my oil and vinegar salad and my applesauce *relishe* my dear and my black coffee and Roquefort cheese and afterdinner nuts, my dear, all in the woods—— (Ten delicate olives slowly chewed at midnight is something no one's ever done in luxurious restaurants)——There's the present moment fraught with tangled woods——There's the bird suddenly quiet on his branch while his wife glances at him—— There's the grace of an axe handle as good as an Eglevsky

ballet——There's "Mien Mo Mountain" in the fog illumined
August moon mist among other heights gorgeous and misty
rising in dimmer tiers somehow rosy in the night like the classic
silk paintings of China and Japan——There's a bug, a helpless
little wingless crawler, drowning in a water can, I get it out and it
wanders and goofs on the porch till I get sick of watching——
There's the spider in the outhouse minding his own business——
There's my side of bacon hanging from a hook on the ceiling of
the shack——There's the laughter of the loon in the shadow of
the moon——There's an owl hooting in weird Bodhidharma
trees——There's flowers and redwood logs——There's the
simple woodfire and the careful yet absentminded feeding of it
which is an activity that like all activities is no-activity (*Wu Wei*)
yet it is a meditation in itself especially because all woodfires, like
snowflakes, are different every time——Yes, there's the resinous
purge of a flame-enveloped redwood log——Yes the cross-sawed
redwood log turns into a coal and looks like a City of the Gandharvas or like a western butte at sunset——There's the bhikku's
broom, the kettle——There's the laced soft fud over the sand, the
sea——There's all these avid preparations for decent sleep like
the night I'm looking for my sleeping socks (so's not to dirty the
sleepingbag inside) and find myself singing "A donde es me
sockiboos?"——Yes, and down in the valley there's my burro,
Alf, the only living being in sight——There's in mid of sleep the
moon appearing——There's universal substance which is divine
substance because where else can it be?——There's the family of
deer on the dirt road at dusk——There's the creek coughing
down the glade——There's the fly on my thumb rubbing its nose
then stepping to the page of my book——There's the humming-
bird swinging his head from side to side like a hoodlum——
There's all that, and all my fine thoughts, even unto my ditty
written to the sea "I took a pee, into the sea, acid to acid, and me
to ye" yet I went crazy inside three weeks.

For who could go crazy that could be so relaxed as that: but
wait: there are the signposts of something wrong.

9

The first signpost came after that marvelous day I went hiking up the canyon road again to the highway at the bridge where there was a rancher mailbox where I could dump mail (a letter to my mother and saying in it give a kiss to Tyke, my cat, and a letter to old buddy Julien addressed to Coaly Rustnut from Runty Onenut) and as I walked way up there I could see the peaceful roof of my cabin way below and half mile away in the old trees, could see the porch, the cot where I slept, and my red handkerchief on the bench beside the cot (a simple little sight: of my handkerchief a half mile away making me unaccountably happy)——And on the way back pausing to meditate in the grove of trees where Alf the Sacred Burro slept and seeing the roses of the unborn in my closed eyelids just as clearly as I had seen the red handkerchief and also my own footsteps in the seaside sand from way up on the bridge, saw, or heard, the words "Roses of the Unborn" as I sat crosslegged in soft meadow sand, heard that awful stillness at the heart of life, but felt strangely low, as tho premonition of the next day—— When I went to the sea in the afternoon and suddenly took a huge deep Yogic breath to get all that good sea air in me but somehow just got an overdose of iodine, or of evil, maybe the sea caves, maybe the seaweed cities, something, my heart suddenly beating——Thinking I'm gonna get the local vibrations instead here I am almost fainting only it isnt an ecstatic swoon by St. Francis, it comes over me in the form of horror of an eternal

condition of sick mortality in me——In me and in everyone——
I felt completely nude of all poor protective devices like
thoughts about life or meditations under trees and the "ultimate" and all that shit, in fact the other pitiful devices of making
supper or saying "What I do now next? chop wood?"——I see
myself as just doomed, pitiful——An awful realization that I
have been fooling myself all my life thinking there was a next
thing to do to keep the show going and actually I'm just a sick
clown and so is everybody else——All all of it, pitiful as it is, not
even really any kind of commonsense animate effort to ease the
soul in this horrible sinister condition (of mortal hopelessness)
so I'm left sitting there in the sand after having almost fainted
and stare at the waves which suddenly are not waves at all, with I
guess what must have been the goopiest downtrodden expression God if He exists must've ever seen in His movie
career——*Éh vache,* I hate to write——All my tricks laid bare,
even the realization that they're laid bare itself laid bare as a lotta
bunk——The sea seems to yell to me GO TO YOUR DESIRE
DONT HANG AROUND HERE——For after all the sea
must be like God, God isnt asking us to mope and suffer and sit
by the sea in the cold at midnight for the sake of writing down
useless sounds, he gave us the tools of self reliance after all to
make it straight thru bad life mortality towards Paradise maybe
I hope——But some miserables like me dont even know it, when
it comes to us we're amazed——Ah, life is a gate, a way, a path to
Paradise anyway, why not live for fun and joy and love or some
sort of girl by a fireside, why not go to your desire and
LAUGH . . . but I ran away from that seashore and never came
back again without that secret knowledge; that it didnt want me
there, that I was a fool to sit there in the first place, the sea has its
waves, the man has his fireside, period.

That being the first indication of my later flip——But also
on the day of leaving the cabin to hitch hike back to Frisco
and see everybody and by now I'm tired of my food (forgot
to bring jello, you need jello after all that bacon fat and cornmeal

in the woods, every woodsman needs jello) (or cokes) (or
something)——But it's time to leave, I'm now so scared by that
iodine blast by the sea and by the boredom of the cabin I take 20
dollars worth of perishable food left and spread it out on a big
board below the cabin porch for the bluejays and the raccoon
and the mouse and the whole lot, pack up, and go——But before
I go I realize this isnt my own cabin (here's the second signpost
of my madness), I have no right to hide Monsanto's rat poison, as
I've been doing, feeding the mouse instead, as I said——So like
a dutiful guest in another man's cabin I take the cover off the rat
poison but compromise by simply leaving the box on the top
shelf, so nobody can complain—And go off like that——But
during my absence, but——You'll see.

10

With my mind even and upright and abiding nowhere, as Hui Neng would say, I go dancing off like a fool from my sweet retreat, rucksack on back, after only three weeks and really after only 3 or 4 days of boredom, and go hankering back for the city——"You go out in joy and in sadness you return," says Thomas à Kempis talking about all the fools who go forth for pleasure like high school boys on Saturday night hurrying clacking down the sidewalk to the car adjusting their ties and rubbing their hands with anticipatory zeal, only to end up Sunday morning groaning in bleary beds that Mother has to make anyway——It's a beautiful day as I come out of that ghostly canyon road and step out on the coast highway, just this side of Raton Canyon bridge, and there they are, thousands and thousands of tourists driving by slowly on the high curves all oo ing and aa ing at all that vast blue panorama of seas washing and raiding at the coast of California——I figure I'll get a ride into Monterey real easy and take the bus there and be in Frisco by nightfall for a big ball of wino yelling with the gang, I feel in fact Dave Wain oughta be back by now, or Cody will be ready for a ball, and there'll be girls, and such and such, forgetting entirely that only three weeks previous I'd been sent fleeing from that gooky city by the horrors—— But hadnt the sea told me to flee back to my own reality?

But it is beautiful especially to see up ahead north a vast expanse of curving seacoast with inland mountains dreaming under slow clouds, like a scene of ancient Spain, or properly really like a scene of the real essentially Spanish California, the old Monterey pirate coast right there, you can see what the Spaniards must've thought when they came around the bend in their magnificent sloopies and saw all that dreaming fatland beyond the seashore whitecap doormat——Like the land of gold—— The old Monterey and Big Sur and Santa Cruz magic——So I confidently adjust my pack straps and start trudging down the road looking back over my shoulder to thumb.

This is the first time I've hitch hiked in years and I soon begin to see that things have changed in America, you cant get a ride any more (but of course especially on a strictly tourist road like this coast highway with no trucks or business)——Sleek long stationwagon after wagon comes sleering by smoothly, all colors of the rainbow and pastel at that, pink, blue, white, the husband is in the driver's seat with a long ridiculous vacationist hat with a long baseball visor making him look witless and idiot——Beside him sits wifey, the boss of America, wearing dark glasses and sneering, even if he wanted to pick me up or anybody up she wouldn't let him——But in the two deep backseats are children, children, millions of children, all ages, they're fighting and screaming over ice cream, they're spilling vanilla all over the Tartan seatcovers——There's no room anymore anyway for a hitch hiker, tho conceivably the poor bastard might be allowed to ride like a meek gunman or silent murderer in the very back platform of the wagon, but here no, alas! here is ten thousand racks of drycleaned and perfectly pressed suits and dresses of all sizes for the family to look like millionaires every time they stop at a roadside dive for bacon and eggs——Every time the old man's trousers start to get creased a little in the front he's made to take down a fresh pair of slacks from the back rack and go on, like that, bleakly, tho he might have secretly wished just a good oldtime fishing trip alone or with his buddies for this year's vacation—— But the P.T.A. has prevailed over every one of his desires by now, 1960's, it's no time for him to yearn for Big Two Hearted River and the old sloppy pants and the string of fish in the tent, or the woodfire with Bourbon at night——It's time for motels, roadside driveins, bringing napkins to the gang in the car, having the car washed before the return trip——And if he thinks he wants to explore any of the silent secret roads of America it's no go, the lady in the sneering dark glasses has now become the navigator and sits there sneering over her previously printed blue-lined roadmap distributed by happy executives in neckties to the vacationists of America who would also wear neckties (after having come along so far) but the vacation fashion is sports shirts, long visored hats, dark glasses, pressed slacks and baby's first shoes dipped in gold oil dangling from the dashboard——So here I am standing in that road with that big woeful rucksack but also probably with that expression of horror on my face after all those nights sitting in the seashore under giant black cliffs, they see in me the very apotheosical opposite of their every vacation dream and of course drive on——That afternoon I say about 5 thousand cars or probably 3 thousand passed me not one of them ever dreamed of stopping——Which didnt bother me anyway because at first seeing that gorgeous long coast up to Monterey I thought "Well I'll just hike right in, it's only 14 miles, I oughta do that easy"—— And on the way there's all kindsa interesting things to see anyway like the seals barking on rocks below, or quiet old farms made of logs on the hills across the highway, or sudden upstretches that go along dreamy seaside meadows where cows grace and graze in full sight of endless blue Pacific——But because I'm wearing desert boots with their fairly thin soles, and the sun is beating hot on the tar road, the heat finally gets through the soles and I begin to deliver heat blisters in my sockiboos——I'm limping along wondering what's the matter with me when I realize I've got blisters—— I sit by the side of the road and look——I take out my first aid kit from the pack and apply unguents and put on cornpads and carry on——But the combination of the heavy pack and the heat of the road increases the pain of the blisters until finally I realize I've got to hitch hike a ride or never make it to Monterey at all.

But the tourists bless their hearts after all, they couldnt know, only think I'm having a big happy hike with my rucksack and they drive on, even tho I stick out my thumb——I'm in despair because I'm really stranded now, and by the time I've walked seven miles I still have seven to go but I cant go on another step——I'm also thirsty and there are absolutely no filling stations or anything along the way——My feet are ruined and burned, it develops now into a day of complete torture, from nine o'clock in the morning till four in the afternoon I negotiate those nine or so miles when I finally have to stop and sit down and wipe the blood off my feet——And then when I fix the feet and put the shoes on again, to hike on, I can only do it mincingly with little twinkletoe steps like Babe Ruth, twisting footsteps every way I can think of not to press too hard on any particular blister——So that the tourists (lessening now as the sun starts to go down) can now plainly see that there's a man on the highway limping under a huge pack and asking for a ride, but still they're afraid he may be the Hollywood hitch hiker with the hidden gun and besides he's got a rucksack on his back as tho he'd just escaped from the war in Cuba——Or's got dismembered bodies in the bag anyway——But as I say I dont blame them.

The only car that passes that might have given me a ride is going in the wrong direction, down to Sur, and it's a rattly old car of some kind with a big bearded "South Coast Is the Lonely Coast" folksinger in it waving at me but finally a little truck pulls up and waits for me 50 yards ahead and I limprun that distance on daggers in my feet——It's a guy with a dog——He'll drive me to the next gas station, then he turns off——But when he learns about my feet he takes me clear to the bus station in Monterey—— Just as a gesture of kindness——No particular reason, and I've made no particular plea about my feet, just mentioned it.

I offer to buy him a beer but he's going on home for supper so I go into the bus station and clean up and change and pack things away, stow the bag in the locker, buy the bus ticket, and go limping quietly in the blue fog streets of Monterey evening feeling light as feather and happy as a millionaire——The last time I ever hitch hiked——And NO RIDES a sign.

11

The next sign is in Frisco itself where after a night of perfect sleep in an old skid row hotel room I go to see Monsanto at his City Lights bookstore and he's smiling and glad to see me, says "We were coming out to see you next weekend you should have waited," but there's something else in his expression——— When we're alone he says "Your mother wrote and said your cat is dead."

Ordinarily the death of a cat means little to most men, a lot to fewer men, but to me, and that cat, it was exactly and no lie and sincerely like the death of my little brother——I loved Tyke with all my heart, he was my baby who as a kitten just slept in the palm of my hand with his little head hanging down, or just purring, for hours, just as long as I held him that way, walking or sitting——He was like a floppy fur wrap around my wrist, I just twist him around my wrist or drape him and he just purred and purred and even when he got big I still held him that way, I could even hold this big cat in both hands with my arms out-stretched right over my head and he'd just purr, he had complete confidence in me——And when I'd left New York to come to my retreat in the woods I'd carefully kissed him and instructed him to wait for me, *"Attends pour mué kitigingoo"*——But my mother said in the letter he had died the NIGHT AFTER I LEFT!——— But maybe you'll understand me by seeing for yourself by reading the letter:-

"Sunday July 20, 1960, Dear Son, I'm afraid you wont like my letter because I only have sad news for you right now. I really dont know how to tell you this but Brace up Honey. I'm going through hell myself. Little Tyke is *gone*. Saturday all day he was fine and seemed to pick up strength, but late at night I was watching T.V. a late movie. Just about 1:30 A.M. when he started belching and throwing up. I went to him and tried to fix him up but to no *availe*. He was shivering like he was cold so I rapped him up in a Blanket then he started to throw up all over me. And that was the last of him. Needless to say how I feel and what I went through. I stayed up till 'day *Break*' and did all I could to revive him but it was useless. I realized at 4 A.M. he was gone so at six I wrapped him up good in a clean blanket——and at 7 A.M. went out to dig his grave. I never did anything in my whole life so heart breaking as to bury my beloved little Tyke who was as human as you and I. I buried him under the Honeysuckle vines, the corner, of the fence. I just cant sleep or eat. I keep looking and hoping to see him come through the cellar door calling *Ma Wow*. I'm just plain sick and the weirdest thing happened when I buried Tyke, all the black Birds I fed all Winter seemed to have known what was going on. Honest Son this is no lies. There was lots and lots of *em* flying over my head and chirping, and settling on the fence, for a whole hour after Tyke was laid to rest——that's something I'll never forget——I wish I had a camera at the time but God and Me knows it and saw it. Now Honey I know this is going to hurt you but I had to tell you somehow. . . I'm so sick not physically but heart sick. . . I just cant believe or realize that my Beautiful little Tyke is no more——and that I wont be seeing him come through his little "Shanty" or Walking through the green grass. . . . P.S. I've got to dismantle Tyke's shanty, I just cant go out there and see it empty——as is. Well Honey, write soon again and be kind to yourself. Pray the real "God"——Your old Mom X X X X XX."

So when Monsanto told me the news and I was sitting there *smiling* with happiness the way all people feel when they come out of a long solitude either in the woods or in a hospital bed, bang, my heart sank, it sank in fact with the same strange idiotic helplessness as when I took the unfortunate deep breath on the seashore——All the premonitions tying in together.

Monsanto sees that I'm terribly sad, he sees my little smile (the smile that came over me in Monterey just so glad to be back in the world after the solitudes and I'd walked around the streets just bemusedly. Mona Lisa'ing at the sight of everything)—— He sees now how that smile has slowly melted away into a mawk of chagrin——Of course he cant know since I didnt tell him and hardly wanta tell it now, that my relationship with my cat and the other previous cats has always been a little dotty: some kind of psychological identification of the cats with my dead brother Gerard who'd taught me to love cats when I was 3 and 4 and we used to lie on the floor on our bellies and watch them lap up milk——The death of "little brother" Tyke indeed—— Monsanto seeing me so downcast says "Maybe you oughta go back to the cabin for a few more weeks——or are you just gonna get drunk again"——"I'm gonna get drunk yes"——Because anyway there are so many things brewing, everybody's waiting, I've been daydreaming a thousand wild parties in the woods—— In fact it's fortunate I've heard of the death of Tyke in my favorite exciting city of San Francisco, if I had been home when he died I might have gone mad in a different way but tho I now ran out to get drunk with the boys and still once in a while that funny little smile of joy came back as I drank, and melted away again because now the smile itself was a reminder of death, the news made me go mad anyway at the end of the three week binge, creeping up on me finally on that terrible day of St. Carolyn By The Sea as I can also call it——All, all confusing till I explain.

Meanwhile anyway poor Monsanto a man of letters wants to enjoy big news swappings with me about writing and what everybody's doing, and then Fagan comes into the store (downstairs to Monsanto's old rolltop desk making me also feel chagrin because it always was the ambition of my youth to end up a kind

of literary businessman with a rolltop desk, combining my
father image with the image of myself as a writer, which Monsanto without even thinking about it has accomplished at the
drop of a hat)——Monsanto with his husky shoulders, big blue
eyes, twinkling rosy skin, that perpetual smile of his that earned
him the name Smiler in college and a smile you often wondered
"Is it real?" until you realized if Monsanto should ever stop
using that smile how could the world go on anyway——It was
that kind of smile too inseparable from him to be believably
allowed to disappear——Words words words but he is a grand
guy as I'll show and now with real manly sympathy he really felt
I should not go on big binges if I felt so bad, "At any rate," sez
he, "you can go back a little later huh"——"Okay Lorry"——
"Did you write anything?"——"I wrote the sounds of the sea,
I'll tell you all about it——It was the most happy three weeks of
my life dammit and now this has to happen, poor little Tyke——
You should have seen him a big beautiful yellow Persian the
kind they call calico"——"Well you still have my dog Homer,
and how was Alf out there?"——"Alf the Sacred Burro, he ha,
he stands in groves of trees in the afternoon suddenly you see
him it's almost scarey, but I fed him apples and shredded wheat
and everything" (and animals are so sad and patient I thought as
I remembered Tyke's eyes and Alf's eyes, ah death, and to think
this strange scandalous death comes also to human beings, yea
to Smiler even, poor Smiler, and poor Homer his dog, and all of
us)——I'm also depressed because I know how horrible my
mother now feels all alone without her little chum in the house
back there 3 thousand miles (and indeed by Jesus it turns out
later some silly beatniks trying to see me broke the windowpane
in the front door trying to get in and scared her so much she bar-
ricaded the door with furniture all the rest of that summer).

But there's old Ben Fagan puffing and chuckling over his pipe
so what the hell, why bother grownup men and poets at that
with your own troubles——So Ben and I and his chum Jonesy
also a chuckly pipesmoker go out to the bar (Mike's Place) and

sip a few beers, at first I vow I'm not going to get drunk after all, we even go out to the park to have a long talk in the warm sun that always turns to delightful cool foggy dusk in that town of towns——We're sitting in the park of the big Italian white church watching kids play and people go by, for some reason I'm bemused by the sight of a blonde woman hurrying somewhere "Where's she going? does she have a secret sailor lover? is she only going to finish her typing afterhours in the office? what if we knew Ben what every one of these people goin by is headed for, some door, some restaurant, some secret romance"—— "You sound like you stored up a lot of energy and innerest in life in those woods"——And Ben knows that for sure because he's been months in the wilderness too, alone——Old Ben, much thinner than he used to be in our madder Dharma Bum days of 5 years ago, a little gaunt in fact, but still the same old Ben who stays up late at night chuckling over the Lankavatara Scripture and writing poems about raindrops——And he knows me very well, he knows I'll get drunk tonight and for weeks on end just on general principles and that a day will come in a few weeks when I'll be so exhausted I wont be able to talk to anybody and he'll come and visit me and just silently at my side be puffing his pipe, as I sleep——The kind of guy he is——I trying to explain about Tyke to him but some people are cat lovers and some aint, tho Ben always has a little kitty around his pad——His pad usually has a straw rug on the floor, with a pillow 'pon which he sits crosslegged, by a smoking teapot, his bookshelves full of Stein and Pound and Wallace Stevens——A strange quiet poet who was only beginning to be recognized as a big rosy secret sage (one of his lines "When I leave town all my friends go back on the sauce")——And I'm on my way to the sauce right now.

Because anyway old Dave Wain is back and Dave I can see him rubbing his hands in anticipation of another big wild binge with me like we had the year before when he drove me back to New York from the west coast, with George Baso the little Japanese Zen master hepcat sitting crosslegged on the back mattress of Dave's jeepster (Willie the Jeep), a terrific trip through Las Vegas, St. Louis, stopping off at expensive motels and drinking nothing but the best Scotch out of the bottle all the way——And what better way to go back to New York, I could have blown 190 dollars on an airplane——And Dave's never met the great Cody and will be looking forward to that——So me and Ben leave the park and slowly walk to the bar on Columbus Street and I order my first double bourbon and gingerale.

The lights are twinkling on outside in that fantastic toy street, I can feel the joy rise in my soul——I now remember Big Sur with a clear piercing love and agony and even the death of Tyke fits in with everything but I dont realize the enormity of what's yet to come——We call up Dave Wain who's back from Reno and he comes blattin down to the bar in his jeepster driving that marvelous way he does (once he was a cab-driver) talking all the time and never making a mistake, in fact as good a driver as Cody altho I cant imagine anybody being that good and asked Cody about it the next day——But old jealous drivers always point out faults and complain, "Ah well that Dave Wain of yours doesnt takes his curves right, he eases up and sometimes even pokes the brake a little instead of just ridin that old curve around on increased power, man you gotta *work* those curves"—— Obvious at this time now, by the way and parenthetically, that there's so much to tell about the fateful following three weeks it's hardly possible to find anyplace to begin.

Like life, actually——And how multiple it all is!——"And what happened to little old George Baso, boy?"——"Little old George Baso is probably dyin of T.B. in a hospital outsida Tulare"——"Gee, Dave, we gotta go see him"——"Yessir, let's do that tomorrow"——As usual Dave has no money whatever but that doesnt bother me at all, I've got plenty, I go out the following day and cash 500 dollars worth of travelers checks just so's me and old Dave can really have a good time——Dave likes good food and drink and so do I——But he's got this young kid he brought back from Reno called Ron Blake who is a goodlook-

ing teenager with blond hair who wants to be a sensational new
Chet Baker singer and comes on with that tiresome hipster
approach that was natural 5 or 10 and even 25 years ago but now
in 1960 is a pose, in fact I dug him as a con man conning Dave
(tho for what, I dont know)——But Dave Wain that lean rangy
red head Welchman with his penchant for going off in Willie to
fish in the Rogue River up in Oregon where he knows an abandoned mining camp, or for blattin around the desert roads, for
suddenly reappearing in town to get drunk, and a marvelous
poet himself, has that certain something that young hip teenagers probably wanta imitate——For one thing is one of the
world's best talkers, and funny too——As I'll show——It was
he and George Baso who hit on the fantastically simple truth
that everybody in America was walking around with a dirty
behind, but everybody, because the ancient ritual of washing
with water after the toilet had not occurred in all the modern
antisepticsm——Says Dave "People in America have all these
racks of drycleaned clothes like you say on their trips, they spatter
Eau de Cologne all over themselves, they wear Ban and Aid or
whatever it is under their armpits, they get aghast to see a spot on
a shirt or a dress, they probably change underwear and socks
maybe even twice a day, they go around all puffed up and inso-
lent thinking themselves the cleanest people on earth and they're
walkin around with dirty azzoles——Isnt that amazing? give
me a little nip on that tit" he says reaching for my drink so I
order two more, I've been engrossed, Dave can order all the
drinks he wants anytime, "The President of the United States,
the big ministers of state, the great bishops and shmishops and
big shots everywhere, down to the lowest factory worker with all
his fierce pride, movie stars, executives and great engineers and
presidents of law firms and advertising firms with silk shirts
and neckties and great expensive traveling cases in which they
place these various expensive English imported hair brushes
and shaving gear and pomades and perfumes are all walkin
around with dirty azzoles! All you gotta do is simply wash

yourself with soap and water! it hasnt occurred to anybody in America at all! it's one of the funniest things I've ever heard of! dont you think it's marvelous that we're being called filthy unwashed beatniks but we're the only ones walkin around with clean azzoles?"——The whole azzole shot in fact had spread swiftly and everybody I knew and Dave knew from coast to coast had embarked on this great crusade which I must say is a good one——In fact in Big Sur I'd instituted a shelf in Monsanto's outhouse where the soap must be kept and everyone had to bring a can of water there on each trip——Monsanto hadnt heard about it yet, "Do you realize that until we tell poor Lorenzo Monsanto the famous writer that he is walking around with a dirty azzole he will be doing just that?"——"Let's go tell him right now!"——"Why of course if we wait another minute . . . and besides do you know what it *does* to people to walk around with a dirty azzole? it leaves a great yawning guilt that they cant understand all day, they go to work all cleaned up in the morning and you can smell all that freshly laundered clothes and Eau de Cologne in the commute train yet there's something gnawing at them, something's wrong, they know something's wrong they dont know just what!"——We rush to tell Monsanto at once in the book store around the corner.

By now we're beginning to feel great——Fagan has retired saying typically "Okay you guys go ahead and get drunk, I'm goin home and spend a quiet evening in a hot bath with a book"——"Home" is also where Dave Wain and Ron Blake live——It's an old roominghouse of four stories on the edge of the Negro district of San Francisco where Dave, Ben, Jonesy, a painter called Lanny Meadows, a mad French Canadian drinker called Pascal and a Negro called Johnson all live in different rooms with their clutter of rucksacks and floor mattresses and books and gear, each one taking turns one day a week to go out and do all the shopping and come back and cook up a big communal dinner in the kitchen——All ten or twelve of them sharing the rent, and with that rotation of dinner, they end up living comfortable lives with wild parties and girls rushing in, people bringing bottles, all at about a minimum of seven dollars a week say——It's a wonderful place but at the same time a little maddening, in fact a whole lot maddening because the painter Lanny Meadows loves music and has installed his Hi Fi speaker in the kitchen altho he applies the records in a back room so the daily cook may be concentrating on his Mulligan stew and all of a sudden Stravinski's dinosaurs start dinning overhead—— And at night there are bottlecrashing parties usually supervised by wild Pascal who is a sweet kid but crazy when he drinks——A regular nuthouse actually and just exactly the image of what the journalists want to say about the Beat Generation nevertheless a harmless and pleasant arrangement for young bachelors and a good idea in the long run——Because you can rush into any room and find the expert, like say Ben's room and ask "Hey what did Bodhidharma say to the Second Patriarch?"——"He said go fuck yourself, make your mind like a wall, dont pant after outside activities and dont bug me with your outside plans"——"So the guy goes out and stands on his head in the snow?"——"No that was Fubar"——Or you go runnin into Dave Wain's room and there he is sitting crosslegged on his mattress on the floor reading Jane Austen, you ask "What's the best way to make beef Stroganoff?"——"Beef Stroganoff is very simple, 't'aint nothin but a good well cooked beef and onion stew that you let cool afterwards then you throw in mushrooms and lotsa sour cream, I'll come down and show way soon's I finish this chapter in this marvelous novel, I wanta find out what happens next"——Or you go into the Negro's room and ask if you can borrow his tape recorder because right at the moment some funny things are being said in the kitchen by Duluoz and McLear and Monsanto and some newspaperman——Because the kitchen was also the main talking room where everybody sat in a clutter of dishes and ashtrays and all kinds of visitors came——The year before a beautiful 16 year old Japanese girl had come there just to interview me, for instance, but

chaperoned by a Chinese painter——The phone rang
consistently——Even wild Negro hepcats from around the
corner came in with bottles (Edward Kool and several
others)——There was Zen, jazz, booze, pot and all the works
but it was somehow obviated (as a supposedly degenerate idea)
by the sight of a 'beatnik' carefully painting the wall of his room
and clean white with nice little red borders around the door and
windowframes——Or someone is sweeping out the livingroom.
Itinerant visitors like me or Ron Blake always had an extra mattress to sleep on.

12

But Dave is Anxious and so am I to see great Cody who is always the major part of my reason for journeying to the west coast so we call him up at Los Gatos 50 miles away down the Santa Clara Valley and I hear his dear sad voice saying "Been waitin for ya old buddy, come on down right away, but I'll be goin to work at midnight so hurry up and you can visit me at work soon's the boss leaves round two and I'll show you my new job of tire recappin and see if you cant bring a little somethin like a girl or sumptin, just kiddin, come on down pal——"

So there's old Willie waiting for us down on the street parked across from the little pleasant Japanese liquor store where as usual, according to our ritual, I run and get Pernod or Scotch or anything good while Dave wheels around to pick me up at the store door, and I get in the front seat right at Dave's right where I belong all the time like old Honored Samuel Johnson while everybody else that wants to come along has to scramble back there on the mattress (a full mattress, the seats are out) and squat there or lie down there and also generally keep silent because when Dave's got the wheel of Willie in his hand and I've got the bottle in mine and we're off on a trip the talking all comes from the front seat——"By God" yells Dave all glad again "it's just like old times Jack, gee old Willie's been sad for ya, waitin for ya to come back——So now I'm gonna show ya how old Willie's even improved with age, had him reconditioned in Reno last month, here he goes, are you ready Willie?" and off we go and

the beauty of it all this particular summer is that the front right
seat is broken and just rocks back and forth gently to every one
of Dave's driving moves——It's like sitting in a rocking chair
on a porch only this is a moving porch and a porch to talk on at
that——And insteada watching old men pitch horseshoes from
this here talking porch it's all that fine white clean line in the
middle of the road as we go flying like birds over the Harrison
ramps and whatnot Dave always uses to sneak out of Frisco real
fast and avoid all the traffic——Soon we're set straight and
pointed head on down beautiful fourlane Bayshore Highway to
that lovely Santa Clara Valley——But I'm amazed that after
only a few years the damn thing no longer has prune fields and
vast beet fields like at Lawrence when I was a brakeman on the
Southern Pacific and even after, it's one long row of houses right
down the line 50 miles to San Jose like a great monstrous Los
Angeles beginning to grow south of Frisco.

   At first it's beautiful to just watch that white line reel in to
Willie's snout but when I start looking around out the window
there's just endless housing tracts and new blue factories
everywhere——Sez Dave "Yes that's right, the population
explosion is gonna cover every bit of backyard dirt in America
someday in fact they'll even have to start piling up friggin levels
of houses and others over that like your cityCityCITY till the
houses reach a hundred miles in the air in all directions of the
map and people looking at the earth from another planet with
super telescopes will see a prickly ball hangin in space——It's
like real horrible when you come to think of it, even us with all
our fancy talks, shit man it's all millions of people and events
piling up almost unimaginable now, like raving babboons we'll
all be piled on top of each other or one another or whatever you're
sposed to say——Hundreds of millions of hungry mouths
raving for more more more——And the sadness of it all is that
the world hasnt any chance to produce say a writer whose life
could really actually touch all this life in every detail like you
always say, some writer who could bring you sobbing thru the

bed fuckin bedcribs of the moon to see it all even unto the god-
damned last gory detail of some dismal robbery of the heart at
dawn when no one cares like Sinatra sings" ("When no one
cares," he sings in his low baritone but resumes):—"Some strict
sweeper sweeping it all up, I mean the incredible helplessness I
felt Jack when Céline ended his Journey To The End Of The
Night by pissing in the Seine River at dawn there I am thinkin
my God there's probably somebody pissing in the Trenton River
at dawn right now, the Danube, the Ganges, the frozen Obi, the
Yellow, the Paraña, the Willamette, the Merrimac in Missouri
too, the Missouri itself, the Yuma, the Amazon, the Thames,
the Po, the so and so, it's so friggin endless it's like poems endless
everywhere and no one knows any bettern old Buddha you know
where he says it's like 'There are immeasurable star misty aeons
of universes more numerous than the sands in all the galaxies,
multiplied by a billion lightyears of multiplication, in fact if I
were to go on you'd be scared and couldnt comprehend and
you'd despair so much you'd drop dead,' that's what he just
about said in one of those sutras——Macrocosms and micro-
cosms and chillicosms and microbes and finally you got all these
marvelous books a man aint even got time to read em all, what
you gonna do in this already piled up multiple world when you
have to think of the Book of Songs, Faulkner, César Birotteau,
Shakespeare, Satyricons, Dantes, in fact long stories guys tell
you in bars, in fact the sutras themselves, Sir Philip Sidney,
Sterne, Ibn El Arabi, the copious Lope de Vega and the uncopi-
ous goddamn Cervantes, shoo, then there's all those Catulluses
and Davids and radio listening skid row sages to contend with
because they've all got a million stories too and you too Ron
Blake in the backseat shut up! down to everything which is so
much that it is of necessity dont you think NOthing anyway,
huh?" (expressing exactly the way I feel, of course).

  And to corroborate all that about the too-much-ness of the
world, in fact, there's Stanley Popovich also in the back mattress
next to Ron, Stanley Popovich of New York suddenly arrived in

San Francisco with Jamie his Italian beauty girl but's going to leave her in a few days to go work for the circus, a big tough Yugoslav kid who ran the Seven Arts Gallery in New York with big bearded beatnik readings but now comes the circus and a whole big on-the-road of his own——It's too much, in fact right this minute he's started telling us about circus work——On top of all that old Cody is up ahead with HIS thousand stories—— We all agree it's too big to keep up with, that we're surrounded by life, that we'll never understand it, so we center it all in by swigging Scotch from the bottle and when it's empty I run out of the car and buy another one, period.

13

But on the way to cody's my madness already began to manifest itself in a stranger way, another one of those signposts of something wrong I mentioned a ways back: I thought I saw a flying saucer in the sky over Los Gatos——From five miles away——I look and I see this thing flying along and mention it to Dave who takes one brief look and says "Ah it's only the top of a radio tower"——It reminds me of the time I took a mescaline pill and thought an airplane was a flying saucer (a strange story this, a man has to be crazy to write it anyway).

But there's old Cody in the livingroom of his fine ranchito home sittin over his chess set pondering a problem and right by the fresh woodfire in the fireplace his wife's set out because she knows I love fireplaces——She a good friend of mine too—— The kids are sleeping in the back, it's about eleven, and good old Cody shakes my hand again——Havent seen him for several years because mainly he's just spent two years in San Quentin on a stupid charge of possession of marijuana——He was on his way to work on the railroad one night and was short on time and his driving license had been already revoked for speeding so he saw two bearded bluejeaned beatniks parked, asked them to trade a quick ride to work at the railroad station for two sticks of tea, they complied and arrested him——They were disguised policemen——For this great crime he spent two years in San Quentin in the same cell with a murderous gunman——His job was sweeping out the cotton mill room——I expect him to be all bitter and out of his head because of this but strangely and magnificently he's become quieter, more radiant, more patient, manly, more friendly even——And tho the wild frenzies of his old road days with me have banked down he still has the same taut eager face and supple muscles and looks like he's ready to go anytime——But actually loves his home (paid for by railroad insurance when he broke his leg trying to stop a boxcar from crashing), loves his wife in a way tho they fight some, loves his kids and especially his little son Timmy John partly named after me——Poor old, good old Cody sittin there with his chess set, wants immediately to challenge somebody to a chess game but only has an hour to talk to us before he goes to work supporting the family by rushing out and pushing his Nash Rambler down the quiet Los Gatos suburb street, jumping in, starting the motor, in fact his only complaint is that the Nash wont start without a push——No bitter complaints about society whatever from this grand and ideal man who really loves me moreover as if I deserved it, but I'm bursting to explain everything to him, not even Big Sur but the past several years, but there's no chance with everybody yakking——And in fact I can see in Cody's eyes that he can see in my own eyes the regret we both feel that recently we havent had chances to talk whatever, like we used to do driving across America and back in the old road days, too many people now want to talk to us and tell us *their* stories, we've been hemmed in and surrounded and outnumbered—— The circle's closed in on the old heroes of the night——But he says "However you guys, come on down round 'bout one when the boss leaves and watch me work and keep me company awhile before you go back to the City"——I can see Dave Wain really loves him at once, and Stanley Popovich too who's come along on this trip just to meet the fabled "Dean Moriarty"——The name I give Cody in "On the Road"——But O, it breaks my heart to see he's lost his beloved job on the railroad and after all the seniority he'd piled up since 1948 and now is reduced to tire recapping and dreary parole visits——All for two sticks of

wild loco weed that grows by itself in Texas because God
wanted it——

And there over the bookshelf is the old photo of me and Cody
arm in arm in the early days on a sunny street——

I rush to explain to Cody what happened the year before
when his religious advisor at the prison had invited me to come
to San Quentin to lecture the religious class——Dave Wain
was supposed to drive me and wait outside the prison walls as
I'd go in there alone, probably with a pepup nip bottle hidden in
my coat (I hoped) and I'd be led by big guards to the lecture
room of the prison and there would be sitting a hundred or so
cons including Cody probably all proud in the front row——
And I would begin by telling them I had been in jail myself once
and that I had no right nevertheless to lecture them on
religion——But they're all lonely prisoners and dont care what I
talk about——The whole thing arranged, in any case, and on
the big morning I wake up instead dead drunk on a floor, it's
already noon and too late, Dave Wain is on the floor also, Willie's parked outside to take us to Quentin for the lecture but it's
too late——But now Cody says "It's alright old buddy I
understand"——Altho our friend Irwin had done it, lectured
there, but Irwin can do all sorta things like that being more
social than I am and capable of going in there as he did and
reading his wildest poems which set the prison yard humming
with excitement tho I think he shouldna done it after all because
I say just to show up for any reason except visiting inside a prison
is still SIGNIFYING——And I tell this to Cody who ponders
a chess problem and says "Drinkin again, hey?" (if there's anything he hates is to see me drink).

We help him push his Nash down the street, then drink
awhile and talk with Evelyn a beautiful blonde woman that
young Ron Blake wants and even Dave Wain wants but she's got
her mind on other things and taking care of the children who
have to go to school and dancing classes in the morning and
hardly gets a word in edgewise anyway as we all yak and yell like

fools to impress her tho all she really wants is to be alone with me to talk about Cody and his latest soul.

Which includes the fact of Billie Dabney his mistress who has threatened to take Cody away completely from Evelyn, as I'll show later.

So we do go out to the San Jose highway to watch Cody recap tires——There he is wearing goggles working like Vulcan at his forge, throwing tires all over the place with fantastic strength, the good ones high up on a pile, "This one's no good" down on another, bing, bang, talking all the time a long fantastic lecture on tire recapping which has Dave Wain marvel with amazement——("My God he can do all that and even explain while he's doing it")——But I just mention in connection with the fact that Dave Wain now realizes why I've always loved Cody——Expecting to see a bitter ex con he sees instead a martyr of the American Night in goggles in some dreary tire shop at 2 A.M. making fellows laugh with joy with his funny explanations yet at the same time to a T performing every bit of the work he's being paid for——Rushing up and ripping tires off car wheels with a jicklo, clang, throwing it on the machine, starting up big roaring steams but yelling explanations over that, darting, bending, flinging, flaying, till Dave Wain said he thought he was going to die laughing or crying right there on the spot.

So we drive back to town and go to the mad boardinghouse to drink some more and I pass out dead drunk on the floor as usual in that house, waking up in the morning groaning far from my clean cot on the porch in Big Sur——No bluejays yakking for me to wake up any more, no gurgling creek, I'm back in the grooky city and I'm trapped.

14

Instead there's the sound of bottles crashing in the livingroom where poor Lex Pascal is holding forth yelling, it reminds of the time a year ago when Jarry Wagner's future wife got sore at Lex and threw a half gallonfull of tokay across the room and hooked him right across the eye, thereupon sailing to Japan to marry Jarry in a big Zen ceremony that made coast to coast papers but all old Lex's got is a cut which I try to fix in the bathroom upstairs saying "Hey, that cut's already stopped bleeding, you'll be alright Lex"——"I'm French Canadian too" he says proudly and when Dave and I and George Baso get ready to drive back to New York he gives me a St.Christopher medal as a goingaway gift——Lex the kind of guy shouldnt really be living in this wild beat boardinghouse, should hide on a ranch somewhere, powerful, goodlooking, full of crazy desire for women and booze and never enough of either——So as the bottles crash again and the Hi Fi's playing Beethoven's Solemn Mass I fall asleep on the floor.

Waking up the next morning groaning of course, but this is the big day when we're going to go visit poor George Baso at the TB hospital in the Valley——Dave perks me up right away bringing coffee or wine optional——I'm on Ben Fagan's floor somehow, apparently I've harangued him till dawn about Buddhism—some Buddhist.

Complicated already but now suddenly appears Joey Rosenberg a strange young kid from Oregon with a full beard and his

hair growing right down to his neck like Raul Castro, once the
California High School high jump champ who was only about 5
foot 6 but had made the incredible leap of six foot nine over the
bar! and shows his highjump ability too by the way he dances
around on light feet——A strange athlete who's suddenly
decided instead to become some sort of beat Jesus and in fact
you see perfect purity and sincerity in his young blue eyes——
In fact his eyes are so pure you dont notice the crazy hair and
beard, and also he's wearing ragged but strangely elegant clothing ("One of the first of the new Beat Dandies," McLear told me
a few days later, "did you hear about that? there's a new strange
underground group of beatniks or whatever who wear special
smooth dandy clothes even tho it may just be a jean jacket with
shino slacks they'll always have strange beautiful shoes or shirts,
or turn around and wear fancy pants unpressed acourse but with
torn sneakers")——Joey is wearing something like brown soft
garments like a tunic or something and his shoes look like Las
Vegas sports shoes——The moment he sees my battered blue
little sneakers that I'd used at Big Sur when my feet go sore, that
is in case my feet got sore on a rocky hike, he wants them for
himself, he wants to swap the snazzy Las Vegas sports shoes
(pale leather, untooled) for my silly little tightfitting tho perfect
sneakers that in fact I was wearing because the Monterey hike
blisters were still hurting me——So we swap——And I ask
Dave Wain about him: Dave says: "He's one of the really strang-
est sweetest guys I've ever known, showed up about a week ago I
hear tell, they asked him what he wanted to do and never
answers, just smiles——He just sorta wants to dig everything
and just watch and enjoy and say nothing particular about
it——If someone's to ask him 'Let's drive to New York' he'd
jump right for it without a word——On a sort of a pilgrimage,
see, with all that youth, us old fucks oughta take a lesson from
him, in faith too, he has faith, I can see it in his eyes, he has faith
in any direction he may take with anyone just like Christ I
guess."

It's strange that in a later revery I imagined myself walking across a field to find the strange gang of pilgrims in Arkansas and Dave Wain was sitting there saying "Shhh, He's sleeping," "He" being Joey and all the disciples are following him on a march to New York after which they expect to keep going walking on water to the other shore——But of course (in my revery even) I scoff and dont believe it (a kind of story daydreaming I often do) but in the morning when I look into Joey Rosenberg's eyes I instantly realize it IS Him, Jesus, because anyone (according to the rules of my revery) who looks into those eyes is instantly convinced and converted——So the revery continues into a long farfetched story ending with thinking I.B.M. machines trying to destroy this "Second Coming" etc. (but also, in reality, a few months later I threw away his shoes in the ashcan back home because I felt they had brought me bad luck and wishing I'd kept my blue sneakers with the little holes in the toes!)

So anyway we get Joey and Ron Blake who's always following Dave and go off to see Monsanto at the store, our usual ritual, then across the corner to Mike's Place where we start off the 10 A.M. with food, drink and a few games of pool at the tables along the bar——Joey winning the game and a stranger pool-shark you never saw with his long Biblical hair bending to slide the cue stick smoothly through completely professionally competent fingerstance and smashing home long straight drives, like seeing Jesus shoot pool of course——And meanwhile all the food these poor starved kids all three of them do pack in and eat!——It's not every day they're with a drunken novelist with hundreds of dollars to splurge on them, they order everything, spaghetti, follow that up with Jumbo Hamburgers, follow that up with ice cream and pie and puddings, Dave Wain has a huge appetite anyway but adds Manhattans and Martinis to the side of his plate——I'm just wailing away on my old fatal double bourbons and gingerale and I'll be sorry in a few days.

Any drinker knows how the process works: the first day you

get drunk is okay, the morning after means a big head but so you can kill that easy with a few more drinks and a meal, but if you pass up the meal and go on to another night's drunk, and wake up to keep the toot going, and continue on to the fourth day, there'll come one day when the drinks wont take effect because you're chemically overloaded and you'll have to sleep it off but cant sleep any more because it was alcohol itself that made you sleep those last five nights, so delirium sets in——Sleeplessness, sweat, trembling, a groaning feeling of weakness where your arms are numb and useless, nightmares, (nightmares of death) . . . well, there's more of that up later.

About noon which is now the peak of a golden blurry new day for me we pick up Dave's girl Romana Swartz a big Rumanian monster beauty of some kind (I mean with big purple eyes and very tall and big but Mae West big), Dave whispers in my ear "You oughta see her walking around that Zen-East House in those purple panties of hers, nothing else on, there's one married guy lives there who goes crazy every time she goes down the hall tho I dont blame him, would you? she's not trying to entice him or anybody she's just a nudist, she believe in nudism and bygod she's going to practice it!" (the Zen-East house being another sort of boardinghouse but this one for all kinds of married people and single and some small bohemian type families all races studying Subud or something, I never was there)——She's a big beautiful brunette anyway in the line of taste you might attribute to every slaky hungry sex slave in the world but also intelligent, well read, writes poetry, is a Zen student, knows everything, is in fact just simply a big healthy Rumanian Jewess who wants to marry a good hardy man and go live on a farm in the valley, that's it——

The T.B. hospital is about two hours away through Tracy and down the San Joaquin Valley, Dave drives beautiful with Romana between us and me holding the bottle again, it's bright beautiful California sunshine and prune orchards out there zipping by——It's always fun to have a good driver and a bottle and dark glasses on a fine sunny afternoon going somewhere interesting, and all the good conversation as I said——Ron and Joey are on the back mattress sitting crosslegged just like poor George Baso had sat on that trip last year from Frisco to New York.

But the main thing I'd liked at once about that Japanese kid was what he told me the first night I met him in that crazy kitchen of the Buchanan Street house: from midnight to 6 A.M. in his slow methodical voice he gave me his own tremendous version of the Life of Buddha beginning with infancy and right down to the end——George's theory (he has many theories and has actually run meditation classes with bells, just really a serious young lay priest of Japanese Buddhism when all is said and done) is that Buddha did not reject amorous love life with his wife and with his harem girls because he was sexually disinterested but on the contrary had been taught in the highest arts of lovemaking and eroticism possible in the India of that time, when great tomes like the Kama Sutra were in the process of being developed, tomes that give you instructions on every act, facet, approach, moment, trick, lick, lock, bing and bang and slurp of how to make love with another human being "male or female" insisted George: "He knew everything there is to know about all kinds of sex so that when he abandoned the world of pleasure to go be an ascetic in the forest everybody of course knew that he wasnt putting it all down out of ignorance——It served to make people of those times feel a marvelous respect for all his words——And he was just no simple Casanova with a few frigid affairs across the years, man he went all the way, he had ministers and special eunuchs and special women who taught him love, special virgins were brought to him, he was acquainted with every aspect of perversity and non perversity and as you know he was also a great archer, horseman, he was just completely trained in all the arts of living by his father's orders because his father wanted to make sure he'd NEVER leave the palace——They used every trick in the books to entice

him to a life of pleasure and as you know they even had him
happily married to a beautiful girl called Yasodhara and he had
a son with her Rahula and he also had his harem which included
dancing boys and everything in the books" then George would
go into every detail of this knowledge, like "He knew that the
phallus is held with the hand and moved inside the vagina with a
rotary movement, but this was only the first of several variations
where there is also the lowering down of the gal's hips so that the
vulva you see recedes and the phallus is introduced with a fast
quick movement like stinging of a wasp, or else the vulva is
protruded by means of lifting up the hips high so that the
member is buried with a sudden rush right to the basis, or then
he can withdraw real teasing like, or concentrate on right or left
side——And then he knew all the gestures, words, expressions,
what to do with a flower, what not to do with a flower, how to
drink the lip in all kinds of kissing or how to crush kiss or soft
kiss, man he was a *genius* in the beginning". . . and so on, George
went all the way telling me this till 6 A.M. it being one of the
most fantastic *Buddha Charitas* I'd ever heard ending with
George's own perfect enunciation of the law of the Twelve Nir-
danas whereby Buddha just logically disconnected all creation
and laid it bare for what it was, under the Bo Tree, a chain of
illusions——And on the trip to New York with Dave and me up
front talking all the way poor George just sat there on the mattress for the most part very quiet and told us he was taking this
trip to find out if HE was traveling to New York or just the CAR
(Willie the Jeep) was traveling to New York or was it just the
WHEELS were rolling, or the tires, or what——A Zen problem
of some kind——So that when we'd see grain elevators on the
Plains of Oklahoma George would say quietly "Well it seems to
me that grain elevator is sorta waitin for the road to approach it"
or he'd say suddenly "While you guys was talkin just then about
how to mix a good Pernod Martini I just saw a white horse
standing in an abandoned storefront"——In Las Vegas we'd
taken a good motel room and gone out to play a little roulette, in

St.Louis we'd gone to see the great bellies of the East St.Louis hootchy kootchy joints where three of the most marvelous young girls performed smiling directly at us as tho they knew all about George and his theories about erogenous Buddha (there sits the monarch observing the donzinggerls) and as tho they knew anyway all about Dave Wain who whenever he sees a beautiful girls says licking his lips "Yum Yum.". . .

But now George has T.B. and they tell me he may even die——Which adds to that darkness in my mind, all these DEATH things piling up suddenly——But I cant believe old Zen Master George is going to allow his body to die just now tho it looks like it when we pass through the lawn and come to a ward of beds and see him sitting dejected on the edge of his bed with his hair hanging over his brow where before it was always combed back——He's in a bathrobe and looks up at us almost displeased (but everybody is displeased by unexpected visits from friends or relatives in a hospital)——Nobody wants to be surprised on their hospital bad——He sighs and comes out to the warm lawn with us and the expression on his face says "Well ah so you've come to see me because I'm sick but what do you really want?" as tho all the old humorous courage of the year before has now given away to a profoundly deep Japanese skepticism like that of a Samurai warrior in a fit of suicidal depression (surprising me by its abject gloomy fearful frown).

15

I mean it was like my first frightened realization of what to be Japanese really meant——To be Japanese and not to believe in life any more and to be gloomy like Beethoven yet to be Japanese in gloom, the gloom of Bashô behind it all, the huge thunderous scowl of Issa or of Shiki, kneeling in the frost with the bowed head like the bowed-head-oblivion of all the old horses of Japan long dust.

He sits there on the lawn bench looking down and when Dave asks him "Well you gonna be alright soon George" he says simply "I dont know"——He really means "I don't care"—— And always warm and courteous with me he now hardly pays any attention to me——He's a little nervous because the other patients, G.I. vets, will see that he's received a visit from a bunch of ragged beatniks including Joey Rosenberg who is bouncing around the lawn looking at flowers with that bemused sincere smile——But little neat George, just 5 feet 5 and a few pounds over that and so clean, with his soft feathery hair like the hair of a child, his delicate hands, he just stares at the ground——His answers come like an old man's (he's only 30)——"I guess all the Dharma talk about everything is nothing is just sorta sinking in my bones," he concedes, which makes me shudder——(On the way Dave's been telling us to be ready because George's changed so)——But I try to keep things going, "Do you remember those dancing girls in St.Louis?"——"Yeh, whore candy" (he's referring to a piece of perfumed cotton one of the girls threw at us in her dance, which we tacked up later to a highway accident cross we'd yanked out of the ground one blood red sunset in Arizona, tacking this perfumed beautiful cotton right where the head of Christ was so that when we brought the cross to New York naturally we had everybody smelling it but George pointed out how beautiful we'd done all this subconsciously because the net result was that all the hepcats of Greenwich Village who came in to see us were picking up the cross and putting their heads (noses) to it)——But George doesnt care any more——And anyway it's time to leave.

But ah, as we're leaving and waving back at him and he's turned around tentatively to go into the hospital I linger behind the others and turn around several times to wave again—— Finally I start to make a joke of it by ducking around a corner and peeking out and waving again——He ducks behind a bush and waves back——I dart to a bush and peek out——Suddenly we're two crazy hopeless sages goofing on a lawn——Finally as we part further and further and he comes closer to the door we are making elaborate gestures and down to the most infinitesimal like when he steps inside the door I wait till I see him sticking a finger out——So from around my corner I stick out a shoe——So from his door he sticks out an eye——So from my corner I stick out nothing but just yell "Wu!"——So from his door he sticks out nothing and says nothing——So I hide in the corner and do nothing——But suddenly I burst out and there HE is bursting out and we start waving gyrations and duck back to our hiding places——Then I pull a big one by simply walking away rapidly but suddenly I turn and wave again——He walking backwards and waving back——The further I go now also walking backwards the more I wave——Finally we're so far apart by about a hundred yards the game is almost impossible but we continue somehow——Finally I see a distant sad little Zen wave of hand——I jump up into the air and gyrate both arms——He does the same——He goes into the hospital but a moment later he's peeking out this time from the ward window!——I'm behind a tree trunk thumbing my nose at him——There's no end to it, in fact——The other kids are all back at the car wondering what's keeping me——What's keeping me is that I know George will get better and live and teach the joyful truth and George knows I know this, that's why he's playing the game with me, the magic game of glad freedom which is what Zen or for that matter the Japanese soul ultimately means I say, "And someday I will go to Japan with George" I tell myself after we've made our last little wave because I've heard the supper bell ring and seen the other patients rush for the chow line and knowing George's fantastic appetite wrapped in that little frail body I dont wanta hang him up tho he nevertheless does one last trick: He throws a glass of water out the window in a big froosh of water and I dont see him any more.

"Wotze mean by that?" I'm scratching my head going back to the car.

16

To complete this crazy day at 3 o'clock in the morning here I am sitting in a car being driven 100 miles an hour around the sleeping streets and hills and waterfronts of San Francisco, Dave's gone off to sleep with Romana and the others are passed out and this crazy nextdoor neighbor of the roominghouse (himself a Bohemian but also a laborer, a housepainter who comes home with big muddy boots and has his little boy living with him the wife has died)——I've been in his pad listening to booming loud Stan Getz jazz on his Hi Fi and happened to mention I thought Dave Wain and Cody Pomeray were the two greatest drivers in the world——"What?" he yells, a big blond husky kid with a strange fixed smile, "man I used to drive the getaway car! come on down I'll show yal!"——So almost dawn and here we are cuttin down Buchanan and around the corner on screeching wheels and he opens her up, goes zipping towards a red light so takes a sudden screeching left and goes up a hill fullblast, when we come to the top of the hill I figger he'll pause awhile to see what's over the top but he goes even faster and practically flies off the hill and we head down one of those incredibly steep San Fran streets with our snout pointed to the waters of the Bay and he steps on the gas! we go sailing down a hundred m.p.h. to the bottom of the hill where there's an intersection luckily with the light on green and thru that we blast with just one little bump where the road crosses and another bump where the street is dipping downhill again——We come

down to the waterfront and screech right——In a minute we're
soaring over the ramps around the Bridge entrance and before I
can gulp up a shot or two from my last late bottle we're already
parked back outside the pad on Buchanan——The greatest driver in the world whoever he was and I never saw him
again——Bruce something or other——What a getaway.

17

I end up groaning drunk on the floor this time beside Dave's floor mattress forgetting that he's not even there.

But a strange thing happened that morning I remember now: before Cody's call from downvalley: I'm feeling hopelessly idiotically depressed again groaning to remember Tyke's dead and remembering that sinking beach but at the side of the radiator in the toilet lies a copy of Boswell's Johnson which we'd been discussing so happy in the car: I open to any page then one more page and start reading from the top left and suddenly I'm in an entirely perfect world again: old Doc Johnson and Boswell are visiting a castle in Scotland belonging to a deceased friend called Rorie More, they're drinking sherry by the great fireplace looking at the picture of Rorie on the wall, the widow of Rorie is there, Johnson suddenly says "Sir, here's what I would do to deal with the sword of Rorie More" (the portrait shows old Rorie with his Highlands flinger) "I'd get inside him with a dirk and stab him to my pleasure like an animal" and bleary with hangover I realize that if there was any way for Johnson to express his sorrow to the widow of Rorie More on the unfortunate circumstance of his death, this was the way——So pitiful, irrational, yet perfect——I rush down to the kitchen where Dave Wain and some others are already eating breakfast of sorts and start reading the whole thing to the lot of them——Jonesy looks at me askance over his pipe for being so literary so early in the morning but I'm not being literary at all——Again I see death, the death of Rorie More, but Johnson's response to death is ideal and so ideal I only wish old Johnson be sitting in the kitchen now——(Help! I'm thinking).

The call comes from Cody in Los Gatos that he lost his job tire recapping——"Because we were there last night?"——"No no something entirely different, he's gotta lay off some men because his mortgage is bleeding him and all that and some girl is tryna sue him for forging a check and all that, so man I've got to find another job but I have to pay the rent and everything's all fucked up down here, Oh old buddy how about, cant you, I plead or I dont plead, or honestly, Jack, ah, lend me a hundred dollars willya?"——"By God Cody I'll be right down and GIVE you a hundred dollars"——"You mean you'll really do that, listen just to lend to me is enough but if you insist, hm" (fluttering his eyelashes over the phone because he knows I mean it) "you old loverboy you, how you gonna get down here there and give me that money there son and make my old heart glad"——"I'll have Dave drive me down"——"Okay I'll pay the rent with it right away and because it's now Friday, why, Thursday or whatever, that's right Thursday, why I dont have to be lookin for a new job till next Monday so you can stay here and we'll have a long weekend just goofin and talkin boy like we used to do, I can demolish you at chess or we can watch a baseball game" and in a whisper "and we can sneak into the City see and see my purty baby"——So I ask Dave Wain and yes he's ready to go anytime, he's just following me like I often follow people myself, and so off we go again.

And on the way we drop in on Monsanto at the bookstore and the idea suddenly comes to me for Dave and me and Cody to go to the cabin and spend a big quiet crazy weekend (how?) but when Monsanto hears this idea he'll come too, in fact he'll bring his little Chinese buddy Arthur Ma and we'll catch McLear at Santa Cruz and go visit Henry Miller and suddenly another big huge ball is begun.

So there's Willie waiting down on the street, I go to the store, buy the bottle, Dave wheels Willie around, Ron Blake and now Ben Fagan are on the back mattress, I'm sitting in my front seat rocking chair as now in broad afternoon we go blattin again down that Bay Shore highway to see old Cody and Monsanto's in back of us in his jeep with Arthur Ma, two jeeps now, and about to be two more as I'll show——Coming to Cody's in mid afternoon, his own house already filled with visitors (local Los Gatos literaries and all kinds of people the phone there ringing continually too) and Cody says to Evelyn "I'll just spend a couple days with Jack and the gang like the old days and look for a job Monday"——"Okay"——So we all go to a wonderful pizza restaurant in Los Gatos where the pizzas are piled an inch high with mushrooms and meat and anchovies or anything you want, I cash a travelers check at the supermarket, Cody takes the 100 in cash, gives it to Evelyn in the restaurant, and later that day the two jeeps resume down to Monterey and down that blasted road I walked on blistered feet back to the frightful bridge at Raton Canyon——And I'd thought I'd never see the place again. But now I was coming back loaded with observers. The sight of the canyon down there as we renegotiated the mountain road made me bite my lip with marvel and sadness.

18

It's as familiar as an old face in an old photograph as tho I'm gone a million years from all that sun shaded brush on rocks and that heartless blue of the sea washing white on yellow sand, those rills of yellow arroyo running down mighty cliff shoulders, those distant blue meadows, that whole ponderous groaning upheaval so strange to see after the last several days of just looking at little faces and mouths of people——As tho nature had a Gargantuan leprous face of its own with broad nostrils and huge bags under its eyes and a mouth big enough to swallow five thousand jeepster stationwagons and ten thousand Dave Wains and Cody Pomerays without a sigh of reminiscence or regret——There it is, every sad contour of my valley, the gaps, the Mien Mo captop mountain again, the dreaming woods below our high shelved road, suddenly indeed the sight of poor Alf again far way grazing in the mid afternoon by the corral fence——And there's the creek bouncing along as tho nothing had ever happened elsewhere and even in the daytime somehow dark and hungry looking in its deeper tangled grass.

Cody's never seen this country before altho he's an old Californian by now, I can see he's very impressed and even glad he's come out on a little jaunt with the boys and with me and is seeing a grand sight——He's like a little boy again now for the first time in years because he's like let out of school, no job, the bills paid, nothing to do but gratefully amuse me, his eyes are shining——In fact ever since he's come out of San Quentin

there's been something hauntedly boyish about him as tho
prison walls had taken all the adult dark tenseness out of
him——In fact every evening after supper in the cell he shared
with the quiet gunman he'd bent his serious head to a daily letter
or at least every-other-day letter full of philosophical and religious musings to his mistress Billie——And when you're in bed
in jail after lights out and you're not sleepy there's ample time to
just remember the world and indeed savor its sweetness if any
(altho it's always sweet to remember it in jail tho harder in prison,
as Genêt shows) with the result that he'd not only come to a
chastisement of his bashing bitternesses (and of course it's
always good to get away from alcohol and excessive smoking for
two years) (and all that regular sleep) he was just like a kid again,
but as I say that haunting kidlikeness I think all ex cons seem to
have when they've just come out——In seeking to severely
penalize criminals society by putting the criminals away behind
safe walls actually provide them with the means of greater
strength for future atrocities glorious and otherwise——"Well
I'll be damned" he keeps saying as he sees those bluffs and cliffs
and hanging vines and dead trees, "you mean to tell me you ben
alone here for three weeks, why I wouldnt dare that . . . must be
awful at night . . . looka that old mule down there . . . man, dig
the redwood country way back in . . . reminds me of old Col-
orady b'god when I used to steal a car every day and drive out to
hills like this with a fresh little high school sumptin"——"Yum
Yum," says Dave Wain emphatically turning that big goofy look
to us from his driving wheel with his big mad feverish shining
eyes full of yumyum and yabyum too——"S'matter with you
boys not making extensive plans to bring a bevy of schoolgirls
down here to wile away our conversation pieces thar" says Cody
real relaxed and talking sadly.

Behind us the Monsanto jeepster follows doggedly——
Passing thru Monterey Monsanto has already called Pat
McLear, staying for the summer with wife and kid in Santa

Cruz, McLear with his own jeepster is following us a few miles down the highway——It's a big Big Sur day.

We wheel downhill to cross the creek and at the corral fence I proudly get out to officially open the gate and let the cars through——We go bumping down the two-rutted lane to the cabin and park——My heart sinks to see the cabin.

To see the cabin so sad and almost human waiting there for me as if forever, to hear my little neat gurgling creek resuming its song just for me, to see the very same blue-jays still waiting in the tree for me and maybe mad at me now they see I'm back because I havent been there to lay out their Cheerios along the porch rail every blessed morning——And in fact first thing I do is rush inside and get them some food and lay it out——But so many people around now they're afraid to try it.

Monsanto all decked out in his old clothes and looking forward to a wine and talkfest weekend in his pleasant cabin takes the big sweet axe down from the wall nails and goes out and starts hammering at a huge log——In fact it's really a half of a tree that fell there years ago and's been hammered at inter-mittently but now he's bound he's going to crack it in half and again in half so we can then start splitting it down the middle for huge bonfire type logs——Meanwhile little Arthur Ma who never goes anywhere without his drawing paper and his Yellow-jack felt tip pencils is already seated in my chair on the porch (wearing my hat now too) drawing one of his interminable pic-tures, he'll do 25 a day and 25 the next day too——He'll talk and go on drawing——He has felt tips of all colors, red, blue, yellow, green, black, he draws marvelous subconscious glurbs and can also do excellent objective scenes or anything he wants on to cartoons——Dave is taking my rucksack and his rucksack out of Willie and throwing them into the cabin, Ben Fagan is wandering around near the creek puffing on his pipe with a happy bhikku smile, Ron Blake is unpacking the steaks we bought enroute in Monterey and I'm already flicking the plastics off the top of bottles with that expert twitch and twist you only get to learn after years of winoing in alleys east and west.

Still the same, the fog is blowing over the walls of the canyon obscuring the sun but the sun keeps fighting back——The inside of the cabin with the fire finally going is still the dear lovable abode now as sharp in my mind as I look at it as an unusually well focused snapshot——The sprig of ferns still stands in a glass of water, the books are there, the neat groceries ranged along the wall shelves——I feel excited to be with the gang but there's a hidden sadness too and which is expressed later by Monsanto when he says "This is the kind of place where a person should really be alone, you know? when you bring a big gang here it somehow desecrates it not that I'm referring to us or anybody in particular? there's such a sad sweetness to those trees as tho yells shouldnt insult them or conversation only"—— Which is just the way I feel too.

In a gang we all go down the path towards the sea, passing underneath "That *sono*fabitch bridge" Cody calls it looking up with horror——"That thing's enough to scare anybody away"——But worst of all for an old driver like Cody, and Dave too, is to see that upended old chassis in the sand, they spend a half hour poking around the wreckage and shaking their heads——We kick around the beach awhile and decide to come back at night with bottles and flashlights and build a huge bonfire, now it's time to get back to the cabin and cook those steaks and have a ball, and there's McLear's jeep already arrived and parked and there's McLear himself and that beautiful blonde wife of his in her tight blue jeans that makes Dave say "Yum yum" and Cody just say "Yes, that's right, yes, that's right, ah hum honey, yes."

19

A roaring drinking bout begins deep in the canyon——Fog nightfall sends cold seeping into the windows so all these softies demand that the wood windows be closed so we all sit there in the glow of the one lamp coughing in the smoke but they dont care——They think it's just the steaks smoking over the fire——I have one of the jugs in my hand and I wont let go—— McLear is the handsome young poet who's just written the most fantastic poem in America, called "Dark Brown," which is every detail of his and his wife's body described in ecstatic union and communion and inside out and everywhichaway and not only that he insists on reading it to us——But I wanta read my "Sea" poem too——But Cody and Dave Wain are talking about something else and that silly kid Ron Blake is singing like Chet Baker——Arthur Ma is drawing in the corner, and it sorta goes like this generally:—

"That's what old men do, Cody, they drive slowly backwards in Safeway Supermarket parking lots"——"Yes that's right, I was tellin you about that bicycle of mine but that's what they do yes you see that's because while the old woman is shoppin in that store they figure they'll park a little closer to the entrance and so they spend a half hour to think their big move out and they back in out slowly from their slot, can hardly turn around to see what's in back, usually nothin there, then they wheel real slow and trembly to that slot they picked but all of a sudden some cat jumps in it with his pickup and them old men is scratchin their

heads sayin and whining 'Owww, these young fellers nowadays'
and all that obvious, ah, yes, but that BICYCLE of mine in
Denver I tell you I had it twisted and that wheel used to wobble
so by necissity I had to invent a new way to maneuver them han-
dlebars see——"——"Hey Cody have a drink," I'm yelling in
his ear and meanwhile McLear is reading: "Kiss my thighs in
darkness the pit of fire" and Monsanto is chuckling saying to
Fagan: "So this crazy character comes down stairs and asking
for a copy of Alisteir Crowley and I didnt know 'bout that till
you told me the other day, then on the way out I see him sneak a
book off the shelf but he puts another one in its place that he got
out of his pocket, and the books is a novel by somebody called
Denton Welch all about this young kid in China wanderin
around the streets like real romantic young Truman Capote
only it's China" and Arthur Ma suddenly yells: "Hold still you
buncha bastards, I got a hole in my eye" and generally the way
parties go, and so on, ending with the steak dinner (I dont even
touch a bite but just drink on), then the big bonfire on the beach
to which we march all in one arm-swinging gang, I've gotten the
idea in my head I'm the leader of a guerilla warfare unit and I'm
marching ahead the lieutenant giving orders, with all our flashlights and yells we come swarming down the narrow path going
"Hup one two three" and challenging the enemy to come out of
hiding, some guerillas.

Monsanto that old woodsman starts a huge bonfire on the
beach that can be seen flaring from miles away, cars passing
across the bridge way up there can see there's a party goin on in
the hole of night, in fact the bonfire lights up the eerie weird
beams and staunches of the bridge almost all the way up, giant
shadows dance on the rocks——The sea swirls up but seems
subdued——It's not like being alone down in the vast hell
writing the sounds of the sea.

The night ending with everybody passing out exhausted on
cots, in sleepingbags outside (McLear goes home with wife) but
Arthur Ma and I by the late fire keep up yelling spontaneous

questions and answers right till dawn like "Who told you you had a hat on your head?"——"My head never questions hats"——"What's the matter with your liver training?"—— "My liver training got involved in kidney work"—(and here again another great gigantic little Oriental friend for me, an eastcoaster who's never known Chinese or Japanese kids, on the west coast it's quite common but for an eastcoaster like me it's amazing and what with all my earlier studies in Zen and Chan and Tao)——(And Arthur also being a gentle small soft-haired seemingly soft little Oriental goofnik)——And we come to great chanted statements, taking turns, without a pause to think, just one then the other, bing and bang, the beauty of them being that while one guy is yelling like (me):- "Tonight the full apogee August moon will out, early with a jaundiced tint, and pop angels all over my rooftop along with Devas sprinkling flowers" (any kind of nonsense being the rule) the other guy has time not only to figure the next statement but can take off from the sub-conscious arousement of an idea from "angels all over my rooftop" and so can yell without thinking an answer the stupider or rather the more unexpectedly in-saner sillier brighter it is the better "Pilgrims dropping turds and sweet nemacular nameless railroad trains from heaven with omnipotent youths bearing monkey women that will stomp through the stage waiting for the moment when by pinching myself I prove that a thought is like a touch"——But this is only the beginning because now we know the routine and get better and better till at dawn I seem to recall we were so fantastically brilliant (while everyone snored) the skies must have shook to hear it and not just foil: let's see if I can recreate at least the style of this game:-

ARTHUR: "When are you going to become the Eighth Patriarch?"

ME: "As soon as you give me that old motheaten sweater"——(Much better than that, forget this for now, because I want to talk first about Arthur Ma and try again to duplicate our feat).

20

As I say my first little Chinese friend, I keep saying "little" George and "little" Arthur but the fact is they were both small anyway——Altho George talked slowly and was a little absent from everything in the way of a Zen Master actually who realizes that everything is indifferent anyway, Arthur was friendlier, warmer in a way, curious and always asking questions, more active than George with his constant drawing, and of course Chinese instead of Japanese——He wanted me to meet his father the following weeks——He was Monsanto's best friend at the time and they made an extremely strange pair going down the street together, the big ruddy happy man with the crewcut and corduroy jacket and sometimes pipe in mouth, and the little childlike Chinese boy who looked so young most bartenders wouldnt serve him tho he was actually 30 years old——Nevertheless the son of a famous Chinatown family and Chinatown is right back there behind the fabled beatnik streets of Frisco——Also Arthur was a tremendous little loverboy who had fabulously beautiful girls on the line and however'd just separated from his wife, a girl I never saw but Monsanto told me she was the most beautiful Negro girl in the world——Arthur came from a large family but as a painter and a Bohemian his family disapproved of him now so he lived alone in a comfortable old hotel on North Beach tho sometimes he went around the corner into Chinatown to visit his father who sat in the back of his Chinese general store brooding among his countless

poems written swiftly in Chinese stroke on pieces of beautiful
colored paper which he then hanged from the ceiling of his little
cubicle——There he sat, clean, neat, almost shiney, wondering
about what poem to write next but his keen little eyes always
jumping to the street door to see who's going by and if someone
came into the shop itself he knew at once who it was and for
what——He was in fact the best friend and trusted adviser of
Chiang Kai Shek in America, true and no lie——But Arthur
himself was in favor of the Red Chinese which was a family
matter and a Chinese matter I had nothing to say about and
didnt interest me except insofar as it gave a dramatic picture of
father and son in an old culture——The pint of the matter
anyway being that he was goofing with me just like George had
done and making me happy somehow like George had done——
Something anciently familiar about his loyal presence made me
wonder if I'd ever lived before in some other lifetime in China or
if he'd been an Occidental himself in a previous lifetime of his
own involved with mine somewhere else than China——The
pity of it is that I have no record of what we were yelling and
announcing back and forth as the birds woke up outside but it
went generally like this:-

ME:- "Unless someone sicks a hot iron in my heart or heaps up
Evil Karma like tit and tat the pile of that and pulls my mother
out her bed to slay her before my damning human eyes——"

ARTHUR:- "And I break my hand on heads——"

ME:- "Everytime you throw a rock at a cat from your glass
house you heap upon yourself the automatic Stanley Gould
winter so dark of death after death, and growing old——"

ARTHUR:- "Because lady those ashcans'll bite you back and be
cold too——"

ME:- "And your son will never rest in the imperturbable
knowledge that what he thinks he thinks as well as what he does
he thinks as well as what he feels he thinks as well as future
that——"

ARTHUR:- "Future that my damn old sword cutter Paisan Pasha lost the Preakness again———"

ME:- "Tonight the moon shall witness angels trooping at the baby's window where inside he gurgles in his pewk looking with mewling eyes for babyside waterfall lambikin hillside the day the little Arab shepherd boy hugged the babylamb to heart while the mother bleeted at his bay heel———"

ARTHUR:- "And so Joe the sillicks killit no not———"

ME:- "Shhhhoww graaa———"

ARTHUR:- "Wind and carstart———"

ME:- "The angels Devas monsters Asuras Devadattas Vedantas McLaughlins Stones will hue and hurl in hell if they dont love the lamb the lamb the lamb of hell lamb-chop———"

ARTHUR:- "Why did Scott Fitzgerald keep a notebook?"

ME:- "Such a marvelous notebook———"

ARTHUR:- "Komi denera ness pata sutyamp anda wanda vesnoki shadakiroo paryoumemga sikarem nora sarkadium baron roy kellegiam myorki ayastuna haidanseetzel ampho andiam yerka yama chelmsford alya bonneavance koroom cemanda versel———"

ME:- "The 26th Annual concert of the Armenian Convention?"

21

Incidentally I forgot to mention that during the three weeks alone the stars had not come out at all, not even for one minute on any night, it was the foggy season, except the very last night when I was getting ready to leave——Now the stars were out every night, the sun shone considerably longer but a sinister wind accompanied the Autumn in Big Sur: it seemed like the whole Pacific Ocean was blowing with all its might right into Raton Canyon and also over the high gap from another end causing all the trees to shudder as the big groaning howl came newsing and noising from downcanyon, when it hit there was raised a roar of noise I didnt like——It seemed ill omened to me somewhere——It was much better to have fog and silence and quiet trees——Now the whole canyon by one blast could be led screaming and waving in all directions in such a confused mass that even the fellows with me were a little surprised to see it——It was too big a wind for such a little canyon.

This development also prevented the constant hearing of the reassuring creek.

One good thing was that when jet planes broke the sound barrier overhead the wind dispersed the clap of empty thunder they caused, because during the foggy season the noise would come down into the canyon, concentrate there, and rock the house like an explosion making me think the first time (alone) that somebody'd set off a blast of dynamite nearby.

While I woke up groaning and sick there was plenty of wine

right there to start me off with the hounds of hair, so okay, but Monsanto had retired early and typically sensibly to sleep by the creek and now he was awake singing swooshing his whole head into the creek and going Brrrrr and rubbing his hands for a new day——Dave Wain made breakfast with his usual lecture "Now the real way to fry eggs is to put a cover over them so that they can have that neat basted white look on the yellows, soon's I get this pancake batter ready we'll start on them"——My list of groceries was so all inclusive in the beginning it was now feeding guerilla troops.

A big axe chopping contest began after breakfast, some of us sitting watching on the porch and the performers down below hacking away at the tree trunk which was over a foot thick—— They were chopping off two foot chunks, no easy job——I realized you can always study the character of a man by the way he chops wood——Monsanto an old lumberman up in Maine as I say now showed us how he conducted his whole life in fact by the way he took neat little short handled chops from both left and right angles getting his work done in reasonably short time without too much sweat——But his strokes were rapid—— Whereas old Fagan pipe-in-mouth slogged away I guess the way he learned in Oregon and in the Northwest fire schools, also getting his job done, silently, not a word——But Cody's fantastic fiery character showed in the way he went at the log with horrible force, when he brought down the axe with all his might and holding it far at the end you could hear the whole tree-trunk groaning the whole length inside, runk, sometimes you could hear a lengthwise cracking going on, he is really very strong and he brought that axe down so hard his feet left the earth when it hit——He chopped off his log with the fury of a Greek god—— Nevertheless it took him longer and much more sweat than Monsanto——"Used to do this in a workgang in southern Arizony" he said, whopping one down that made the whole tree-trunk dance off the ground——But it was like an example of vast but senseless strength, a picture of poor Cody's life and in a sense my own——I too chopped with all my might and got madder and went faster and raked the log but took more time than Monsanto who watched us smiling——Little Arthur thereupon tried his luck but gave up after five strokes——The axe was like to carry him away anyway——Then Dave Wain demonstrated with big easy strokes and in no time we had five huge logs to use——But now it was time to get in the cars (McLear had rearrived) and go driving south down the coast highway to a hot springs bath house down there, which sounded good to me at first.

But the new Big Sun Autumn was now all winey sparkling blue which made the terribleness and giantness of the coast all the more clear to see in all its gruesome splendor, miles and miles of it snaking away south, our three jeeps twisting and turning the increasing curves, sheer drops at our sides, further ghostly high bridges to cross with smashings below——Tho all the boys are wowing to see it——To me it's just an inhospitable madhouse of the earth, I've seen it enough and even swallowed it in that deep breath——The boys reassure me the hot springs bath will do me good (they see I'm gloomy now hungover for good) but when we arrive my heart sinks again as McLear points out to sea from the balcony of the outdoor pools: "Look out there floating in the sea weeds, a dead otter!"——And sure enough it is a dead otter I guess, a big brown pale lump floating up and down mournfully with the swells and ghastly weeds, my otter, my dear otter I'd written poems about——"Why did he die?" I ask myself in despair——"Why do they do that?"——"What's the sense of all this?"——All the fellows are shading their eyes to get a better look at the big peaceful tortured hunk of seacow out there as tho it's something of passing interest while to me it's a blow across the eyes and down into my heart——The hot water pools are steaming, Fagan and Monsanto and the others are all sitting peacefully up to their necks, they're all naked, but there's a gang of fairies also there naked all standing around in various bath house postures that make me hesitate to take my

clothes off just on general principles——In fact Cody doesnt
even bother to do anything but lie down with his clothes on in
the sun, on the balcony table, and just smoke——But I borrow
McLear's yellow bathingsuit and get in——"What ya wearing
a bathingsuit in a hot springs pool for boy?" says Fagan
chuckling——With horror I realize there's spermatazoa floating in the hot water——I look and I see the other men (the
fairies) all taking good long looks at Ron Baker who stands there
facing the sea with his arse for all to behold, not to mention
McLear and Dave Wain too——But it's very typical of me and
Cody that we wont undress in this situation (we were both raised
Catholics?)——Supposedly the big sex heroes of our generation, in fact——You might think——But the combination of
the strange silent watching fairy-men, and the dead otter out
there, and the spermatozoa in the pools makes me sick, not to
mention that when somebody informs me this bath house is
owned by the young writer Kevin Cudahy whom I knew very
well in New York and I ask one of the younger strangers where's
Kevin Cudahy he doesnt even deign to reply——Thinking he
hasnt heard me I ask again, no reply, no notice, I ask a third time,
this time he gets up and stalks out angrily to the locker
rooms——It all adds up to the confusion that's beginning to
pile up in my battered drinking brain anyway, the constant
reminders of death not the least of which was the death of my
peaceful love of Raton Canyon now suddenly becoming a horror.

From the baths we go to Nepenthe which is a beautiful cliff
top restaurant with vast outdoor patio, with excellent food,
excellent waiters and management, good drinks, chess tables,
chairs and tables to just sit in the sun and look at the grand
coast——Here we all sit at various tables and Cody starts
playing chess with everybody will join while he's chomping
away at those marvelous hamburgers called Heavenburgers
(huge with all the side works)——Cody doesnt like to just sit
around and lightly chat away, he's the kind of guy if he's going to
talk he has to do all the talking himself for hours till everything

is exhaustedly explained, sans that he just wants to bend over a
chessboard and say "He he heh, old Scrooge is saving up a pawn
hey? cak! I got ya!"——But while I'm sitting there discussing
literature with McLear and Monsanto suddenly a strange couple
of gentlemen nearby strike up an acquaintance——One of them
is a youngster who says he is a lieutenant in the Army——I
instantly (drunk on fifth Manhattan by now) go into my theory
of guerilla warfare based on my observations the night before
when it did seriously occur to me that if Monsanto, Arthur,
Cody, Dave, Ben, Ron Blake and I were all members of one
fighting unit (and all carrying canteens of booze on our belts) it
would be very difficult for the enemy to hurt any of us because
we'd be, as dear friends, watching so desperately closely over
one another, which I tell the first lieutenant, which attracts the
interest of the older man who admits that he's a GENERAL in
the Army——There are also some further homosexuals at a
separate table which prompts Dave Wain to look up from the
chess game at one quiet drowsy point and announce in his dry
twang "Under redwood beams, people talking about homosex-
uality and war . . . call it my Nepenthe Haiku"——"Yass" says
Cody checkmating him "see what you can *ku* about that m'boy
and get out of there and I'll noose you with my queen, dear."

   I mention the general only because there are also something
sinister about the fact that during this long binge I came across
him and *another* general, two strange generals, and I'd never
met any generals in my life——This first general was strange
because he seemed too polite and yet there was something sinister about his steely eyes behind goof darkglasses——Something
sinister too about the first lieutenant who guessed who we were
(the San Francisco poets, a major nucleus of them indeed) and
didn't seem at all pleased tho the general seemed amused——
Nevertheless in a sinister way the general seemed to take great
interest in my theory about buddy units for guerilla warfare and
when President Kennedy about a year later ordered just such a
new scheme for part of our armed forces I wondered (still crazy

even then but for new reasons) if the general had got an idea from me——The second general, even stranger, coming up, occurred when I was even more far gone.

Manhattans and more Manhattans and finally when we got back to the cabin in late afternoon I was feeling good but realized I was going to be finished tomorrow——But poor young Ron Blake asked me if he could stay with me in the cabin, the others were all going back to the city in the three cars, I couldnt think of any way to reject his request in a harmless way so said yes——So when they all left suddenly I was alone with this mad beatnik kid singing me songs and all I wanta do is sleep——But I've got to make the best of it and not disappoint his believing heart.

Because after all the poor kid actually believes that there's something noble and idealistic and kind about all this beat stuff, and I'm supposed to be the King of the Beatniks according to the newspapers, so but at the same time I'm sick and tired of all the endless enthusiasms of new young kids trying to know me and pour out all their lives into me so that I'll jump up and down and say yes yes that's right, which I cant do any more——My reason for coming to Big Sur for the summer being precisely to get away from that sort of thing——Like those pathetic five highschool kids who all came to my door in Long Island one night wearing jackets that said "Dharma Bums" on them, all expecting me to be 25 years old according to a mistake on a book jacket and here I am old enough to be their father——But no, hep swinging young jazzy Ron wants to dig everything, go to the beach, run and romp and sing, talk, write tunes, write stories, climb mountains, go hiking, see everything, do everything with everybody——But having one last quart of port with me I agree to follow him to the beach.

We go down the old sad path of the bhikku and suddenly I see a dead mouse in the grass——"A wee dead mousie" I say cleverly poetically but suddenly I realize and remember now for the first time how I've left the cover off the rat poison in

Monsanto's shelf and so this is *my mouse*——It's lying there *dead*——Like the otter in the sea——It's my own personal mouse that I've carefully fed chocolate and cheese all summer but once again I've unconsciously sabotaged all these great plans of mine to be kind to living beings even bugs, once again I've murdered a mouse one way or the other——And on top of that when we come to the place where the garter snake usually lies sunning itself, and I bring it to Ron's attention, he suddenly yells "LOOKOUT! you never can tell what kind of snake it is!" which really scares me, my heart pounds with horror——My little friend the garter snake turns therefore with my head from a living being with a long green body into the evil serpent of Big Sur.

On top of that, at the surf, where long streamers of hollow sea weed always lie around drying in the sun some of them huge, like living bodies with skin, pieces of living material that always made me sad somehow, here's the young hepcat lifting them up and dancing a dervish around the beach with them, turning my Sur into something seachange——Something brainchange.

All that night by lamplight we sing and yell songs which is okay but in the morning the bottle is gone and I wake up with the "final horrors" again, precisely the way I woke up in the Frisco skidrow room before escaping down here, it's all caught up with me again, I can hear myself again whining "Why does God torture me?"——But anybody who's never had delirium tremens even in their early stages may not understand that it's not so much a physical pain but a mental anguish indescribable to those ignorant people who dont drink and accuse drinkers of irresponsibility——The mental anguish is so intense that you feel you have betrayed your very birth, the efforts nay the birth pangs of your mother when she bore you and delivered you to the world, you've betrayed every effort your father ever made to feed you and raise you and make you strong and my God even educate you for "life," you feel a guilt so deep you identify yourself with the devil and God seems far away abandoning you to your sick silliness——You feel sick in the greatest sense of the word, *breathing without believing in it*, sicksicksick, your soul groans, you look at your helpless hands as tho they were on fire and you cant move to help, you look at the world with dead eyes, there's on your face an expression of incalculable repining like a constipated angel on a cloud——In fact it's actually a cancerous look you throw on the world, through browngray wool fuds over your eyes——Your tongue is white and disgusting, your teeth are stained, your hair seems to have dried out overnight, there are huge mucks in the corners of your eyes, greases on your nose, froth at the sides of your mouth: in short that very disgusting and wellknown hideousness everybody knows who's walked past a city street drunk in the Boweries of the world——But there's no joy at all, people say "Oh well he's drunk and happy let him sleep it off"——The poor drunkard is *crying*——He's crying for his mother and father and great brother and great friend, he's crying for help——He tries to pull himself together by moving one shoe nearer to his foot and he cant even do that properly, he'll drop the shoe, or knock something over, he'll do something invariably that'll start him crying again——He'll want to bury his face in his hands and moan for mercy and he knows there is none——Not only because he doesnt deserve it but there's no such thing anyway——Because he looks up at the blue sky and there's nothing there but empty space making a big face at him——He looks at the world, it's sticking its tongue out at him and once that mask is removed it's looking at him with hollow big red eyes like his own eyes——He may see the earth move but there's no significance of any particular kind to attach to that——One little unexpected noise behind him will make him snarl in rage——He'll pull and tug at his poor stained shirt——He feels like rubbing his face into something that isnt.

His socks are thick tired moisty slimes——The beard on his cheeks itches the running sweats and annoys the tortured mouth——There's a twisted feeling of no-more, never-again,

agh——What was beautiful and clean yesterday has irrationally
and unaccountably changed into a big dreary crock of shit——
The hairs on his fingers stare at him like tomb hairs——The
shirt and trousers have become glued to his person as tho he was
to be drunk forever——The ache of remorse sinks in as tho somebody was pushing it in from above——The pretty white clouds in
the sky hurt his eyes only——The only thing to do is turn over
and lie face down and weep——The mouth is so blasted there's
not even a chance to gnash the teeth——There's not even strength
to tear the hair.

And here comes Ron Blake starting off his new day singing at
the top of his voice——I go down by the creek and throw myself
in the sand and lie looking with sad eyes at the water which no
longer friends me but sorta wants me to go away——There isnt
a drop to drink left in the cabin, all the goddamn jeeps are gone
with all its healthy cargo of people and I'm alone with an enthu-
siastic kid on a lark——The little bugs I'd saved from drowning
just because I was bemused and alone and glad, now drown
unnoticed within my reach anyway——The spider is still
minding his own business in the outhouse——Alf lows mournfully in the valley far away to express just the way I feel——The
bluejays yak around me as tho because I'm too tired and helpless
to feed them any more they're figuring on trying me if they can,
"They're friggin vultures anyway" I moan with my mouth in
the sand——The once pleasant thumpthump gurgle slap of the
creek is now an endless jabbering of blind nature which doesnt
understand anything in the first place——My old thoughts
about the slit of a billion years covering all this and all cities and
generations eventually is just a dumb old thought, "Only a silly
sober fool could think it, imagine gloating over such nonsense"
(because in one sense the drinker learns wisdom, in the words of
Goethe or Blake or whichever it was "The pathway to wisdom
lies through excess")——But in this condition you can only say
"Wisdom is just another way to make people sick"——"I'm
SICK" I yell emphatically to the trees, to the woods around, to

the hills above, looking around desperately, nobody cares——I
can even hear Ron singing at his lunch inside.

What's even more horrible he tries to show compunction and
wants to help me, "Anything I can do"——Later he goes for a
lone walk so I go in the cabin and lie on the cot and spend about
two hours groaning out a lament: *"O mon Dieux, pourquoi Tu
m'laisse faire malade comme ça——Papa Papa aide mué——Aw
j'ai mal au coeur——J'envie d'aller à toilette 'pi ça m'interesse
pas——Aw 'shu malade*——Owaowaowao——" (I go into a
long "awaowaowoa" that I guess lasted a whole minute)——I
toss over and find new reasons to groan——I think I'm alone
and I'm letting it all go a whole lot like I'd heard my father do
when he was dying of cancer in the night in the bed next to
mine——When I do manage to stagger up and go lean on the
door I realize with double upon double horror that Ron Blake
has been sitting there all this time listening to everything over a
book——(I wonder now what he told people about this later, it
must have sounded horrible)——(Idiotic too, cretinous even,
maybe only French Canadian who knows?)——"Ron I'm sorry
you had to hear all that, I'm sick"——"I know, man, it's okay, lie
down and try to sleep"——"I cant sleep!" I yell in a rage——I
feel like yelling "Fuck yourself you little idiot what do you know
what Im going through!" but then I realize how oldman disgusting and hopeless all that is, and here he is enjoying his big
weekend with the big writer he was supposed to tell all his
friends what a great swinging ball it was and what I did and
said——But methinks and mayhap he took away a lesson in
temperance, or a lesson in beatness really——Because the only
time I've ever been sicker and madder was a week later when
Dave and I came back with the two girls leading to the final horrible night.

22

But look at this: in the afternoon restless youngster Ron wants to go hitch hiking to Monterey of all things to go see McLear and I say "Okay go ahead"——"Aint you coming with me?" he asks surprised to see the champion on-the-roader wont even hitch hike any more, "No I'll stay here and get better——I gotta be alone," which is true, because as soon as he's gone and has yelled one final hoot from the canyon road directly above and gone on, and I've sat in the sun alone on the porch, fed my birds finally again, washed my socks and shirt and pants and hung them up to dry on bushes, slurped up tons of water kneeling at the creek race, stared silently at the trees, soon as the sun goes down I swear on my arm I'm as well as I ever was: just like that suddenly.

"Can it be that Ron and all these other guys, Dave and McLear or somebody, the other guys earlier are all a big bunch of witches out to make me go mad?" I seriously consider this——Remembering that childhood revery I always had, which I used to ponder seriously as I walked home from St. Joseph's Parochial School or sat in the parlor of my home, that everybody in the world is making fun of money me and I dont know it because everytime I turn around to see who's behind me they snap back into place with regular expressions, but soon's I look away again they dart up to my nape of neck and all whisper there giggling and plotting evil, silently, you cant hear them, and when I turn quickly to catch them they've already snapped back perfectly in place and are saying "Now the proper way to cook eggs is" or they're singing Chet Baker songs looking the other way or they're saying "Did I ever tell you about Jim that time?"——But my childhood revery also included the fact that everybody in the world was making this fun of me because they were all members of an eternal secret society or Heaven society that knew the secret of the world and were seriously fooling me so I'd wake up and see the light (i.e., become enlightened, in fact)——So that I, "Ti Jean," was the LAST Ti Jean left in the world, the last poor holy fool, those people at my neck were the devils of the earth among whom God had cast me, an angel baby, as tho I was the last Jesus in fact! and all these people were waiting for me to realize it and wake up and catch them peeking and we'd all laugh in Heaven suddenly——But animals werent doing that behind my back, my cats were always adornments licking their paws sadly, and Jesus, he was a sad witness to this, somewhat like the animals——He wasnt peeking down my neck——There lies the root of my belief in Jesus——So that actually the only reality in the world was Jesus and the lambs (the animals) and my brother Gerard who had instructed me——Meanwhile some of the peekers were kindly and sad, like my father, but had to go along with everybody else in the same boat——But my waking up would take place and then everything would vanish except Heaven, which is God—— And that was why later in life after these rather strange you must admit childhood reveries, after I had that fainting vision of the Golden Eternity and others before and after it including Samadhis during Buddhist meditations in the woods, I conceived of myself as a special solitary angel sent down as a messenger from Heaven to tell everybody or show everybody by example that their peeking society was actually the Satanic Society and they were all on the wrong track.

With all this in my background, now at the point of adulthood disaster of the soul, through excessive drinking, all this was easily converted into a fantasy that everybody in the world was witching me to madness: and I must have believed it sub-consciously because as I say as soon as Ron Blake left I was well again and in fact content.

In fact very contented——I rose that following morning with more joy and health and purpose than ever, and there was me old Big Sur Valley all mine again, here came good old Alf and I gave him food and patted his big rough neck with its various cocotte's manes, there was the mountain of Mien Mo in the distance just a dismal old hill with funny bushes around the sides and a peaceful farm on top, and nothing to do all day but amuse myself undisturbed by witches and booze——And I'm singing ditties again "My soul aint snow, wouldnt you know, the color of my soul, is interpole" and such silly stuff——And I yell "If Arthur Ma is a witch he sure is a funny witch! har har!"—— And there's the bluejay idiot with one foot on the bar of soap on the porch rail, pecking at the soap and eating it, leaving the cereal unattended, and when I laugh and yell at him he looks up cute with an expression that seems to say "What's the matter? wotti do wong?"——"Wo wo, got the wong place," said another bluejay landing nearby and suddenly leaving again——And everything of my life seems beautiful again, I even start remembering the nutty things of the binge and go back even farther and remember nutty things all through my life, it's just amazing how inside our own souls we can lift out so much strength I think it would be enough strength to move mountains at that, to lift our boots up again and go clomping along happy out of nothing but the good source power in our own bones——And when I visit the sea it doesnt scare me anymore, I just sing out "Seventy thousand schemers in the sea" and go back to my cabin and just quietly pour my coffee in the cup, afternoon, how pleasant!

I make a wood run, axe and yank logs outa everywhichawhere and leave em by the side of the road to leisurely carry home——I investigate a cabin down the creek that has 15 wood matches in it for my emergency——Take a shot of sherry, hate it——Find

an old San Francis Chronicle with my name in it all over——
Hack a giant redwood log in half in the middle of the creek——
That kind of day, perfect, ending up sewing my holy sweater
singing "There's no place like home" remembering my
mother——I even plunge into all the books and magazines
around, I read up on 'Pataphysics and yell contemptuously in
the lamplight " 'T'sa'n intellectual excuse for facetious joking,"
throwing the magazine away, adding "Peculiarly attractive to
certain shallow types"——Then I turn my rumbling attention
to a couple of unknown *Fin du Siècle* poets called Theo Marzials
and Henry Harland——I take a nap after supper and dream of
the U.S. Navy, a ship anchored near a war scene, at an island,
but everything is drowsy as two sailors go up the trail with
fishing-poles and a dog between them to go make love quietly in
the hills: the captain and everybody know they're queer and
rather than being infuriated however they're all drowsily
enchanted by such gentle love: you see a sailor peeking after
them with binoculars from the poop: there's supposed to be a
war but nothing happens, just laundry. . .

I wake up from this silly but strangely pretty dream feeling
exhilirated——Besides now the stars come out every night and
I go out on that porch and sit in the old canvas chair and turn my
face up to all that mooching going on up there, starmooched fir-
mament, all those stars crying with happy sadness, all that ream
and cream of mocky ways with alleyways of lightyears old as
Dame Mae Whitty and the hills——I go walking towards Mien
Mo mountain in the moon illuminated August night, see gorgeous misty mountains rising the horizon and like saying to me
"You dont have to torture your consciousness with endless
thinking" so I sit in the sand and look inward and see those old
roses of the unborn again——Amazing, and in just a few hours
this change——And I have enough physical energy to walk
back to the sea suddenly realizing what a beautiful oriental silk
scroll painting this whole canyon would make, those scrolls you

open slowly at one end and keep unrolling and unrolling as the valley unfolds towards sudden cliffs, sudden Bodhisattvas sitting alone in lamplit huts, sudden creeks, rocks, trees, then sudden white sand, sudden sea, out to sea and you've reached the end of the scroll——And with all those misty rose darknesses of varying tint and tuckaway shades to express the actual ephemerality of night——One long roll unfurling from the range fence among the misty hills, moon meadows, even the hay rick near the creek, down to the trail, the narrowing creek, then the mystery of the AW SEA——So I investigate the scroll of the valley but I'm singing "Man is a busy little animal, a nice little animal, his thoughts about everything, dont amount to shit."

In fact back at the cabin to make my bedtime hot Ovaltine I even sing "Sweet Sixteen" like an angel (by God bettern Ron Blake) and all the old memories of Ma and Pa, the upright piano in old Massachusetts, the old summernight sings——That's how I go to sleep, under the stars on the porch, and at dawn I turn over with a blissful smile on my face because the owls are callin and answering from two different huge dead trunks across the valley, hoo hoo hoo.

So maybe it's true what Milarepa says: "Though you youngsters of the new generation dwell in towns infested with deceitful fate, the link of truth still remains"——(and said this in 890!)——"When you remain in solitude, do not think of the amusements in the town. . . You should turn your mind inwardly, and then you'll find your way. . . The wealth I found is the inexhaustible Holy Property. . . The companion I found is the bliss of perpetual Voidness. . . Here in the place of Yolmo Tag Pug Senge Dzon, the tigress howling with a pathetic trembling voice reminds me that her piteous cubs are playing lively. . . Like a madman I have no pretension and no hope. . . I am telling you the honest truth. . . These are the crazy words of mine. . . Oh you innumerable motherlike beings, by the force of imaginary destiny you see a myriad visions and experience endless emotions. . . I smile. . . To a Yogi, everything is fine and splendid!. . . . . In the goodly quiet of this Self-Benefitting sky Enclosure, the timely sounds I hear are all my fellows' sounds. . . At such a pleasant place, in solitude, I, Milarepa, happily remain, meditating upon the void-illuminating mind——The more Ups and Downs the more Joy I feel——The greater the fear, the greater the happiness I feel. . ."

23

But in the morning (and I'm no Milarepa who could also sit naked in the snow and was seen flying on one occasion) here comes Ron Blake back with Pat McLear and Pat's wife the beautiful one, and by God their little sweet 5 year old girl who is such a pleasant sight to see as she goes jongling and jiggling through the fields to look for flowers, everything to her is perfectly new beautiful primordial Garden of Eden morning here in this tortured human canyon——And a rather beautiful morning develops——There's fog so we close the blinds and light the fire and the lamp, me and Pat, and sit there drinking from the jug he brought talking about literature and poetry while his wife listens and occasionally gets up to heat more coffee and tea or goes out to play with Ron and the little girl——Pat and I are in a serious talkative mood and I feel that lonely shiver in my chest which always warns me: you actually love people and you're glad Pat is here.

Pat is one if not THE most handsome man I've ever seen—— Strange that he's announced in a preface to his poems that his heroes, his Triumvirate, are Jean Harlow, Rimbaud and Billy the Kid because he himself is handsome enough to play Billy the Kid in the movies, that same darkhaired handsome slightly slit-eyed look you expect from the myth appearance of Billy the Kid (I suppose not the actual real life William Bonnie who's said to've been a pimply cretin monster).

So we launch on a big discussion of everything in the

comfortable gloom of the cabin by the warm red glow of the girly fire, I'm wearing dark glasses anyway for fun, Pat says "Well Jack I didnt have a chance to talk to you yesterday or even last year or even ten years ago when I first met you, I remember I was terrified of you and Pomeray when you ran up my steps one night with sticks of tea, you looked like a couple of car thieves or bank robbers——And you know a lot of this sneery stuff they've written against us, against San Francisco or beat poetry and writers is because a lot of us dont LOOK like writers or intellecuals or anything, you and Pomeray I must say look awful in a way, I'm sure I dont fill the bill either"——"Man you oughta go to Hollywood and play Billy the Kid"——"Man I'd rather go to Hollywood and play Rimbaud"——"Well you cant play Jean Harlow"——"I'd really like to just get my 'Dark Brown' published in Paris, do you know that when you think it's possible a word from you to Gallimard or Girodias would help"——"I dunno"——"Do you know that when I read your poems Mexico City Blues I immediately turned around and started writing a brand new way, you enlightened me with that book"——"But it's nothing like what you do, in fact it's miles away, I am a language spinner and you're idea man" and so on we talk till about noon and Ron's been in and out, 's'made jaunts to the beach with the little ladies and Pat and I dont realize the sun has come out but still sit there deep in the cabin by now talking about Villon and Cervantes.

Suddenly, boom, the door of the cabin is flung open with a loud crash and a burst of sunlight illuminates the room and I see an Angel standing arm outstretched in the door!——It's Cody! all dressed in his Sunday best in a suit! beside him are ranged several graduating golden angels from Evelyn golden beautiful wife down to the most dazzling angel of them all little Timmy with the sun striking off his hair in beams!——It's such an incredible sight and surprise that both Pat and I rise from our chairs involuntarily, like we've been lifted up in awe, or scared, tho I dont feel scared so much as ecstatically amazed as tho I've

seen a vision——And the way Cody stands there not saying a
word with his arm outstretched for some reason, struck a pose of
some sort to surprise us or warn us, he's so much like St. Michael
at the moment it's unbelievable especially as I also suddenly
realize what he's just actually done, he's had wife and kiddies
sneak up ever so quiet up the porch steps (which are noisy and
creaky), across the wood planks, easy and tiptoeing, stood there
awhile while he prepared to fling the door open, all lined up and
stood straight, then pow, he's opened the door and thrown the
golden universe into the dazzled mystic eyes of big hip Pat
McLear and big amazed grateful me——It reminds me of the
time I once saw a whole tiptoeing gang of couples sneaking into
our back kitchen door on West Street in Lowell the leader telling
me to shush as I stand there 9 years old amazed, then all bursting in on my father innocently listening to the Primo
Camera-Ernie Schaaft fight on the old 1930's radio——For a
big roaring toot——But Cody's oldfashioned family tiptoe
sneak carries that strange apocalyptic burst of gold he somehow
always manages to produce, like I said elsewhere the time in
Mexico he drove an old car over a rutted road very slowly as we
were all high on tea and I saw golden Heaven, or the other times
he's always seemed so golden like as I say in a davenport of some
sort in Heaven in the golden top of Heaven.

Not that he means to produce this effect: he's just standing
there with innate dramatic mystery holding forth his arm as if to
say Behold, the sun! and Behold, the angels! sorta pointing at all
the golden heads of his family and Pat and I stand aghast.

"Happy birthday Jack!" yells Cody or some such ordinary
crazy inane greeting "I've come to you with good news! I've
brought Evelyn and Emily and Gaby and Timmy because we're
all so grateful and glad because everything has worked out absolutely dead perfect, or living perfect, boy, with that little old
hunnerd dollars you gave me let me tell you the fantastic story of
what happened" (to him it was utterly fantastic), "I went out and
traded in my Nash that as you know wont even start but I have

to have m'old buddies push it down the road for me, this guy had a perfect gem of a purple or what color is it Maw? magenty, slamelty, a *jeepster* station-wagon Jack but a perfect beauty mind you listen with a beautiful radio, a brand new set of backup lights, thisa and thata down to the perfect new tires and that wonderful shiney paint job, that color'll knock you out, that's what it is, Grape!" (as Evelyn murmurs the color) "Grape color for all the old grape wine jacks, so we've come here to not only thank you and see you again but to celebrate this, and on top of all that, occasion, goo me I'm all so gushy and girly, hee hee hee, yes that's right come on in children and then go out and get that gear in the car and get ready to sleep outdoors tonight and get that good open fresh air, Jack on top of all that and my heart is jess OVERflowin I got a NEW JOB!! along with that splissly little old beautiful new jeep! a new job right downtown in Los Gatos in fact I dont even have to drive to work any more, I can walk it, just half a mile, now Ma you come in here, meet old Pat McLear here, start up some eggs or some of that steak we brought, open up that vieen roossee wine we brought for drunk old Jack that good old boy while I personally private take him to walk with me back down the road where the jeep is parked, unlock that gate, you got the corral key Jack, okay, and we'll talk and walk just like old times and drive back real slow in my new slowboat to China."

So it's a whole new day, a whole new situation the way it is with Cody, in fact a whole new universe as suddenly we're alone again really for the first time in ages walking rapidly down the road to go get the car and he looks at me with that hand-rubbing wicked look like he's about to spring a surprise on me that's the top surprise of them all, "You guessed it old buddy I have here the LAST, the absolutely LAST yet most perfect of all black-haired seeded packed tight superbomber joints in the world which you and I are now going to light up, 's'why I didnt want you to bring any of that wine right away, why boy we got time to drink wine and wine and dance" and here he is lighting up, says

"Now dont walk too fast, it's time to stroll along like we used to do remember sometimes on our daysoff on the railroad, or walkin across that Third and Townsend tar like you said and the time we watched the sun go down so perfect holy purple over that Mission cross——Yessir, slow and easy, lookin at this gone valley" so we start to puff the pot but as usual it creates doubtful paranoias in both our minds and we actually sort of fall silent on the way to the car which is a beautiful grape color at that, a brand new shiney Jeepster with all the equipments, and the whole golden reunion deteriorates into Cody's matter-of-fact lecture on why the car is going to be such a honey (the technical details) and he even yells at me to hurry up with that corral gate, "Cant wait here all day, hor hor hor."

But that's not the point, about pot paranoia, yet maybe it is at that——I've long given it up because it bugs me anyway—— But so we drive back slowly to the shack and Evelyn and Pat's wife have met and are having woman talk and McLear and I and Cody talk around the table planning excursions with the kids to the beach.

And there's Evelyn and I havent had a chance to talk to her for years either, Oh the old days when we'd stay up late by the fireplace as I say discussing Cody's soul, Cody this and Cody that, you could hear the name Cody ringing under the roofs of America from coast to coast almost to hear his women talking about him, always pronouncing "Cody" with a kind of anguish yet there was girlish squealing pleasure in it, "Cody has to learn to control the enormous forces in him" and Cody "will always modify his little white lies so much that they turn into black ones," and according to Irwin Garden Cody's women were always having transcontinental telephone talks about his dong (which is possible.)

Because he was always tremendously generated towards complete relationship with his women to the point where they ended up in one convoluted octopus mess of souls and tears and fellatio and hotel room schemes and rushing in and out of cars and doors and great crises in the middle of the night, wow that madman you can at least write on his grave someday "He Lived, He Sweated"——No halfway house is Cody's house——Tho now as I say sorta sweetly chastised and a little bored at last with the world after the crummy injustice of his arrest and sentence he's sorta quieted down and where he'd launch into a tremendous explanation of every one of his thoughts for the benefit of everybody in the room as he's putting on his socks and arranging his papers to leave, now he just flips it aside and may make a stale shrug——A Jesuit at work——Tho I remember one crazy moment in the shack that was typically Cody-like: complicated and simultaneous with a million nuances as though the whole of creation suddenly exploded and imploded together in one moment: at the moment that Pat's pretty little angel daughter is coming in, to hand me an extremely tiny flower ("It's for you," she says direct to me) (for some reason the poor little thing thinks I need a flower, or else her mother instructed her for charming reasons, like adornment) Cody is furiously explaining to his little son Tim "Never let the right hand know what your left hand is doing" and at that moment I'm trying to close my palm around the incredibly small flower and it's so small I cant even do that, cant feel it, cant hardly see it, in fact such a small flower only that little girl could have found it, but I look up to Cody as he says that to Tim, and also to impress Evelyn who's watching me, I announced "Never let the left hand know what the right hand is doing but this right hand cant even hold this flower" and Cody only looks up "Yass yass."

So what started as a big holy reunion and surprise party in Heaven deteriorates to a lot of showoff talk, actually, at least on my part, but when I get to drink the wine I feel lighter and we all go down to the beach——I walk in front with Evelyn but when we get to the narrow path I walk in front like an Indian to show her what a big Indian I've been all summer——I'm bursting to tell her everything——"See that grove there, once in a while you'll be surprised out of your shoes to see the mule quietly standing there with locks of hair like Ruth's over his forehead, a big Biblical mule meditating, or over there, but up here, and look at that bridge, now what do you think of that?"——All the kids are fascinated by the upsidedown car wreck——At one point I'm sitting in the sand as Cody walks up my way, I say to him him imitating Wallace Beery and scratching my armpits "Cuss a man for dyin in Death Valley" (the last lines of that great movie *Twenty Mule Team*) and Cody says "That's right, if anybody can imitate old Wallace Beery that's the only way to do it, you had just the right timber there in the tone of your voice there, *Cuss a man for dyin in Death Valley* hee hee yes" but he rushes off to talk to McLear's wife.

Strange sad desultory the way families and people sorta scatter around a beach and look vaguely at the sea, all disorganized and picnic sad——At one point I'm telling Evelyn that a tidal wave from Hawaii could very easily come someday and we'd see it miles away a huge wall of awful water and "Boy it would take some doing to run back and climb up these cliffs, huh?" but Cody hears this and says, "What?" and I say "It would wash over us and take us all to Salinas I bet" and Cody says "What? that brand new jeep? I'm goin back and move it!" (an example of his strange humor).

"How'd'st rain rule here?" says I to Evelyn to show her what a big poet I am——She really loves me, used to love me in the old days like a husband, for awhile there she had two husbands Cody and me, we were a perfect family till Cody finally got jealous or maybe I got jealous, it was wild for awhile I'd be coming home from work on the railroad all dirty with my lamp and just as I came in for my Joy bubblebath old Cody was rushing off on a call so Evelyn had her new husband in the second shift then when Cody come home at dawn all dirty for his Joy bubblebath, ring, the phone's run and the crew clerk's asked me out and I'm rushing off to work, both of us using the same old clunker car in shifts——And Evelyn always maintaining that she and I were really made for each other but her

Karma was to serve Cody in this particular lifetime, which I really believe and I believe she loves him, too, but she'd say "I'll get you, Jack, in another lifetime. . . And you'll be very happy"——"What?" I'd yell to joke, "me running up the eternal halls of Karma tryina get away from you hey?"——"It'll take you eternities to get rid of me," she adds sadly, which makes me jealous, I want her to say I'll never get rid of her——I wanta be chased for eternity till I catch her.

"Ah Jack" she says putting her arm around me on the beach, "it's nice to see you again, Oh I wish we could be quiet again and just have our suppers of homemade pizza all together and watch T.V. together, you have so many friends and responsibilities now it's sad, and you get sick drinking and everything, why dont you just come stay with us awhile and rest"——"I will"——But Ron Blake is redhot for Evelyn and keeps coming over to dance with seaweeds and impress her, he's even asked me to ask Cody to let him spend some time alone with Evelyn, Cody's said "Go ahead man."

Having run out of liquor in fact Ron does get his opportunity to be alone with Evelyn as Cody and me and the kids in one car, and McLear and family in the other start for Monterey to stock up for the night and also more cigarettes——Evelyn and Ron light a bonfire on the beach to wait for us——As we're driving along little Timmy says to Paw "We shoulda brought Mommy with us, her pants got wet in the beach"——"By now they oughta be steamin," says Cody matter-of-factly in another one of his fantastic puns as he lockwallops that awful narrow dirt canyon road like a getaway car in the mountains in a movie, we leave poor McLear miles back——When Cody comes to a narrow tight curve with all our death staring us in the face down that hole he just swerves the curve saying "The way to drive in the mountains is, boy, no fiddlin around, these roads dont move, you're the one that moves"——And we come out on the highway and go right battin up to Monterey in the Big Sur dusk where down there on the faint gloamy frothing rocks you can hear the seals cry.

24

McLear exhibits another strange facet of his handsome but faintly "decadent" Rimbaud-type personality at his summer camp by coming out in the livingroom with a goddamn HAWK on his shoulder——It's his pet hawk, of all things, the hawk is black as night and sits there on his shoulder pecking nastily at a clunk of hamburg he holds up to it——In fact the sight of that is so rarely poetic, McLear whose poetry is really like a black hawk, he's always writing about darkness, dark brown, dark bedrooms, moving curtains, chemical fire dark pillows, love in chemical fiery red darkness, and writes all that in beautiful long lines that go across the page irregularly and aptly somehow——Handsome Hawk McLear, in fact I suddenly yell out "Now I know your real name! it's M'Lear! M' Lear the Scotch Highland moorhaunter with his hawk about to go mad and tear his white hair in a tempest"——Or some such silly thing, feeling good again now we've got new wine—— Time to go back to the cabin and fly down that dark highway the way only Cody can fly (even bettern Dave Wain but you feel safer with Dave Wain tho the reason Cody gives you a sense of dooming boom as he pushes the night out the wheels is not because he'll lose perfect control of the car but you feel the car will take off suddenly up to Heaven or at least just up into what the Russians call the Dark Cosmos, there's a booming rushing sound out the window when Cody bats her down the white line at night, with Dave Wain it's all conversation and smooth

sailing, with Cody it's a crisis about to get worse)——And now
he's saying to me "Not only today but the other day with the
boys, that beautiful McLear woman there, wow, with her tight
blue jeans, man I cried under a tree to see that poppin around so
innocent like, whoo, so I tell you what we're gonna do old buddy:
tomorrow we go back to Los Gatos the whole family and we've
dropped Evelyn and the kids home after the hiss-the-villain play
we're all gonna see at seven——"——"The what?"——"It's a
play," he says suddenly imitating the tired whiney voice of an old
P.T.A. Committee woman, "you go there and you sit down and
out comes this old 1910 play about villains foreclosing the mortgage, mustaches, you know, calico tears, you can sit there you
see and hiss the villain all you want even for all I know yell
obscenities or something I dunno——But it's Evelyn's world,
you know, she's designing the sets and that's the work she's done
while I was in the can so I cant begrudge her that, in fact I aint
got a word in edgewise, when you're the father of a family you go
along with the little woman acourse, and the kids enjoy it, after
that plan and after you've hissed the villain we'll drop them
home and then old buddy" zooming up the car even of all thinks,
the hawk is black as night and sits there faster in lieu of rubbing
his hands with zeal, so to say Zoom, "you and me gonna go flyin
down that Bay Shore highway and as usual you're gonna ask
your usual dumb almost Okie wino questions, *Hey Cody*"
(whining like a old drunk) "*I b'lieve we're comin into Burlingame
aint it?* and you're always wrong, hee hee, old crazy dumb fuckin
old Jack, then we go rubbin shoulders into that City and go
poppin right up to my sweet little old baby Willamine that I
want you to meet inasmuch and also I want you go dig because
she's gonna dig YOU my dear old sonumbitch Jack, and I'm
gonna leave you two little lovebirds together for days on end
alone, you can live there and just enjoy that gone little woman
because also" (his tone now businesslike) "I want her to dig as
much as possible everything you got to tell her about what YOU
know, hear me? she's my soulmate and confidante and mistress

and I want her to be happy and learn"——"What's she look like?" I ask grossly——And I see the grimace on his face, he really knows me, "Eh well she looks alright, she has a gone little body that's all I can say and in bed she is by far the first and only and last possible greatest everything you dig"——This being just another of a long line of occasions when Cody gets me to be a sub-beau for his beauties so that everything can tie in together, he really loves me like a brother and more than that, he gets annoyed at me sometimes especially when I fumble and blumble like with a bottle or the time I almost stripped the gears of the car because I forgot I was driving, in which case actually I remind him of his old wino father but the fantastic thing is that HE reminds ME of MY father so that we have this strange eternal father-image relationship that goes on and on sometimes with tears, it's easy for me to think of Cody and almost cry, sometimes I can see the same tearful expression in his eyes when he sometimes looks at me——He reminds me of my father because he too blusters and hurries and fills all his pockets with Racing Forms and papers and pencils and we're all ready to go on some mission in the night he takes with ultimate seriousness as tho we were going on the last trip of them all but it always ends up being a hilarious meaningless Marx Brothers adventure which gives me even more reason to love him (and my father too)——That way——And finally in the book I wrote about us ("On The Road") I forgot to mention two important things, that we were both devout little Catholics in our childhood, which gives us something in common tho we never talk about it, it's just there in our natures, and secondly and most important that strange business when we shared another girl (Marylou, or that is, let's call her Joanna) and Cody at the time announced "That's what we'll be old buddy, you and me, double husbands, later on we'll have whole Harreeeem and reams of Hareems boy, and we'll call ourselves or that is" (flutter) "ourself Duluomeray, see Duluoz and Pomeray, Duluomeray, see, hee hee hee" tho he was younger then and really silly but that gives an indication of the way he felt about me: some kind of new thing in the world actually where men can really be angelic friends and not be homosexual and not fight over girls——But alas the only thing we'd ever fought about was money, or the ridiculous time we fought about a little line of marijuana dust running down the middle of a page where we were separating our shares with a knife, when I objected I wanted some of the dust he yelled "Our original agreement had nothing to do with the dust!" and he slumps it all into his pocket and stalks off redfaced so I jump up and pack and announce I'm leaving and Evelyn drives me to the City but the car wont start (this is years ago) so Cody redfaced and crazy and ashamed now has to push us with the clunker, there we go down San Jose boulevard with Cody behind us pushing us and with Cody behind us pushing us and bumping us not just to give us a start but to chastise me for being so greedy and I shouldnt leave at all——In fact he'd back up and come up on our rear and really wham us——That night ending me dead drunk on Mal Damlette's floor on North Beach——And in any case the whole question of us, the two most advanced men friends in the world still fighting over money after all being, as Julien says in New York, indication of the fact that "Money is the only thing Canucks ever fight about, and Okies too I guess" but Julien I suppose imagining and fantasizing himself as a noble Scotsman who fights about honor (tho I tell him "Ah you Scotchmen save your spit in your watchpocket").

Lacrimae rerum, the tears of things, all the years behind me and Cody, the way I always say "me and Cody" instead of "Cody and I" or some such, and Irwin watching us across the world night now with a bite of marvel on his lower lip saying "Ah, angels of the West, Companions in Heaven" and writing letters asking "What now, what's the latest, what visions, what arguments, what sweet agreements?" and such.

That night the kids end up sleeping in the jeep anyway because they're afraid of the big black woods and I sleep by the creek in my bag and in the morning we're all set to go back to

Los Gatos and see the villain play——Frustrated Ron is casting
sad eyes at Evelyn, apparently she's put him off because she says
to me (and I dont blame her) "Really the way Cody presses
people on me it's awful, at least I should have my own choice"
(but she's laughing because it's funny and it is funny the way
Cody does it anxious and harried wondering if that's what she
really wants and wants no such thing)——"At least not with
utter strangers," says I to be funny——She:-"Besides I'm so
sick of all this sex business, that's all he talks about, his friends,
here they are all open channels to do good as co creators with
God and all they think about is behinds——that's why you're so
refreshing" she adds——"But I aint so refreshing as all that?
hey!"——But that's my relationship with Evelyn, we're real pals
and we can kid about anything even the first night I met her in
Denver in 1947 when we danced and Cody watched anxiously, a
kind of romantic pair in fact and I shudder sometimes to think
of all that stellar mystery of how she IS going to get me in a
future lifetime, wow——And I seriously do believe that will be
my salvation, too.

A long way to go.

25

The silly stupid hiss-the-villain play is alright in itself but just as we arrive at the scene of the chuck wagons and tents all done up real old western style there's a big fat sheriff type with two sixshooters standing at the admission gate, Cody says "That's to give it color see" but I'm drunk and as we all pile out of the car I go up to the fat sheriff and start telling him a Southern joke (in fact just the plot of an Erskine Caldwell short story) which he receives with a witless smiling expression or really like the expression of an executioner or a Southern constable listening to a Yankee talk——So naturally I'm surprised later when we go into the cute old west saloon and the kids start banging on the old piano and I join them with big loud Stravinsky chords, here comes two gun sheriff fatty coming in and saying in a menacing voice like T.V. western movies "You cant play that piano"——I'm surprised, turning to Evelyn, to learn that he's the blasted proprietor of the whole place and if he says I cant play the piano there's nothing I can do about it legally——But besides that he's got actual bullets in those six guns——He's going all out to play the part——But to be yanked from joyful pianothumping with kids to see that awful dead face of negative horror I just jump up and say "Alright, the hell with it I'm leaving anyway" so Cody follows me to the car where I take another swig of white port——"Let's get the hell out of here" I say——"Just what I was thinkin about," says Cody, "in fact I've already arranged with the director of the play to drive Evelyn

and the kids home so we'll just go to the City now"——
"Great!"——"And I've told Evelyn we're cuttin out so let's go."

"I'm sorry Cody I screwed up your little family party"——
"No No" he protests "Man I have to come to these things you
know and be a big hubby and father type and you know I'm on
parole and I gotta put up appearances but it's a drag"——To
show what a drag it is we go scootin down that road passing six
cars easy as pie——"And I'm GLAD this happened because it
gave us an excuse, hee hee titter you know to get outa there, I
was thinking for an excuse when it happened, that old fart is
crazy you know! he's a millionaire you know! I've talked to him,
that little beady brain, and you be glad you missed hangin
around till that performance, man, and that AUDIENCE, ow,
ugh, I almost wish I was back in San Quentin but here we go,
son!"

So of old we're alone in a car at night bashing down the line to
a specific somewhere, nothing nowhere about it whatever, especially this time, in a way——That white line is feeding into our
fender like an anxious impatient electronic quiver shuddering in
the night and how beautifully sometimes it curves one side or
the other as he smoothly swerves for passing or for something
else, avoiding a bump or something——And on the big highway
Bay Shore how beautifully he just swings in and out of lanes
almost effortlessly and completely unnoticeable passing to the
right and to the left without a flaw all kinds of cars with anxious
eyes turning to us, altho he's the only one on the road who knows
how to drive completely well——It's blue dusk all up and down
the California world——Frisco glitters up ahead——Our radio
plays rhythm and blues as we pass the joint back and forth in
jutjawed silence both looking ahead with big private thoughts
now so vast we cant communicate them any more and if we tried
it would take a million years and a billion books——Too late,
too late, the history of everything we've seen together and sepa-
rately has become a library in itself——The shelves pile
higher——They're full of misty documents or documents of the

Mist——The mind has convoluted in every tuckaway every-whichaway tuckered hole till there's no more the expressing of our latest thoughts let alone old——Mighty genius of the mind Cody whom I announce as the greatest writer the world will ever know if he ever gets down to writing again like he did earlier—— It's so enormous we both sit here sighing in fact——"No the only writing I done," he says, "a few letters to Willamine, in fact quite a few, she's got em all wrapped in ribbons there, I figgered if I tried to write a book or sumptin or prose or sumptin they'd just take it away from me when I left so I wrote her 'bout three letters a week for two years——and the trouble of course and as I say and you've heard a million times is the mind flows the mind rises and nobody can by any possible c——oh hell, I dont wanta talk about it"——Besides I can see from glancing at him that becoming a writer holds no interest for him because life is so holy for him there's no need to do anything but live it, writing's just an afterthought or a scratch anyway at the surface—— But if he could! if he would! there I am riding in California miles away from home where my poor cat's buried and my mother grieves and that's what I'm thinking.

It always makes me proud to love the world somehow—— Hate's so easy compared——But here I go flattering myself helling headbent to the silliest hate I ever had.

26

Altho Cody's said these things I'm very well aware that the real arrangement of the evening is that we're just going to see Billie together so she can get her kicks meeting me (after hearing about me from him and after reading my books etc.) and in fact Cody has already conferred with Evelyn about how I'm going to be staying at their house in Las Gatos for a month, as of old sleeping in my bag in the backyard not because they dont want me to sleep in the house but it's my idea, but it's beautiful anyway to sleep under the stars and anyway I therefore keep out of the way of the family when they get up to go to work and school——At noon they see me shambling in from the big back field yard yawning for coffee——And I'm in line for that, i.e., that's what I want to do and that's my plan——But when we run upstairs to Willamine's apartment and come bursting in to this neat little well arranged pad with goldfish bowl, books, strange doodads, neat kitchen, the whole clean as a pin, and there's Billie herself a blonde with arched eyebrows exactly like the male Julien blond with arched eyebrows and I yell out "It's JUlien by God it's Julien!" (and by now I'm drunk anyway because we've as of old picked up an old hitch hiker on Bay Shore who says his name is Joe Ihnat and we bought him a bottle and I bought me one too, never will forget old Joe Ihnat in fact somehow because he said he was a Russian and his was an ancient Russian name and when I wrote out our names he said *my* name was an ancient Russian name also) (tho it's Breton) (and also told us he'd just been beaten up by a young Negro for no reason in a public toilet and Cody gasps and says to me "I've met those Negroes that beat up old men, they're called the Strongarms in San Quentin, they're all put away among themselves away from the other prisoners, they're all Negroes and it seems all they wanta do is beat up old defenseless men, he's tellin the absolute truth"——"But why do they do that?"——"Oh man I dont know they just wanta hit up on some old man that cant hit back and just beat him and beat him till he's dead" and Oh the horror of Cody's knowledge of the world when all is said and done)——So now we're sitting with Billie in her pad, outside the window you see the glittering lights of the city again, ah Urbi y Roma, the world again, and she's got these mad blue eyes, arched eyebrows, intelligent face, just like Julien, I keep saying "Julien goddamit!" and I see even in my drunkenness a little worried flutter in Cody's eyes—— The fact of the matter being, Billie and I go for each other like two tons of bricks right there in front of Cody so that when he rises and announces he's going back to Los Gatos to get some sleep to go to work it's already well agreed I'm staying right where I am and not only for tonight but for weeks months years.

Poor Cody——Yet you see I've already explained why actually subconsciously this is what he really wants to happen but he wont admit it ever and always invents reasons around this to get mad at me and call me a bastard——But aside from Cody I find Billie to be a very companionable strange kid in this lonesome night and I actually NEED to stay with her awhile——In fact both Billie and I explain to Cody why——But there's nothing evil, man-against-man or sinister about any of it, it's just a strange innocence, a spontaneous burst of love in fact and Cody understands that bettern anybody else anyway so he leaves at midnight saying he'll be back tomorrow night and all of a sudden I'm alone with a charming woman and we're talking a blue streak sitting crosslegged facing each other on the floor in a litter of books and bottles.

It gives me a pang of pain and remorse really now to recall

that on this first night her apartment was so neat and clean and charming——The chair by the goldfish bowl which I quickly appropriated as my old man chair, where I sat constantly sipping port for a whole week, the kitchen with its intelligent arrangements of spices and eggs in the icebox, and for that matter too the poor little son of Billie sleeping in a well arranged back room (her son from her deceased husband who was also a railroad man)——Elliott the child's name and I didnt get to see him till later that night——And with the huge packet of Cody's San Quentin letters in her hand she launches forth on her theories about Cody and eternity but all I can keep saying as I swig from my bottle is "Julien, you're talking too much! Julien, Julien, my God who'd ever dream I'd run into a woman who looks like Julien . . . you look like Julien but you're not Julien and on top of that you're a woman, how goddam strange"——In fact she had to pack me off to bed drunk——But not before our first lovely undertaking of love and everything Cody said about her being absolutely true——But the main thing being that tho she looked like Julien etc. and had Cody's big sad abstract letters about Karma in a ribbon and actually went out in the morning and earned a hundred a week in fashion modeling she had the most musical beautiful and sad voice I've ever heard in my life—— The things she's saying are really rather inane because after all her education is based on really Californian hysterias like the earlier mistress of Cody Rosemarie who also was thin and pale haired and crazy and kept talking abstract——(Like she's saying "I thought I could do something to ease the contradiction between immanent and universal ethics which I thought was my problem and was what I hoped to gain thru therapy, like, any evolution presupposes an involution and all that kind of thinking" as I sigh, but she does say something interesting once in a while like "While Cody was in prison my main occupation was praying for him, I had an all day going, there was also a bit we did together every evening from 9:00 to 9:09 but he's out now and something else is happening I'm not sure what . . . but I'm

sure we aid the storm when we transcend time in one respect
and cant even keep up with it in others. . .")——But also all
kinds of to-me-unimportant and uninteresting crap about channels about people being either closed or open channels and Cody
is a big open channel pouring out all his holy gysm on Heaven, I
really cant remember, or the destinies, the sighs, the rooftops of
all that, the stars are shining down on their poor heads as they
draw breath to explain inanities really——Like the letters to her
(I glance at them) are all about how they've met and their souls
have collided in this dimension because of some unfulfilled
Karma on another planet and in another plane that is, and now
they have to gird themselves to assume this big responsibility to
meet some measure of this and that, I dont even wanta go into
it——Because also the fact of the matter being, when Willamine talks to me I'm utterly bored, I'm only interested in the sad
music of her voice and in the strange circumstance (I guess
Karma-like too) that she looks like poor Julien.

Her voice is the main point——She talks with a broken
heart——Her voice lutes brokenly like a heart lost, musically
too, like in a lost grove, it's almost too much to bear sometimes
like some fantastic futuristic Jerry Southern singer in a night
club who steps up to the mike in the spotlight in Las Vegas but
doesnt even have to sing, just talk, to make men sigh and women
wonder I guess (if women ever wonder)——So that as she's
trying to explain all that nonsense to me (all that philosophy of
hers and Cody's and Cody's new buddy Perry, coming up the
next day) I just sit and marvel and stare at her mouth wondering
where all the beauty is coming from and why——And we
end up making love sweetly too——A little blonde well experienced in all the facets of lovemaking and sweet with compassion
and just too much so that b'dawn we're already going to get
married and fly away to Mexico in a week——In fact I can see it
now, a great big four way marriage with Cody and Evelyn.

For she is the great enemy of Evelyn——She's not satisfied
just to be Cody's lover and soul heart she wants to go right over

there and lay Evelyn down on the line and take Cody away with her forever and to do this she'll even have a deadend heaven deep love affair with old Jack (same pattern of old)——There's not much difference between her and Evelyn when you listen to their talk about Cody except in Evelyn's case I'm always fascinatedly interested——Billie actually bores me tho of course I cant tell her that——Evelyn is still the champ and I wonder about Cody.

O the ups and downs and juggling of women, blondes at that, all in the great magical City of the Gandharvas of San Francisco and here I am alone on a magic carpet with one of em, whee, at first of course it's a great ball, a great new eye-shattering explosion of experience——Not dreaming, I, what's to come——For with sad musical Billie in my arms and my name Billie too now, Billie and Billie arm in arm, oh beautiful, and Cody has given his consent in a way, we go roaming the Genghiz Khan clouds of soft love and hope and anybody who's never done this is crazy—— Because a new love affair always gives hope, the irrational mortal loneliness is always crowned, that thing I saw (that horror of snake emptiness) when I took the deep iodine deathbreath on the Big Sur beach is now justified and hosannah'd and raised up like a sacred urn to Heaven in the mere fact of the taking off of clothes and clashing wits and bodies in the inexpressibly nervously sad delight of love——Dont let no old fogies tell you otherwise, and on top of that nobody in the world even ever dares to write the true story of love, it's awful, we're stuck with a 50% incomplete literature and drama——Lying mouth to mouth, kiss to kiss in the pillow dark, loin to loin in unbelievable surrendering sweetness so distant from all our mental fearful abstractions it makes you wonder why men have termed God antisexual somehow——The secret underground truth of mad desire hiding under fenders under buried junkyards throughout the world, never mentioned in newspapers, written about haltingly and like corn by authors and painted tongue in cheek by artists, agh, just listen to *Tristan und Isolde* by Wagner and think of him in a Bavarian field with his beloved naked beauty under the fall leaves.

How strange in all, and making everything that's happened in the past weeks, the backs and forths and pains of me in City and Sur, all piled up now rationally like a big construction whereon could be built a divingboard which would enable me clumsily to dive into Billie's soul and therefore why complain?

In the middle of the night she fetches the little 4 year old boy to show me the spiritual beauty of her son——He is one of the weirdest persons I've ever met——He has large liquid brown eyes very beautiful and he hates anybody who comes near his mother and keeps asking her questions constantly like "Why do you stay with him? why is he here, who is he?" or "Why is it dark outside?" or "Why does the sun shine yesterday?" or anything, he'll just ask questions about everything and she answers every one of them with extreme delight and patience till I say "Doesnt he bother you with all these questions? why dont you let him croon and goof like a little child, he's tugging at your knee asking EVERYTHING man why dont you just let him singsong?"—— She answers "I answer him because I may be missing his next question, everything he asks me and says to me represents something important about the absolute I may be missing"—— "What do you mean the absolute?"——"You yourself said everything is the absolute" but of course she's right and I realize that in my dirty old soul I'm already jealous of Elliott.

27

The mat of night admits the groaning glory godlike love I guess but at the same time it's also boring in a way and we both laugh to discuss that——We stay awake that first night till dawn discussing everything in the books from Cody in every detail down to me in every detail to her in every detail to Evelyn to books and philosophies and religions and the absolute and I end up whispering her poems——Poor kid has to get up in the morning and go to work and I'm left there snoring drunk—— But she makes her neat breakfast and takes Elliott off to the daily babysitter lady and I wake up at one in the afternoon alone and take a swig of wine and get in the hot bath to read a book—— The phone keeps ringing, everybody from Monsanto to Fagan to McLear to the Moon Man has somehow found out where I am and what the number is, tho none of them have previously even met Billie let alone seen her——I shudder to realize Cody will get mad for making his secret life so public.

But here comes Perry——Like me Perry has that strange brotherly relationship with Cody whereby he gets to be *confidant* and sometimes lover of all Cody's gals——And I can see why——He looks just like me only he's young and looks like I did when first Cody met me but the point is not that so much, he is a tempestuous lost tossed soul just out of Soledad State Prison for attempted robbery with a boyish face and black hair falling over it but powerful thick muscular arms that I realize he could break a man in half with——His name is strange too,

Perry Yturbide, I immediately say: "I know what you are, Basque"——"Basque? is that it? I never found out! let's call my mother longdistance in Utah and tell her that!"——And he rings up his mother way over there, on Billie's phone bill, and here I am bottle of port wine in one hand and butt in mouth talking to a Basque ex con's mother in Utah telling her in fact reassuring her "Yes I believe it's a Basque name"——She's saying "Hey, what you say? who are you?" and there's Perry smiling all glad——A very strange kid——It's been a long time in fact in my literary sort of life that I've met a real tough hombre like that out of jails and with those arms of steel and that fevered concern that scares governments and makes officials pale, that's why he's always put away in prison this type of man——Yes yet the type of man the country always needs when there's a little old war started by an aging governor——A real dangerous character, in fact, Perry, because tho I appreciate his poetic soul and everything I realize looking at him he's capable of exploding and killing somebody for an idea maybe or for love.

Some of his own friends ring Billie's doorbell, everybody seems to know I'm there, they come up, they are strange anarchistic Negroes and ex cons, it seems to be some sort of gang, I begin to wonder——Like a ring of fevered sages, the Negroes are intense and crazy and intellectual but they've all got those strong muscular arms again and all have jail records yet they all talk as tho the end of the world depended on their words—— Hard to explain (but will do).

Billie and her gang in fact, with all that fancy rigamarole about spiritual matters I wonder if it isnt just a big secret hustler outfit tho I also realize that I've noticed it before in San Francisco a kind of ephemeral hysteria that hides in the air over the rooftops among certain circles there leading always to suicide and maim——Me just an innocent lost hearted meditator and Goop among strange intense criminal agitators of the heart—— It reminds me in fact of a nightmare I had just before coming out to the Coast, in the dream I'm back in San Francisco but there's something funny going on: there's dead silence throughout the entire city: men like printers and office executives and house-painters are all standing silently in second floor windows looking down on the empty streets of San Francisco: once in a while some beatniks walk by below, also silent: they're being watched but not only by the authorities but by everybody: the beatniks seem to have the whole street system to themselves: but nobody's saying anything: and in this intense silence I take a ride on a self propelled platform right downtown and out to the farms where a woman running a chicken farm invites me to join her and live with her——The little platform rolling quietly as the people are watching from windows in groups of profile like the profiles in old Van Dyck paintings, intense, suspicious, momentous—— This Billie business reminding me of that but because to me the only thing that matters is the conceptions in my own mind, there has to be no reality anyway to what I suppose is going on——But this also an indication of the coming madness in Big Sur.

28

Strange——and Perry Yturbide that first day while Billie's at work and we've just called his mother now wants me to come with him to visit a general of the U.S. Army——"Why? and what's all these generals looking out of silent windows?" I say——But nothing surprises Perry——"We'll go there because I want you to dig the most beautiful girls we ever saw," in fact we take a cab——But the "beautiful girls" turn out to be 8 and 9 and 10 years old, daughters of the general or maybe even cousins or daughters of a nextdoor strange general, but the mother is there, there are also boys playing in a backroom, we have Elliott with us whom Perry has carried on his shoulders all the way——I look at Perry and he says "I wanted you to see the most beautiful little cans in town" and I realize he's dangerously insane——In fact he then says "See this perfect beauty?" a pony tailed 10 year old daughter of the general (who aint home yet) "I'm going to kidnap her right now" and he takes her by the hand and they go out on the street for an hour while I sit there over drinks talking to the mother——There's some vast conspiracy to make me go mad anyway——The mother is polite as ordinarily——The general comes home and he's a rugged big baldheaded general and with him is his best friend a photographer called Shea, a thin well combed welldressed ordinary downtown commercial photographer of the city——I dont understand anything——But suddenly little Elliott is crying in the other room and I rush in there and see that the two boys have

whacked him or something because he did something wrong so
I chastise them and carry Elliott back into the livingroom on my
shoulders like Perry does, only Elliott wants to get down off my
shoulders at once, in fact he wont even sit on my lap, in fact he
hates my guts——I call Billie desperately at her agency and she
says she'll be over to pick us all up and adds "How's Perry
today?"——"He's kidnapping little girls he says are beautiful,
he wants to marry 10 year old girls with pony tails"——"That's
the way he is, be sure to dig him"——In her musical sad voice
over the phone.

I turn my poor tortured attention to the general who says he
was an anti-Fascist fighter with the Maquis during World War
II and also a guerilla in the South Pacific and knows one of the
finest restaurants in San Francisco where we can all go feast, a
Fillipino restaurant near Chinatown, I say okay, great——He
gives me more booze——Seeing the amusing Irish face of Shea
the photographer I yell "You can take my picture anytime you
want" and he says sinister: "Not for propaganda reasons, anything but propaganda reasons"——"What the hell do you mean
propaganda reasons, I aint got nothin to do with propaganda"
(and here comes Perry back through the door with Poo-poo
holding his hand, they've gone to dig the street and have a coke)
and I realize everybody is just living their lives quietly but it's
only me that's insane.

In fact I yearn to have old Cody around to explain all this to
me tho it soon becomes apparent to me not even Cody could
explain, I'm beginning to go seriously crazy, just like Subterra-
nean Irene went crazy tho I dont realize it yet——I'm beginning
to read plots into every simple line——Besides the "general"
scares me even further by turning out to be a strange affluent
welldressed civilian who doesnt even help me to pay the tab for
the Fillipino dinner which we have, meeting Billie at the restaurant, and the restaurant itself is weird especially because of a big
raunchy mad thicklipped sloppy young Fillipino woman sitting
alone at the end of the restaurant gobbling up her food obscenely

and looking at us insolently as tho to say "Fuck you, I eat the way I like" splashing gravy everywhere—I cant understand what's going on——Because also the general has suggested this dinner but I have to pay for everybody, him, Shea, Perry, Billie, Elliott, me, others, strange apocalyptic madness is now shuddering in my eyeballs and I'm even running out of money in their Apocalypse which they themselves have created in this San Francisco silence anyway.

I yearn to go hide and cry in Evelyn's arms but I end up hiding in Billie's arms and here she goes again, the second evening, explaining all her spiritual ideas——"But what about Perry? what's he up to? and who's that strange general? what are you, a bunch of communists?"

29

The little child refuses to sleep in his crib but has to come trotting out and watch us make love on the bed but Billie says "That's good, hell learn, what other way will he ever learn?"——I feel ashamed but because Billie is there and she's the mother I must go along and not worry——Another sinister fact——At one point the poor child is drooling long slavers of spit from his lips watching, I cry "Billie, look at him, it's not good for him" but she says again "Anything he wants he can have, *even us.*"

"But kid it's not fair, why doesn't he just sleep?"——"He doesnt wanta sleep, he wants to be with us"——"Ooh," and I realize Billie is insane and I'm not as insane as I thought and there's something wrong——I feel myself skidding: also because during the following week I keep sitting in that same chair by the goldfish bowl drinking bottle after bottle of port like an automaton, worrying about something, Monsanto comes to visit, McLear, Fagan, everybody, they call to me dashing up the stairs and we have long drunken days talking but I never seem to get out of that chair and never even take another delightful warm bath reading books——And at night Billie comes home and we pitch into love again like monsters who dont know what else to do and by now I'm too blurry to know what's going on anyway tho she reassures me everything is alright, and meanwhile Cody has completely disappeared—In fact I call him up and say "Are you gonna come back and get me here?"——"Yes yes yes in a few days, stay there" as tho maybe he wants me to learn what's happening like putting me through an ordeal to see what I have to say about it because he's been through the ordeal himself.

In fact everything is going crazy.

Perry's visits scare me: I begin to think he must be one of those "strong armers" who beat up old men: I watch him warily——All this time he's pacing back and forth saying "Man dont you appreciate those sweet little cans? what does it matter how old a woman is, 9 or 19, those little pony tails jiggling as they walk with those little jigglin cans"——"Did you ever kidnap one?"——"You out of wine, I'll make a run for you get some more, or would you rather have pot or sumptin? what's wrong with you?"——"I dont know what's goin on!"—— "You're drinking too much maybe, Cody told me you're falling apart man, dont do it"——"But what's goin on?"——"Who cares, pops, we're all swingin in love and tryin to go from day to day with self respect while all the squares are puttin us down"——"Who?"——"The Squares, puttin down Us . . . we wanta swing and live and carry across the night like when we get to L.A. I'm goin to show you the maddest scene some friends of mine down there" (in my drunkenness I've already projected a big trip with Billie and Elliott and Perry to Mexico but we're going to stop in L.A. to see a rich woman Perry knows who's going to give him money and if she doesnt he's going to get it anyway, and as I say Billie and I are going to get married too)——The insanest week of my life——Billie at night saying "You're worried that I cant handle marrying you but of course we can, Cody wants it too, I'll talk to your mother and make her love me and need me: Jack!" she suddenly cries with anguished musical voice (because I've just said "Ah Billie go get yourself a he-man and get married"), "You're my last chance to marry a He Man!"——"Whattayou mean He Man, dont you realize I'm crazy?"——"You're crazy but you're my last chance to have an understanding with a He Man"——"What about Cody?"—— "Cody will never leave Evelyn"——Very strange——But more, tho I dont understand it.

30

I do understand the strange day Ben Fagan finally came to visit me alone, bringing wine, smoking his pipe, and saying "Jack you need some sleep, that chair you say you've been sitting in for days have you noticed the bottom is falling out of it?"——I get on the floor and by God look and it's true, the springs are coming out——"How long have you been sitting in that chair?"—— "Every day waiting for Billie to come home and talking to Perry and the others all day. . . My God let's go out and sit in the park," I add——In the blur of days McLear has also been over on a forgotten day when, on nothing but his chance mention that maybe I could get his book published in Paris I jump up and dial longdistance for Paris and call Claude Gallimard and only get his butler apparently in some Parisian suburb and I hear the insane giggle on the other end of the line——"Is this the home, *c'est le chez eux de Monsieur Gallimard?"*——Giggle——*"Où est Monsieur Gallimard?"*——Giggle——A very strange phone call——McLear waiting there expectantly to get his "Dark Brown" published——So in a fury of madness I then call London to talk to my old buddy Lionel just for no reason at all and I finally reach him at home he's saying on the wire "You're calling me from San Francisco? buy why?"——Which I cant answer any more than the giggling butler (and to add to my madness, of course, why should a longdistance call to Paris to a publisher end up with a giggle and a longdistance call to an old friend in London end up with the friend getting mad?)——So

Fagan now sees I'm going overboard crazy and I need sleep——
"We'll get a bottle!" I yell——But end up, he's sitting in the
grass of the park smoking his pipe, from noon to 6 P.M., and I'm
passed out exhausted sleeping in the grass, bottle unopened,
only to wake up once in a while wondering where I am and by
God I'm in Heaven with Ben Fagan watching over men and me.

And I say to Ben when I wake up in the gathering 6 P.M. dusk
"Ah Ben I'm sorry I ruined our day by sleeping like this" but he
says: "You needed the sleep, I told ya"——"And you mean to tell
me you been sitting all afternoon like that?"——"Watching
unexpected events," says he, "like there seems to be sound of a
Bacchanal in those bushes over there" and I look and hear children yelling and screaming in hidden bushes in the park——
"What they doing?"——"I dont know: also a lot of strange people
went by"——"How long have I been sleeping?"——"Ages"——
"I'm sorry"——"Why should be sorry, I love you anyway"——
"Was I snoring?"——"You've been snoring all day and I've been
sitting here all day"——"What a beautiful day!"——"Yes it's
been a beautiful day"——"How strange!"——"Yes, strange . . .
but not so strange either, you're just tired"——"What do you
think of Billie?"——He chuckles over his pipe: "What do
you expect me to say? that the frog bit your leg?"——"Why
do you have a diamond in your forehead?"——"I dont have a
diamond in my forehead damn you and stop making arbitrary
conceptions!" he roars——"But what am I doing?"——"Stop
thinking about yourself, will ya, just float with the world"——
"Did the world float by the park?"——"All day, you should have
seen it, I've smoked a whole package of Edgewood, it's been a very
strange day"——"Are you sad I didnt talk to you?"——"Not at
all, in fact I'm glad: we better be starting back," he adds, "Billie be
coming home from work soon now"——"Ah Ben, Ah
Sunflower"——"Ah shit" he says——"It's strange"——"Who
said it wasnt"——"I dont understand it"——"Dont worry about
it"——"Hmm holy room, sad room, life is a sad room"——"All
sentient beings realize that," he says sternly——Benjamin my

real Zen Master even more than all our Georges and Arthurs actually——"Ben I think I'm going crazy"——"You said that to me in 1955"——"Yeh but my brain's gettin soft from drinkin and drinkin and drinkin"——"What you need is a cup of tea I'd say if I didnt know that you're too crazy to know how really crazy you are"——"But why? what's going on?"——"Did you come three thousand miles to find out?"——"Three thousand miles from where, after all? from whiney old me"——"That's alright, everything is possible, even Nietzsche knew that"——"Aint nothin wrong with old Nietzsche"——" 'Xcept he went mad too"——"Do you think I'm going mad?"——"Ho ho ho" (hearty laugh)——"What's that mean, laughing at me?"——"Nobody's laughing at you, dont get excited"——"What'll we do now?"——"Let's go visit the museum over there"——There's a museum of some sort across the grass of the park so I get up wobbly and walk with old Ben across the sad grass, at one point I put my arm over his shoulder and lean on him——"Are you a ghoul?" I ask——"Sure, why not?"——"I like ghouls that let me sleep?"——"Duluoz it's good for you to drink in a way 'cause you're awful stingy with yourself when You're sober"——"You sound like Julien"——"I never met Julien but I understand Billie looks like him, you kept saying that before you went to sleep"——"What happened while I was asleep?"——"Oh, people went by and came back and forth and the sun sank and finally sank down and's gone now almost as you can see, what you want, just name it you got it"——"Well I want sweet salvation"——"What's sposed to be sweet about salvation? maybe it's sour"——"It's sour in my mouth"——"Maybe your mouth is too big, or too small, salvation is for little kitties but only for awhile"——"Did you see any little kitties today?"——"Shore, hundreds of em came to visit you while you were sleeping"——"Really?"——"Sure, didnt you know you were saved?"——"Now come on!"——"One of them was real big and roared like a lion but he had a big wet snout and kissed you and you said *Ah*"——"What's this museum up here?"——"Let's go in and find out"——That's the way Ben is, he doesnt know what's going on either but at least he waits to find out maybe——But the museum is closed——We stand there on the steps looking at the closed door——"Hey," I say, "the temple is closed."

So suddenly in red sundown me and Ben Fagan arm in arm are walking slowly sadly back down the broad steps like two monks going down the esplanade of Kyoto (as I imagine Kyoto somehow) and we're both smiling happily suddenly——I feel good because I've had my sleep but mainly I feel good because somehow old Ben (my age) has blessed me by sitting over my sleep all day and now with these few silly words——Arm in arm we slowly descend the steps without a word——It's been the only peaceful day I've had in California, in fact, except alone in the woods, which I tell him and says "Well, who said you werent alone now?" making me realize the ghostliness of existence tho I feel his big bulging body with my hands and say: "You sure some pathetic ghost with all that ephemeral heavy crock a flesh"——"I didnt say nottin" he laughs——"Whatever I say Ben, dont mind it, I'm just a fool"——"You said in 1957 in the grass drunk on whiskey you were the greatest thinker in the world"——"That was before I fell asleep and woke up: now I realize I'm no good at all and that makes me feel free"——"You're not even free being no good, you better stop thinking, that's all"——"I'm glad you visited me today, I think I might have died"——"It's all your fault"—— "What are we gonna do with our lives?"——"Oh," he says, "I dunno, just watch em I guess"——"Do you hate me? . . . well, do you like me? . . . well, how are things?"——"The hicks are alright"——"Anybody hex ya lately . . . ?"——"Yeh, with card-board games?"——"Cardboard games?" I ask——"Well you know, they build cardboard houses and put people in them and the people are cardboard and the magician makes the dead body twitch and they bring water to the moon, and the moon has a strange ear, and all that, so I'm alright, Goof."

"Okay."

31

So there I am as it starts to get dark standing with one hand on the window curtain looking down on the street as Ben Fagan walks away to get the bus on the corner, his big baggy corduroy pants and simple blue Goodwill workshirt, going home to the bubble bath and a famous poem, not really worried or at least not worried about what I'm worried about tho he too carries that anguishing guilt I guess and hopeless remorse that the potboiler of time hasnt made his early primordial dawns over the pines of Oregon come true——I'm clutching at the drapes of the window like the Phantom of the Opera behind the masque, waiting for Billie to come home and remembering how I used to stand by the windows like this in my childhood and look out on dusky streets and think how awful I was in this development everybody said was supposed to be "my life" and "their lives."—— Not so much that I'm a drunkard that I feel guilty about but that others who occupy this plane of "life on earth" with me dont feel guilty at all——Crooked judges shaving and smiling in the morning on the way to their heinous indifferences, respectable generals ordering soldiers by telephone to go die or drop dead, pickpockets nodding in cells saying "I never hurt anybody," "that's one thing you can say for me, yes sir," women who regard themselves saviors of men simply stealing their substance because they think their swan-rich necks deserve it anyway (though for every swan-rich neck you lose there's another ten waiting, each one ready to lay for a lemon), in fact awful hugefaced monsters of men just because their shirts are clean deigning to control the lives of working men by running for Governor saying "Your tax money in my hands will be aptly used," "You should realize how valuable I am and how much you need me, without me what would you be, not led at all?"——Forward to the big designed mankind cartoon of a man standing facing the rising sun with strong shoulders with a plough at his feet, the necktied governor is going to make hay while the sun rises——?——I feel guilty for being a member of the human race——Drunkard yes and one of the worst fools on earth——In fact not even a genuine drunkard just a fool——But I stand there with hand on curtain looking down for Billie, who's late, Ah me, I remember that frightening thing Milarepa said which is other than those reassuring words of his I remembered in the cabin of sweet loneness on Big Sur: "When the various experiences come to light in meditation, do not be proud and anxious to tell other people, else to Goddesses and Mothers you will bring annoyance" and here I am a perfectly obvious fool American writer doing just that not only for a living (which I was always able to glean anyway from railroad and ship and lifting boards and sacks with humble hand) but because if I dont write what actually I see happening in this unhappy globe which is rounded by the contours of my deathskull I think I'll have been sent on earth by poor God for nothing——Tho being a Phantom of the Opera why should that worry me?——In my youth leaning my brow hopelessly on the typewriter bar, wondering why God ever was anyway?——Or biting my lip in brown glooms in the parlor chair in which my father's died and we've all died a million deaths——Only Fagan can understand and now he's got his bus——And when Billie comes home with Elliott I smile and sit down in the chair and it utterly collapses under me, blang, I'm sprawled on the floor with surprise, the chair has gone.

"How'd that happen?" wonders Billie and at the same time we both look at the fishbowl and both the goldfishes are upside-down floating dead on the surface of the water.

I've been sitting in that chair by that fishbowl for a week drinking and smoking and talking and now the goldfish are dead.

"What killed them?"——"I dont know"——"Did I kill the because I gave them some Kelloggs corn flakes?"——"Mebbe, you're not supposed to give them anything but their fish food"——"But I thought they were hungry so I gave them a few flicks of corn flakes"——"Well I dont know what killed them"——"But why dont anybody know? what happened? why do they do this? otters and mouses and every damn thing dyin on all sides Billie, I cant stand it, it's all my goddam fault every time!"——"Who said it was your fault dear?"——"Dear? you call me dear? why do you call me dear?"——"Ah, let me love you" (kissing me), "just because you dont deserve it"—— (Chastised):-"Why dont I deserve it"——"Because you say so. . ."——"But what about the fish"——"I dont know, really"——"Is it because I've been sitting in that crumbling chair all week blowing smoke on their water? and all the others smoking and all the talk?"——But the little kid Elliott comes crawling up his mommy's lap and starts asking questions: "Billie," he calls her, "Billie, Billie, Billie," feeling her face, I'm almost going mad from the sadness of it all——"What did you do all day?"——"I was with Ben Fagan and slept in the park. . . Billie what are we gonna do?"——"Anytime you say like you said, we'll get married and fly to Mexico with Perry and Elliott"——"I'm afraid of Perry and I'm afraid of Elliott"—— "He's only a little boy"——"Billie I dont wanta get married, I'm afraid. . ."——"Afraid?"——"I wanta go home and die with my cat." I could be a handsome thin young president in a suit sitting in an oldfashioned rocking chair, no instead I'm just the Phantom of the Opera standing by a drape among dead fish and broken chairs——Can it be that no one cares who made me or why?——"Jack what's the matter, what are you talking about?" but suddenly as she's making supper and poor little Elliott is waiting there with spoon upended in fist I realize it's just a little

family home scene and I'm just a nut in the wrong place——
And in fact Billie starts saying "Jack we should be married and
have quiet suppers like this with Elliott, something would sanc-
tify you forever I'm positive."

"What have I done wrong?"——"What you've done wrong
is withhold your love from a woman like me and from previous
women and future women like me——can you imagine all the
fun we'd have being married, putting Elliott to bed, going out
to hear jazz or even taking planes to Paris suddenly and all
the things I have to teach you and you teach me——instead
all you've been doing is wasting life really sitting around sad
wondering where to go and all the time it's right there for
you to take"——"Supposin I dont want it"——"That's part
of the picture where you say you dont want it, of course
you want. . ."——"But I dont, I'm a creepy strange guy you
dont even know"——("Cweepy? what's cweepy? Billie? what's
cweepy?" is asking poor little Elliott)——And meanwhile Perry
comes in for a minute and I pointblank say to him "I dont understand you Perry, I love you, dig you, you're wild, but what's all
this business where you wanta kidnap little girls?" but suddenly
as I'm asking that I see tears in his eyes and I realize he's in love
with Billie and has always been, wow——I even say it, "You're
in love with Billie aint ya? I'm sorry, I'm cuttin out"——"What
are you talkin about man?"——It's a big argument then about
how he and Billie are just friends so I start singing *Just Friends*
like Sinatra "Two friends but not like before" but goodhearted
Perry seeing me sing runs downstairs to get another bottle for
me——But nevertheless the fish are dead and the chair is
broken.

Perry in fact is a tragic young man with enormous potentials
who's just let himself swing and float to hell I guess, unless
something else happens to him soon, I look at him and realize
that besides loving Billie secretly and truly he must also love old
Cody as much as I do and all the world bettern I do yet he is the
character who is always being put away behind bars for this——

Rugged, covered with woe, he sits there with his black hair always over his brow, over his black eyes, his iron arms hanging helplessly like the arms of a powerful idiot in the madhouse, with the beauty of lostness pasted all over him——Who is he? in fact?——And why doesnt blonde Billie washing the homey dishes there acknowledge his love?——In fact me and Perry end up we're both sitting with hanging heads when Billie comes back in the livingroom and sees us like that, like two repentant cata- tonics in hell——Some Negro comes in and says if I give him a few dollars he'll get some pot but as soon as I give him five dollars he suddenly says "Well I aint gonna get nothin"—— "You got five dollars, go out and get it"——"I aint sure I can get any"——I dont like him at all——I suddenly realize I can leap up and throw him on the floor and take the five dollars away from him but I dont even care about the money but I am mad about him doing that——"Who is that guy?"——I know that if I start fighting him he has a knife and we'll wreck Billie's livingroom too——But suddenly another Negro comes in and turns out a sweet visit talking about jazz and brotherhood and they all leave and me and Jacky are alone to wonder some more.

All the muscular gum of sex is such a bore, but Billie and I have such a fantastic sexball anyway that's why we're able to philosophize like that and agree and laugh together in sweet nakedness "Oh baby we're together crazy, we could live in an old log cabin in the hills and never say anything for years, it was meant that we'd meet"——She's saying all kinds of things as an idea begins to dawn on me: "Say I know Billie, let's leave the City and take Elliott with us and go to Monsanto's cabin in the woods for a week or two and forget everything"——"Yes I can call up my boss right now and get a coupla weeks off, Oh Jack let's do it"——"And it'll be good for Elliott, get away from all these sinister friends of yours, my God"——"Perry aint sin- ister."

"We'll get married and go away and have a lodge in the Adirondacks, at night by the lamp we'll have simple suppers

with Elliott"——"I'll make love to you always"——"But you
wont even have to because we both realize we're bugs . . . our
lodge will have truth written all over it but tho the whole world
come smear it with big black paints of hate and lies we'll be
falling dead drunk in truth"——"Have some coffee"——"My
hands'll grow numb and I wont be able to handle the axe but still
I'll be the truth man. . . I'll stand by the drape of the window
night listening to the babble of all the world and I'll tell you
about it"——"But Jack I love you and that's not the only reason
why, dont you see that we're meant for each other from the
beginning, didnt you see that when you came in with Cody and
started calling me Julien for that silly reason you told me about
where I look like some old buddy you know in New York"——
"Who hates Cody's guts and Cody hates him"——"But dont
you see what a waste it is?"——"But what about Cody? you
want me to marry you but you love Cody and in fact Perry loves
you too?"——"Sure but what's wrong with that or all that?
there's perfect love between us forever there's no doubt about it
but we only have two bodies"——(a strange statement)——I
stand by the window looking out on the glittering San Francisco
night with its magic cardboard houses saying "And you have
Elliott who doesnt like me and I dont like him and in fact I dont
like you and I dont like myself either, how about that?" (Billie
says nothing to this but only stores up an anger that comes out
later)——"But we can call Dave Wain and he'll drive us to Big
Sur cabin and we'll be alone in the woods at least"——"I'm
telling you that's what I wanta do!"——"Call him now!"——I
tell her the number and she dials it like a secretary——"O the
sad music of it all, I've done it all, seen it all, done everything
with everybody" I say phone in hand, "the whole world's coming
on like a high school sophomore eager to learn what he calls New
things, mind you, the same old singsong sad song truth of
death . . . because the reason I yell death so much is because I'm
really yelling life, because you cant have death without life, hello
Dave? there you are? know what I'm callin you about? listen

pal . . . take that big brunette Romana that Rumanian mad-woman and pack her in Willie and come down to Billie's here and pick us up, we'll pack while you's en route, honey's on, and we'll all go spend two weeks of bliss in Monsanto's cabin"——"Does Monsanto agree?"——"I'll call him right now and ask him, he'll say sure"——"Well I thought I'd be painting Romana's wall tomorrow but maybe I'd a just got drunk doin that anyway: sure you wanta do all this now?"——"Yes yeh yeh, come on——" "And I can bring Romana?"——"Yes but why not?"——"And what's the purpose of all this?"——"Ah Daddy, maybe just to see you again and we can talk about purposes anywhere: you wanta go on a lecture tour to Utah university and Brown university and tell the well scrubbed kids?"——"Scrubbed with what?"——"Scrubbed with hopeless perfection of pioneer puritan hope that leaves nothing but dead pigeons to look at?"——"Okay I'll be right out . . . first I gotta get Willie's tank filled up and an oil change too"——"I'll pay you when you get here"——"I heard you were eloping with Billie"——"Who told you that?"——"It was in the paper today"——"Well we'll start off by getting into Willie again and dont bring Ron Blake, we'll be just two couples dig?"——"Yeh——and lissen I'll bring my surf castin rod and catch some fish down there"——"We'll have a ball——and listen Dave I'm grateful you're free and willing to drive us down there, I'm down in the mouth, I've been sitting here for a week drinking and the chair broke and the fish died and I'm all screwed up again"——"Well you shouldnt oughta drink that sweet stuff all the time and you never eat"——"But that's not the real trouble"——"Well we'll decide what the real trouble is"——"That's right"——"Methinks the real trouble is those pigeons"——"Why?"——"I dunno, remember when we were in East St. Louis with George, and Jack you said you'd love those beautiful dancing girls if you knew they would live forever as beautiful as they are?"——"But that's only a quote from Buddha"——"Yeh, but the girls didn't expect all that"——"How ya feeling Dave? what's Fagan doing tonight"——"Oh he's sitting in his room writing something, calls it his GOOFBOOK, has big wild drawings in it, and Lex Pascal is drunk again and the music is playing and I'm real sad and I'm glad you called"——"You like me Dave?"——"I aint got nothin else to do, kid"——"But you really have somethin else to do really?"——"Lissen never mind, I'll be up, you call Monsanto right away tho because we also gotta get the corral gate keys from him"——"I'm glad I know you Dave"——"Me too Jack"——"Why?"——"Maybe I wanted to stand on my head in the snow to prove it but I do, am glad, will be glad, after all that's right there's nothing else for us to do but solve these damn problems and I've got one right here in my pants for Romana"——"But that's so sick and tired to call life a problem that can be solved"——"Yes but I'm just repeating what I read in the dead pigeon textbooks"——"But Dave I love you"—— "Okay I'll be right over."

32

We pack up little Elliott's pathetic warmclothes and put food together and get the hamper all set and wait for Dave to come sadly in the night——And we have a big talk—— "Billie but why did the fish die?" but she knows already they probably died because I gave them Kelloggs cornflakes or something went wrong, one thing sure is that she didnt forget to feed them or anything, it's all me, all my fault, I'd as soon be rusted by autumn too-much-think than be dead-fisher cause of those poor little hunks of golden death floating on that scummy water——It reminds me of the otter——But I cant explain it to Billie who's all abstract and talking about our abstract soul-meetings in hell, and little Elliott is pulling at her asking "Where we going? where we going? what for? what for?"—— She's saying "And all because you think you dont deserve to be loved because you think you caused the death of the goldfish tho they probably just died on their own accord"——"Why would they do that? why? What kind of logic is that for fish to have?"——"Or because you think you drink too much and therefore every time you're feeling good on a little booze you give up and say your hands hang helpless, like you said last night when you were holding me with those hands blessing my heart and my body with your love, O Jack it's time for you to wake up and come with me or at least come with somebody and open your eyes to why God's put you here, stop all that staring at the floor, you and Perry both you're crazy——I'll draw you magic moon circles'll change all your luck"——I look her dead in the eye and it is blue and I say "O Billie, forgive me"——"But you see you go there talkin guilty again"——"Well I dont know all those big theories about how everything should be goddamit all I know is that I'm a helpless hunk of helpful horse manure looking in your eye saying Help me"——"But when you make those big final statements it doesnt help you"——"Of course I know that but what do you want?"——"I want us to get married and settle down to a sensible understanding about eternal things"——"And you may be right"——I see it all raving before me the endless yakking kitchen mouthings of life, the long dark grave of tomby talks under midnight kitchen bulbs, in fact it fills me with love to realize that life so avid and misunderstood nevertheless reaches out skinny skeleton hand to me and to Billie too——But you know what I mean.

And this is the way it begins.

33

It sounds all so sad but it was actually such a gay night as Dave and Romana came over and there's all the business of packing boxes and clothes down to the car, nipping out of bottles, getting ready in fact to sing all the way to Big Sur "Home On the Range" and "I'm Just a Lonsome Old Turd" by Dave Wain——Me sitting up front next to Dave and Romana for some reason maybe because I wanted to identify with my old broken front rockingchair and lean there flapping and singing but with Romana between us the seat is pinned down and no longer flaps——Meanwhile Billie is on the back mattress with sleeping child and off we go booming down Bay Shore to that other shore whatever it will bring, the way people always feel whenever they essay some trip long or short especially in the night——The eyes of hope looking over the glare of the hood into the maw with its white line feeding in straight as an arrow, the lighting of fresh cigarettes, the buckling to lean forward to the next adventure something that's been going on in America ever since the covered wagons clocked the deserts in three months flat——Billie doesnt mind that I dont sit in back with her because she knows I wanta sing and have a good time—— Romana and I hit up fantastic medleys of popular and folk songs of all kinds and Dave contributes his New York Chicago blue light nightclub romantic baritone specialties——My wavering Sinatra is barely heard in fact——Beat on your knees and yell and sing Dixie and Banjo On My Knee, get raucous and moan

out Red River Valley, "Where's my harmonica, I been meanin
to buy me a eight dollar harmonica for eight years now."

It always starts out good like that, the bad moments——
Nothing is gained or lost also by the fact that I insist we stop at
Cody's en route so I can pick up some clothes I left there but
secretly I want Evelyn to finally come face to face with Billie——
It surprises me more however to see the look of absolute fright
on Cody's face as we pour into his livingroom at midnight and I
announce that Billie's in the jeep sleeping——Evelyn is not perturbed at all and in fact says to me privately in the kitchen "I
guess it was bound to happen sometime she'd come here and see
it but I guess it was destined to be you who'd bring her"——
"What's Cody so worried about?"——"You're spoiling all his
chance to be real secretive"——"He hasnt come and seen us for
a whole week, that's in a way what happened, he just left me
stranded there: I've been feeling awful, too"——"Well if you
want you can ask her to come in"——"Well we're leaving in a
minute anyway, you wanta see her at least?"——"I dont
care"——Cody is sitting in the livingroom absolutely rigid,
stiff, formal, with a big Irish stone in his eye: I know he's really
mad at me this time tho I dont really know why——I go out and
there's Billie alone in the car over sleeping Elliott biting her
fingernail——"You wanta come in and meet Evelyn?"——"I
shouldnt, she wont like that, is Cody there?"——"Yah"——So
Willamine climbs out (I remember just then Evelyn telling me
seriously that Cody always calls his women by their full first
names, Rosemarie, Joanna, Evelyn, Willamine, he never gives
them silly nicknames nor uses them).

The meeting is not eventful, of course, both girls keep their
silence and hardly look at each other so it's all me and Dave
Wain carrying on with the usual boloney and I see that Cody is
really very sick and tired of me bringing gangs arbitrarily to his
place, running off with his mistress, getting drunk and thrown
out of family plays, hundred dollars or no hundred dollars he
probably feels I'm just a fool now anyway and hopelessly lost

forever but I dont realize that myself because I'm feeling good——I want us to resume down that road singing bawdier and darker songs till we're negotiating narrow mountain roads at the pitch of the greatest songs.

I try to ask Cody about Perry and all the other strange characters who visit Billie in the City but he just looks at me out of the corner eye and says "Ah, yah,hm,"——I dont know and I never will know what he's up to anyway in the long run: I realize I'm just a silly stranger goofing with other strangers for no reason far away from anything that ever mattered to me whatever that was——Always an ephemeral "visitor" to the Coast never really involved with anyone's lives there because I'm always ready to fly back across the country but not to any life of my own on the other end either, just a traveling stranger like Old Bull Balloon, an exemplar of the loneliness of Doren Coit actually waiting for the only real trip, to Venus, to the mountain of Mien Mo——Tho when I look out of Cody's livingroom window just then I do see my star still shining for me as it's done all these 38 years over crib, out ship windows, jail windows, over sleepingbags only now it's dummier and dimmer and getting blurreder damnit as tho even my own star be now fading away from concern for me as I from concern for it——In fact we're all strangers with strange eyes sitting in a midnight livingroom for nothing——And small talk at that, like Billie saying "I always wanted a nice fireplace" and I'm yelling "Dont worry we got one at the cabin hey Dave? and all the wood's chopped!" and Evelyn:- "What does Monsanto think of you using his cabin all summer, weren't you supposed to go there alone in secret?"——"It's too late now!" I sing swigging from the bottle without which I'd only drop with shame face flat on the floor or on the gravel driveway——And Dave and Romana look a little uneasy finally so we all get up to go, zoom, and that's the last time I see Cody or Evelyn anyway.

And as I say our songs grow mightier as the road grows darker and wilder, finally here we are on the canyon road the headlights just reaching out there around bleak sand shoulders——Down to the creek where I unlock the corral gate——Across the meadow and back to the haunted cabin——Where on the strength of that night's booze and getaway gladness Billie and I actually have a good time lighting fires and making coffee and *gong* to be together in the one sleepingbag easy as pie after we've bundled up little Elliott and Dave and Romana have retired in his double nylon bag by the creek in the moonlight.

No, it's the next day and night that concerns me.

34

The whole day begins simply enough with me getting up feeling fair and going down to the creek to slurp up water in my palms and wash up, seeing the languid waving of one large brown thigh over the mass of Dave's nylons indicative of an early morning love scene, in fact Romana telling us later at breakfast "When I woke up this morning and saw all those trees and water and clouds I told Dave 'It's a beautiful universe we created' "——A real Adam and Eve waking up, in fact this being one of Dave's gladdest days because he'd really wanted to get away from the City again anyway and this time with a pretty doll, and's brought his surf casting gear planning a big day—— And we've brought a lot of good food——The only trouble is there's no more wine so Dave and Romana go off in Willie to get some more anyway at a store 13 miles south down the highway——Billie and I are alone talking by the fire——I begin to feel extremely low as soon as last night's alcohol wears off.

Everything is trembly again, the trembling hand, I cant for a fact even light the fire and Billie has to do it——"I cant light a fire any more!" I yell——"Well I can" she says in a rare instance when she lets me have it for being such a nut——Little Elliott is constantly pulling at her asking this and that, "What is that stick for, to put in the fire? why? how does it burn? why does it burn? where are we? when are we leaving" and the pattern develops where she begins to talk to him instead of me anyway because I'm just sitting there staring at the floor sighing——

Later when he takes his nap we go down the path to the beach, about noon, both of us sad and silent——"What's the matter I wonder" I say out loud——She:- "Everything was alright last night when we slept in the bag together now you wont even hold my hand . . . goddamit I'm going to kill myself!"——Because I've begun to realize in my soberness that this thing has come too far, that I dont love Billie, that I'm leading her on, that I made a mistake dragging everyone here, that I simply wanta go home now, I'm just plumb sick and tired just like Cody I guess of the whole nervewracking scene bad enough as it is always pivoting back to this poor haunted canyon which again gives me the willies as we walk under the bridge and come to those heartless breakers busting in on sand higher than earth and looking like the heartlessness of wisdom——Besides I suddenly notice as if for the first time the awful way the leaves of the canyon that have managed to be blown to the surf are all hesitantly advancing in gusts of wind then finally plunging into the surf, to be dispersed and belted and melted and taken off to sea——I turn around and notice how the wind is just harrying them off trees and into the sea, just hurrying them as it were to death——In my condition they look human trembling to that brink——Hastening, hastening——In that awful huge roar blast of autumn Sur wind.

Boom, clap, the waves are still talking but now I'm sick and tired of whatever they ever said or ever will say——Billie wants me to stroll with her down towards the caves but I dont want to get up from the sand where I'm sitting back to boulder——She goes alone——I suddenly remember James Joyce and stare at the waves realizing "All summer you were sitting here writing the so called sound of the waves not realizing how deadly serious our life and doom is, you fool, you happy kid with a pencil, dont you realize you've been using words as a happy game——all those marvelous skeptical things you wrote about graves and sea death it's ALL TRUE YOU FOOL! Joyce is dead! The sea took him! it will take YOU!" and I look down the beach and there's

Billie wading in the treacherous undertow, she's already groaned several times earlier (seeing my indifference and also of course the hopelessness at Cody's and the hopelessness of her wrecked apartment and wretched life) "Someday I'm going to commit suicide," I suddenly wonder if she's going to horrify the heavens and me too with a sudden suicide walk into those awful under-tows——I see her sad blonde hair flying, the sad thin figure, alone by the sea, the leaf-hastening sea, she suddenly reminds me of something——I remember her musical sighs of death and I see the words clearly imprinted in my mind over her figure in the sand:- ST. CAROLYN BY THE SEA——"You were my last chance" she's said but dont all women say that?——But can it be by "last chance" she doesnt mean mere marriage but some profoundly sad realization of something in me she really needs to go on living, at least that impression coming across anyway on the force of all the gloom we've shared——Can it be I'm with-holding from her something sacred just like she says, or am I just a fool who'll never learn to have a decent eternally minded deep-down relation with a woman and keep throwing that away for a song at a bottle?——In which case my own life is over anyway and there are the Joycean waves with their blank mouths saying "Yes that's so," and there are the leaves hurrying one by one down the sand and dumping in——In fact the creek is freight-ing hundreds more of them a minute right direct from the back hills——That big wind blasts and roars, it's all yellow sunny and blue fury everywhere——I see the rocks wobble as it seems God is really getting mad for such a world and's about to destroy it: big cliffs wobbling in my dumb eyes: God says "It's gone too far, you're all destroying everything one way or the other wobble boom the end is NOW."

"The Second Coming, tick tock," I think shuddering——St. Carolyn by the Sea is going in further——I could run and go see her but she's so far away——I realize that if that nut is going to try this I'll have to make an awful run and swim to get her——I get up and edge over but just then she turns around and starts back. . . "And if I call her 'that nut' in my secret thoughts wonder what she calls me?"——O hell, I'm sick of life——If I had any guts I'd drown myself in that tiresome water but that wouldnt be getting it over at all, I can just see the big transformations and plans jellying down there to curse us up in some other wretched suffering form eternities of it——I guess that's what the kid feels——She looks so sad down there wandering Ophelialike in bare feet among thunders.

On top of that now here come the tourists, people from other cabins in the canyon, it's the sunny season and they're out two three times a week, what a dirty look I get from the elderly lady who's apparently heard about the "author" who was secretly invited to Mr. Monsanto's cabin but instead brought gangs and bottles and today worst of all trollopes——(Because in fact earlier that morning Dave and Romana have already made love on the sand in broad daylight visible not only to others down the beach but from that high new cabin on the shoulder of the cliff) (tho hidden from sight from the bridge by cliffwall)——So it's all well known news now there's a ball going on in Mr. Monsanto's cabin and him not even here——This elderly lady being accompanied by children of all kinds——So that when Billie returns from the far end of the beach and starts back with me down the path (and I'm silly with a big footlong wizard pipe in my mouth trying to light it in the wind to cover up) the lady gives her the once over real close but Billie only smiles lightly like a little girl and chirps hello.

I feel like the most disgraceful and nay disreputable wretch on earth, in fact my hair is blowing in beastly streaks across my stupid and moronic face, the hangover has now worked paranoia into me down to the last pitiable detail.

Back at the cabin I cant chop wood for fear I'll cut a foot off, I cant sleep, I cant sit, I cant pace, I keep going to the creek to drink water till finally I'm going down there a thousand times making Dave Wain wonder as he's come back with more wine——We sit there slugging out of our separate bottles, in

my paranoia I begin to wonder why I get to drink just the one
bottle and he the other——But he's gay "I am now going out
surf castin and catch us a grabbag of fish for a marvelous supper;
Romana you get the salad ready and anything else you can think
of; we'll leave you alone now" he adds to gloomy me and Billie
thinking he's in our way, "and say, why dont we go to Nepenthe
and *private* our grief tonight and enjoy the moonlight on the
terrace with Manhattans, or go see Henry Miller?"——"No!" I
almost yell, "I mean I'm so exhausted I dont wanta do anything
or see anybody"——(already feeling awful guilt about Henry
Miller anyway, we've made an appointment with him about a
week ago and instead of showing up at his friend's house in Santa
Cruz at seven we're all drunk at ten calling long distance and
poor Henry just said "Well I'm sorry I dont get to meet you Jack
but I'm an old man and at ten o'clock it's time for me to go to
bed, you'd never make it here till after midnight now") (his voice
on the phone just like on his records, nasal, Brooklyn, goodguy
voice, and him disappointed in a way because he's gone to the
trouble of writing the preface to one of my books) (tho I suddenly now think in my remorseful paranoias "Ah the hell with it
he was only gettin in the act like all these guys write prefaces so
you dont even get to read the author first") (as an example of
how really psychotically suspicious and loco I was getting).

Alone with Billie's even worse——"I cant see anything to do
now," she says by the fire like an ancient Salem housewife ("Or
Salem witch?" I'm leering)——"I could have Elliott taken care
of in a private home or an orphanage and just go to a nunnery
myself, there's a lot of them around——or I could kill myself
and Elliott both"——"Dont talk like that"——"There's no
other way to talk when there's no more directions to take"——
"You've got me all wrong I wouldnt be any good for you"——"I
know that now, you want to be a hermit you say but you dont do
it much I noticed, you're just tired of life and wanta sleep, in a
way that's how I feel too only I've got Elliott to worry about. . . I
could take both our lives and solve that"——"You, creepy

talk"——"You told me the first night you loved me, that I was most interesting, that you hadnt met anyone you liked so much then you just went on drinking, I really can see now what they say about you is true: and all the others like you: O I realize you're a writer and suffer through too much but you're really ratty sometimes . . . but even that I know you cant help and I know you're not really ratty but awfully broken up like you explained to me, the reasons . . . but you're always groaning about how sick you are, you really dont think about others enough and I KNOW you cant help it, it's a curious disease a lot of us have anyway only better hidden sometimes . . . but what you said the first night and even just now about me being St. Carolyn in the Sea, why dont you follow through with what your heart knows is Good and best and true, you give up so easy to discouragement . . . then I guess too you dont really want me and just wanta go home and resume your own life maybe with Louise your girlfriend"——"No I couldn't with her either, I'm just bound up inside like constipation, I cant move emotionally like you'd say emotionally as tho that was some big grand magic mystery everybody saying 'O how wonderful life is, how miraculous, God made this and God made that,' how do you know he doesnt hate what He did: He might even be drunk and not noticing what he went and done tho of course that's not true"—— "Maybe God is dead"——"No, God cant be dead because He's the unborn"——"But you have all those philosophies and sutras you were talking about"——"But dont you see they've all become empty words, I realize I've been playing like a happy child with words words words in a big serious tragedy, look around"——"You could make some effort, damn it!"

But what's even ineffably worse is that the more she advises me and discussed the trouble the worse and worse it gets, it's as tho she didnt know what she was doing, like an unconscious witch, the more she tries to help the more I tremble almost too realizing she's doing it on purpose and knows she's witching me but it's all gotta be formally understood as "help" dingblast it——She must be some kind of chemical counterpart to me, I just cant stand her for a minute, I'm racked with guilt because all the evidence there seems to say she's a wonderful person sympathizing in her quiet sad musical voice with an obvious rogue nevertheless none of these rational guilts stick——All I feel is the invisible stab from her——She's hurting me!——At some points in our conversation I'm a veritable ham actor jumping up to twitch my head, that's the effect she has——"What's the matter?" she asks softly——Which makes me almost scream and I've never screamed in my life——It's the first time in my life I'm not confident I can hold myself together no matter what happens and be inly calm enough to even smile with condescension at the screaming hysterias of women in madwards——I'm in the same madward all of a sudden——And what's happened? what's caused it——"Are you driving me mad on purpose?" I finally blurt——But naturally she protests I'm talking out of my head, there's no such evident intention anywhere, we're just on a happy weekend in the country with friends, "Then there's something wrong with ME!" I yell——"That's obvious but why dont you try to calm down and for instance like make love to me, I've been begging you all day and all you do is groan and turn away as tho I was an ugly old bat"——She comes and offers herself to me softly and gently but I just stare at my quivering wrists——It's really very awful——It's hard to explain—— Besides then the little boy is constantly coming at Billie when she kneels at my lap or sits on it or tries to soothe my hair and comfort me, he keeps saying in the same pitiful voice "Dont do it Billie dont do it Billie dont do it Billie" till finally she has to give up that sweet patience of hers where she answers his every little pathetic question and yell "Shut up! Elliott will you shut up! DO I have to beat you again!" and I groan "No!" but Elliott yells louder "Dont do it Billie dont do it Billie dont do it Billie!" so she sweeps him off and starts whacking him screamingly on the porch and I am about to throw in the towel and gasp up my last, it's horrible.

Besides when she beats Elliott she herself cries and then will
be yelling madwoman things like "I'll kill both of us if you dont
stop, you leave me no alternative! O my child!" suddenly picking
him up and embracing him rocking tears, and gnashing of hair
and all under those old peaceful bluejay trees where in fact the
jays are still waiting for their food and watching all this——
Even so Alf the Sacred Burro is in the yard waiting for somebody to give him an apple——I look up at the sun going down
golden throughout the insane shivering canyon, that blasted
rogue wind comes topping down trees a mile away with an
advancing roar that when it hits the broken cries of mother and
son in grief are blown away with all those crazy scattering
leaves——The creek screeches——A door bangs horribly, a
shutter follows suit, the house shakes——I'm beating my knees
in the din and cant even hear that.

"What's I got to do with you committing suicide anyway?"
I'm yelling——"Alright, it has nothing to do with you"——
"So okay you have no husband but at least you've got little
Elliott, he'll grow up and be okay, you can always meanwhile
go on with your job, get married, move away, do something,
maybe it's Cody but more than that I'd say it's all those mad characters making you insane and wanta kill yourself like that——
Perry——"——"Dont talk about Perry, he's wonderful and
sweet and I love him and he's much kinder to me than you'll ever
be: at least he gives of himself"——"But what's all this giving of
ourselves, what's there to give that'll help anybody"——"You'll
never know you're so wrapped up in yourself"——We're now
starting to insult each other which would be a healthy sign
except she keeps breaking down and crying on my shoulder more
or less again insisting I'm her last chance (which isnt true)——
"Let's go to a monastery together," she adds madly——"Evelyn,
I mean Billie you might go to a nunnery at that, by God get thee
to a nunnery, you look like you'd make a nun, maybe that's what
you need all that talk about Cody about religion maybe all this
worldly horror is just holding you back from what you call your

true realizing, you could become a big reverend mother someday with not a worry on your mind tho I met a reverend mother once who cried . . . ah it's all so sad"——"What did she cry about?"——"I dont know, after talking to me, I remember I said some silly thing like 'the universe is a woman because it's round' but I think she cried because she was remembering her early days when she had a romance with some soldier who died, at least that's what they say, she was the greatest woman I ever saw, big blue eyes, big smart woman . . . you could do that, get out of this awful mess and leave it all behind"——"But I love love too much for that"——"And not because you're sensual either you poor kid"——In fact we quiet down a little and do actually make love in spite of Elliott pulling at her "Billie dont do it dont do it Billie dont do it" till right in the middle I'm yelling "Dont do what? what's he mean?——can it be he's right and Billie you shouldnt do it? can it be we're sinning after all's said and done? O this is insane!——but he's the most insane of them all," in fact the child is up on bed with us tugging at her shoulder just like a grownup jealous lover tryin to pull a woman off another man (she being on top indication of exactly how helpless and busted down I've become and here it is only 4 in the afternoon)—— A little drama going on in the cabin maybe a little different than what cabins are intended for or the local neighbors are imagining.

35

But there's an awful paranoiac element sometimes in orgasm that suddenly releases not sweet genteel sympathy but some token venom that splits up in the body——I feel a great ghastly hatred of myself and everything, the empty feeling far from being the usual relief is now as tho I've been robbed of my spinal power right down the middle on purpose by a great witching force——I feel evil forces gathering down all around me, from her, the kid, the very walls of the cabin, the trees, even the sudden thought of Dave Wain and Romana is evil, they're all coming now——I leave poor Billie face in hand and rush off to drink water in the creek but every time I do something like that I have to run back to be sorry and say so, but the moment I see her again "She's doing something else" I leer and I dont feel sorry at all——She's mumbling face in hands and the little boy's crying at her side——"My God she should get to a nunnery!" I think rushing back to the creek——Suddenly the water in the creek tastes different as tho somebody's thrown gasoline or kerosene in it upstream——"Maybe those neighbors wanta get back at me that's what!"——I taste the water carefully and I'm positive that's what happened.

Like an idiot I'm sitting by the creek staring when Dave Wain comes striding down with one fish on the line and his big cheerful western twang as tho nothing unusual's happened "Well boy I spent a whole two hours and look what I got! one measly but beautiful pathetic as you'll see holy little rainbow sea trout that

I'm now going to clean——Now the way to clean fish is as
follows," and he kneels innocently by the creek to show me
how——I have nothing else to do but watch and smile——He
says: "Be prepared to be taken on tour of Farollone Island within
next two years, boy, with wild canaries actually lighting on your
boat hundreds of miles out at sea——See I'm tryna to save
money for a fishboat of my own, I think fishing is bettern anything and I intend to entirely reorganize my life for this tho I see
the stern image of Fagan shrieking with a Roshi stick, but you
ought to see how fast you can bait up hundreds of herring and
clean salmon in one and a half minutes, it's a fact, and you walk
around in hickory shirts and wool knit caps——Man I know all
about it and I'm writing a final definitive article on how clean
hard work is the saviour of us all—When you're out there it's a
very primal light, fishing is——You're a hunter——Birds find
fish for you——Weather drives you——Foolish mind-hangs
dissolve before utter fatigue and everything comes in"——As I
squat there I imagine maybe Billie is telling Romana what happened in the cabin and Dave'll know in a while tho he seems to
know a lot that's going on——He's hinted several times, like
now, "You look like you're having the worse time of your life,
that kid Elliott is enough to drive anybody crazy and Billie is
sure a nervous little wench——Now here's the way you scale,
with this here knife"——And I marvel that I cant be so useful
and humanly simple and good enough to make small talk to
make others feel better, like Dave, there he is long and hollow of
cheeks from long drinking himself the past few weeks, but he's
not complaining or moaning in the corner like me, at least he
does something about it, he puts himself to the test——He
gives me that feeling again that I'm the only person in the world
who is devoid of human-beingness, damn it, that's true, that's
the way I feel anyway——"Ah Dave someday you and me'll go
fishing in your abandoned mining camp on the Rogue River,
huh, we'll be feeling better by then somehow gaddamit"——
"Well we've got to cut down on the sauce a whole lot, Jack,"

saying "Jack" sadly a lot like Jarry Wagner used to do on our Dharmabumming mountain climbs where we'd confide dolors, "yes, and we drink too many SWEET drinks in a way, you know all that sugar and no food is bound to upset your metabolism and fill your blood with sugar to the point where you aint got the strength of a hen; you especially you've been drinking nothin but sweet port and sweet Manhattans now for weeks——I promise you the holy flesh of this little fish will heal you," (chuckle).

I suddenly look at the fish and feel horrible all over again, that old death scheme is back only now I'm gonna put my big healthy Anglosaxon teeth into it and wrench away at the mournful flesh of a little living being that only an hour ago was swimming happily in the sea, in fact even Dave thinking this and saying: "Ah yes that little muzzling mouth was blindly sucking away in the glad waters of life and now look at it, here's where the fittin head's chopped off, you dont have to look, us big drunken sinners are now going to use it for our sacrificial supper so in fact when we cook it I'm going to say an Indian prayer for it hoping it's the same prayer the local Indians used——Jack in a way we might even start havin fun here and make a great week out of it!"——"Week?"——"I thought we was coming here for a week"——"Oh I said that didnt I . . . I feel awful about everything . . . I dont think I can make it . . . I'm going crazy with Billie and Elliott and me too . . . maybe I'll have to, maybe we'll have to leave or something, I think I'll die here"——And Dave is disappointed naturally and here I've already routed him up out of his own affairs to drive down here anyway, another matter to make me feel like a rat.

36

But Dave's making the best of clomping up and down the cabin preparing the bag of cornmeal and starting the corn oil in the frying pan, Romana too she's making an exquisite big salad with lots of mayonnaise and in fact poor Billie is mutely helping her setting the table and the little boy is crooning by the stove it's almost like a happy domestic scene suddenly——Only I watch it from the porch with horrified eyes——Also because their shadows in the lamplight gone casting on the walls look huge and monsterlike and witch-like and warlock-like, I'm alone in the woods with happy ghosts——The wind is howling as the sun goes down so I go in, but I go out at once again madly to my creek, always thinking the creek itself will give me water that will clear away everything and reassure me forever (also remembering in my distress Edgar Cayce's advice "Drink a lot of water") but "There's kerosene in the water!" I yell in the wind, nobody hearing——I feel like kicking the creek and screaming——I turn around and there's the cabin with its warm interiors, the silent people inside all noticeably glum because they cant understand anyway what's with the nut wandering in and out from cabin to creek, silent, wan faced, stupefacted, trembling and sweating like midsummer was on the roof and instead it's even cold now——I sit in the chair with my back to the door and watch Dave as he lectures on bravely.

"What we're having is a sacrificial banquet with all kinds of goodies you see laid in a regal spread around one little delicious fish so that we all have to pray to the fish and take tiny little bites, we only have about four bites apiece and there's all kinds of parts of the fish where the bites are more significant——But beyond that the way to properly fry a freshcaught fish is to be sure the oil is burning and furiously so when you lay the fish in it, not burning but real hot oil, well yeh even burning, hand me the spat, you then gently lay the fish into the oil and create a tremendous crackling racket" (which he does as Romana cheers) (and I glance at Billie and she's thinking of something else like a nun in the corner) but Dave keeps on making jokes till he actually has us all smiling——While the fish is cooking, tho, Romana as she's been doing all day is constantly handing me a bite to eat, some *hors d'oeuvres* or piece of tomato or other, apparently trying to help me feel better——"You've got to EAT" she and Dave keep saying but I dont want to eat and yet they're always holding out bites to my mouth until finally now I begin to frown thinking "What's all these bites they keep throwing at me, poison?——and what's wrong with my eyes, they're all dilated black like I've had drugs, all I've had is wine, did Dave put drugs in my wine or something? thinking it will help or something? or are they members of a secret society that dopes people secretly the idea being to enlighten them or something?" even as Romana is handing me a bite and I take it from her big brown hands and chew——She's wearing purple panties and purple bras, nothing else, just for fun, Dave's slappin her on the can joyfully as he cooks the supper, it's some big erotic natural thing to do for Romana, she believes in showing her beautiful big body anyway——In fact at one point when Billie's up leaning over a chair Dave goes behind Billie and playfully touches *her* and winks at me, but I'm not of all this like a moron and we could all be having fun such as soldiers dream the day away imagining, dammit——But the venoms in the blood are asexual as well as asocial and a-everything——"Billie's so nice and thin, like I'm used to Romana maybe I should switch around here for variety," says Dave at the sizzling frying pan——I look over my shoulder and see at first with a leap of joy but then with ominous fear an enormous full moon at full fat standing there between Mien Mo mountain and the north canyon wall, like saying to me as I look over my trembling shoulder "Hoo doo you."

But I say "Dave, look, as if all this wasnt enough" and I point out the moon to him, there's dead silence in the trees and also among us inside, there she is, vast lugubrious fullmoon that frights madmen and makes waters wave, she's got one or two treetops silhouetted and's got that whole side of the canyon lit up in silver——Dave just looks at the moon with his tired madness eyes (overexcited eyes, my mother'd said) and says nothing——I go out to the creek and drink water and come back and wonder about the moon and suddenly the four shadows in the cabin are all dead silent as tho they had conspired with the moon.

"Time to eat, Jack," says Dave coming out on the porch suddenly——No one's saying anything——I go in and sheepishly sit at the table like the useless pioneer who doesnt do anything to help the men or please the women, the idiot in the wagon train who nevertheless has to be fed——Dave stands there saying "Oh full moon, here is our little fish which we are now going to partake of to feed us so that we shall be stronger; thank you Fish people, thank you Fish god; thank you moon for making our light tonight; this is the night of the fullmoon fish which we now consecrate with the first delicate bite"——He takes his fork and opens the little fish carefully, it's beautifully breaded and fried and centered in a dazzle of salads and vegetables and cornmeal johnnycakes, he opens a funny gill, goes under, removes a strange bite and projects it to my mouth saying "Take the first bite Jack, just a little bite, and be sure to chew very slowly"——I do so, oily delicious bite but nothing delicious any more in my tongue——Then the others take their little holy bites, little Elliott's eyes shining with delight at this wonderful game that however has started to frighten me——For obvious reasons by now.

As we eat Dave announces that he and I are sick from too

much drinking and by God we're going to reform and see to it
that we shape up, then he launches into stories as usual, ending
in a talkative ordinary supper that I think will sorta straighten
me out at first but after supper I feel even worse, "That fish has
all the death of otters and mouses and snakes right in it or something" I'm thinking——Billie is quietly washing the dishes
without complaint, Dave is gladly smoking after-dinner cigarettes on the porch, but here I am again mooning by the creek
hiding from all of them each five minutes tho I cant understand
what makes me do it——I HAVE to get out of there——But I
have no right to STAY AWAY——So I keep coming back but
it's all an insane revolving automatic directionless circle of
anxiety, back and forth, around and around, till they're really by
now so perturbed by my increasing silent departures and creepy
returns they're all sitting without a word by the stove but now
their heads are together and they're whispering——From the
woods I see those three shadowy heads whispering me by the
stove——What's Dave saying?—And why do they look like
they're plotting something further?——Can it be it was all
arranged by Dave Wain via Cody that I would meet Billie and
be driven mad and now they've got me alone in the woods and
are going to give me final poisons tonight that will utterly
remove all my control so that in the morning I'll have to go to a
hospital forever and never write another line?——Dave Wain is
jealous because I wrote 10 novels?——Billie has been assigned
by Cody to get me to marry her so he'll get all my money?
Romana is a member of the expert poisoning society (I've heard
her mention tree spirits already, earlier in the car, and she's sung
some strange songs the night before)——The three of them,
Dave Wain in fact the chief conspirator because I know he does
have amphetamine on his person and the needles in a little box,
just one injection of a tomato, or of a portion of fish, or drops
into a bottle of wine, and my eyes become mad wide and black
like they are now, my nerves OO ouch, this is what I'm
thinking——Still they sit there by the fire in dead silence, when

I tromp into the cabin in fact they all start up again talking:
sure sign——I walk out again, "I'm going down the road a
ways"——"Okay"——But the moment I'm alone on the path a
million waving moony arms are thrashing around me and every
hole in the cliffs and burnt out trees I'd calmly passed a hundred
times all summer in dead of fog, now has something moving in
it quickly——I hurry back——Even on the porch I'm scared to
see the familiar bushes near the outhouse or down by the broken
treetrunk——And now a babble in the creek has somehow
entered my head and with all the rhythm of the sea waves going
"Kettle blomp you're up, you rop and dop, ligger lagger ligger" I
grab my heat but it keeps babbling.

Masks explode before my eyes when I close them, when I look
at the moon it waves, moves, when I look at my hands and feet
they creep——Everything is moving, the porch is moving like
ooze and mud, the chair trembles under me——"Sure you dont
wanta go to Nepenthe for a Manhattan Jack?"——"No" ("Yeh
and you'd dump poison in it" I think darkly but seriously hurt I
could ever allow myself to think that about poor Dave)——And
I realize the unbearable anguish of insanity: how uninformed
people can be thinking insane people are "happy," O God, in
fact it was Irwin Garden once warned me not to think the mad-
houses are full of "happy nuts," "There's a tightening around
the head that hurts, there's a terror of the mind that hurts even
more, they're so unhappy and especially because they cant
explain it to anybody or reach out and be helped through all the
hysterical paranoia they are really suffering more than anyone in
the world and I think in the universe in fact," and Irwin knew,
this from observing his mother Naomi who finally had to have a
lobotomy——Which sets me thinking how nice to cut away
therefore all that agony in my forehead and STOP IT! STOP
THAT BABBLING!——Because now the babbling's not only
in the creek, as I say it's left the creek and come in my head, it
would be alright for coherent babbling meaning something but
it's all brilliantly enlightened babble that does more than mean

something: it's telling me to die because everything is over——
Everything is swarming all over me.

Dave and Romana retire again by the creek for a night's sweet
sleep under the moon while Billie and I sit there gloomy by the
fire——Her voice is crying: "It might make you feel better to
just come in my arms"——"I've got to try something, Billie
after all I've told you I cant make you see what's happening to
me, you dont understand"——"Come into our sleepingbag
again like last night, just sleep"——We get in naked but now
I'm not drunk I'm aware of the real tight squeeze in there and
besides in my fever I'm perspiring so much it's unbearable, her
own skin is soaking wet from mine, yet our arms are outside in
the cold——"This won't do!"——"What'll you do?"——"Let's
try the cot inside" but maniacally I arrange the cot all screwy
with a board on top of it forgetting to put sleepingbag pads
underneath like I'd done all summer, I simply forget all that,
Billie, poor Billie lies down with me on this absurd board thinking I'm trying to drive my madness away by self torturing
ordeals——It's ridiculous, we lie there stiff as boards on a
board——I roll off and saying "We'll try something else"——I
try laying out the sleepingbag on the floor of the porch but the
moment she's in my arms a mosquito comes at me, or I burst
out sweating, or I see a flash of lightning, or I hear a big
roaring Hymn in my head, or imagine a thousand people are
coming down the creek talking, or the roar of the wind is bringing flying treetrunks that will crush us——"Wait a minute," I
yell and get up to pace awhile and run down to drink water by
the creek where Dave and Romana are peacefully entangled—
—I start cursing Dave "Bastard's got the only decent spot there
is to sleep in anyway, right there in that sand by the creek, if he
wasnt here I could sleep there and the creek would cover the
noise in my head and I could sleep there, with Billie even, all
night, bastard's got my spot," and I kick back to the porch——
Poor Billie's arms are outstretched to me: "Please Jack, come on,
love me, love me"——"I CANT"——"But why cant you, if

even we'll never see each other again let us our last night be beautiful and something to remember forever."

"Like a big ideal memory for both of us, cant you give me just that?"——"I would if I could" I'm muttering around like a fussy old nut inside the cabin looking for a match——I cant even light my cigarette, something sinister blows it out, when it's lit it mortifies my hot mouth anyway like a mouthful of death——I grab up another batch of bags and blankets and start piling myself up on the other side of the porch saying to Billie who's sighing now realizing it's hopeless "First I'll try to take a nap by myself here then when I wake up I'll feel better and come over to you"——So I try that, turning over rigidly my eyes wide open staring full fright into the dark like the time in the movie Humphrey Bogart who's just killed his partner trying to sleep by the fire and you see his eyes staring into the fire rigid and insane——That's just the way I'm staring——If I try to close my eyes some elastic pulls them open again——If I try to turn over the whole universe turns over with me but it's no better on the other side of the universe——I realize I may never come out of this and my mother is waiting for me at home praying for me because she must know what's happening tonight, I cry out to her to pray and help me——I remember my cat for the first time in three hours and let out a yell that scares Billie——"All right Jack?"——"Give me a little time"——But now she's started to sleep, poor girl is exhausted, I realize she's going to abandon me to my fate anyway and I cant help thinking she and Dave and Romana are all secretly awake waiting for me to die——"For what reason?" I'm thinking "this secret poisoning society, I know, it's because I'm a Catholic, it's a big anti-Catholic scheme, it's Communists destroying everybody, systematic individuals are poisoned till finally they'll have everybody, this madness changes you completely and in the morning you no longer have the same mind——the drug is invented by Airapa-tianz, it's the brainwash drug, I always thought that Romana was a Communist being a Rumanian, and as for Billie that gang

of hers is strange, and Cody dont care, and Dave's all evil just
like I always figured maybe" but soon my thoughts arent even as
"rational" as that any more but become hours of raving——
There are forces whispering in my ear in rapid long speeches
advising and warning, suddenly other voices are shouting, the
trouble is all the voices are longwinded and talking very fast like
Cody at his fastest and like the creek so that I have to keep up
with the meaning tho I wanta bat it out of my ears——I keep
waving at my ears——I'm afraid to close my eyes for all the tur-
moiled universes I see tilting and expanding suddenly exploding suddenly clawing in to my center, faces, yelling mouths, long
haired yellers, sudden evil confidences, sudden rat-tat-tats of
cerebral committees arguing about "Jack" and talking about
him as if he wasnt there——Aimless moments when I'm
waiting for more voices and suddenly the wind explodes huge
groans in the million treetop leaves that sound like the moon
gone mad——And the moon rising higher, brighter, shining
down in my eyes now like a streetlamp——The huddled
shadowy sleeping figures over there so coy——So human and
safe, I'm crying "I'm not human any more and I'll never be safe
any more, Oh what I wouldnt give to be home on Sunday afternoon yawning because I'm bored, Oh for that again, it'll never
come back again——Ma was right, it was all bound to drive me
mad, now it's done——What'll I say to her?——She'll be terrified and go mad herself——*Oh ti Tykey, aide mué*——me who's
just eaten fish have no right to ask for brother Tyke again——"
——An argot of sudden screamed reports rattles through my
head in a language I never heard but understand immediately——
For a moment I see blue Heaven and the Virgin's white veil but
suddenly a great evil blur like an ink spot spreads over it, "The
devil!——the devil's come after me tonight! tonight is the night!
that's what!"——But angels are laughing and having a big barn
dance in the rocks of the sea, nobody cares any more——
Suddenly as clear as anything I ever saw in my life, I see the
Cross.

37

I see the cross, it's silent, it stays a long time, my heart goes out to it, my whole body fades away to it, I hold out my arms to be taken away to it, by God I am being taken away my body starts dying and swooning out to the Cross standing in a luminous area of the darkness, I start to scream because I know I'm dying but I dont want to scare Billie or anybody with my death scream so I swallow the scream and just let myself go into death and the Cross: as soon as that happens I slowly sink back to life——— Therefore the devils are back, commissioners are sending out orders in my ear to think anew, babbling secrets are hissed, suddenly I see the Cross again, this time smaller and far away but just as clear and I say through all the noise of the voices "I'm with you, Jesus, for always, thank you"——I lie there in cold sweat wondering what's come over me for years my Buddhist studies and pipesmoking assured meditations on emptiness and all of a sudden the Cross is manifested to me——My eyes fill with tears——"We'll all be saved——I wont even tell Dave Wain about it, I wont go wake him up down there and scare him, he'll know soon enough——now I can sleep."

I turn over but it's only begun——It's only one o'clock in the morning and the night wears on to the wheeling moon worse and worse till dawn by which time I've seen the Cross again and again but there's a battle somewhere and the devils keep coming back——I know if I could only sleep for an hour the whole complex of noisy brains would settle down, some control would

come back somewhere inside there, some blessing would soothe
the whole issue——But the bat comes silently flapping around
me again, I see him clearly in the moonlight now his little head
of darkness and wings that zigzag maddeningly so you cant even
get a look at them——Suddenly I hear a hum, a definite flying
saucer is hovering right over those trees where the hum must be,
there are orders in there, "They're coming to get me O my
God!"——I jump up and glare at the tree, I'm going to defend
myself——The bat flaps in front of my face——"The bat is
their representative in the canyon, his radar message they got,
why dont they leave? doesnt Dave hear that awful hum?"——
Billie is dead asleep but little Elliott suddenly thumps his foot,
once——I realize he's not even asleep and knows everything
that's going on——I lie down again and peek at him across the
porch floor: I suddenly realizing he's staring at the moon and there
he goes again, thumping his foot: he's sending messages——He's a
warlock disguised as a little boy, he's also destroying Billie!——I
get up to look at him feeling guilty too realizing this is all nonsense probably but he is not properly covered, his little bare
arms are outside the blankets in the cold night, he hasnt even got
a nightshirt, I curse at Billie——I cover him up and he whim-
pers——I go back and lie down with mad eyes looking deep
inside me, suddenly a bliss comes over me as the sleep mecha-
nism takes sinking hold——And there I am dreaming me and
two kids are hired to work in the mountains on the same "ridge"
as Desolation Peak (i.e. Mien Mo Mountain again) and start
with a cliffside river crew who tell us two workers have apparently sunk in the cliffside snow and we must lean over sheer
drops and see if we can "dump them out" or haul them in——
All we do is lie there on crumbly snow a thousand foot fall to the
river crumbling the snow off in slabs so big you wouldnt know if
men were trapped in em or not——Not only that the bosses
have special shoes on sliders that are holding them to the safe
shore (like ski clamps) so I begin to realize they're only fooling
us poor kids and we could have fallen too (I almost do)——

(did)——(almost)——As observer of the story I see it's just an
annual ritualistic joke to fool the new kids on the job who are
then dispatched to the other side of the river to slump off *more*
snow from sheer banks in hopes of finding the lost workmen—
—So we start there on a big trip, downriver first, but en route all
the peasants tell us stories of the God Monster Machine on the
other shore who makes sounds like certain birds and owls and
has a million infernal contraptions enough to make you sick
with all the slipshod windmill rickety details, as "Observer of
the story" again I see it's just a trick to make us scared when we
get there at night and hear actual natural sounds of birds, owls,
etc. thinking as green rookies in the country it's that "Monster"—
—Meanwhile we sign on to go to the main mountain but I
promise myself if I dont like the work there I'll come back get my
old job on Desolation——Already our employers have shown a
murderous sense of humor——I arrive at Mien Mo Mountain
which is like Raton Canyon again but has a large tho dry rot
river running in the wide hole and down there on many rocks are
huge brooding vultures——Old bums row out to them and pull
them clumsily off the rocks and start feeding them like pets,
bites of red meat or red mite, tho at first I thought the eccentric
old town bums wanted them to eat or to sell (still maybe so)
because before I study this I look and see hundreds of slowly fornicating vulture couples on the town dump——These are now
humanly formed vultures with human shaped arms, legs, heads,
torsos, but they have rainbow colored feathers, and the men are
all quietly sitting *behind* Vulture Women slowly somehow fornicating at them in all the same slow obscene movement——Both
man and woman sit facing the same direction and somehow
there's contact because you can see all their feathery rainbow
behinds slowly dully monotonously fornicating on the dump-
slopes——As I pass I even see the expression on the face of a
youngish blond vulture man eternally displeased because his
Vulture Mistress is an old Yakker who's been arguing with him
all the time——His face is completely human but inhumanly

pasty like uncooked pale pie dough with dull seamed buggy
horror that he's doomed to all this enough to make me shudder
in sympathy, I even see her awful expression of middleaged pie
dough tormentism——They're so human!——But suddenly me
and the two kid workers are taken to the Vulture People respectable quarter of town to our apartment where a Vulture Woman
and her daughter show us our rooms——Their faces are leprous
thick with softy yeast but painted with makeup to make them
like thick Christmas dolls and dull and fuzzy but human expressions, like with thick lips of rubber muzz, fat expressions all
crumbly like cracker meal, yellow pizza puke faces, disgusting
us tho we say nothing——The apartment has dirty beatnik
beds and mattresses everywhere but I walk thru the back looking
for a sink——It's *huge*——An endless walk thru long greasy
pantries and vast washrooms a block long with single filthy little
sink all dark and slimey like underground Lowell High School
crumbling basements——Finally I come to the Kitchen where
we "new workers" are s'posed to cook little meals all summer——
It's vast stone fireplaces and stone stoves all rancid and greasy
from a month-old Vulture People Banquet Orgy with still
dozens of uncooked chickens lying around on the floor, among
garbage and bottles——Rancid stale grease everywhere,
nobody's ever cleaned it up or knew how and the place as big as a
garage——I push my way out of there pushing a huge greasy-
stink foodstained tray of some sort hurrying away from the big
stinky emptiness and horror——The fat golden chickens lie
rotten upsidedown on littered stone slabs——I hurry out never
having seen such a dirty sight in my life. Meanwhile I learn the
two boys are studying a hamper full of Vulture Food for us and
one of them wisely says "Blisters in our sugar," meaning the
Vultures put their blisters in our sugar so we'll "die" but instead
of being really dead we'll be taken to the Underground Slimes to
walk neck deep in steaming mucks pulling huge groaning
wheels (among small forked snakes) so the devil with the long
ears can mine his Purple Magenta Square Stone that is the secret

of all this Kingdom——You end up down there groaning and
pulling thru dead bodies of other people even your own family
floating in the ooze——If you succeed you can become a pasty
Vulture Person obscenely fornicating slowly on the dump above,
I think, either that or the devil just invents the Vulture People
with what's left over out of the underground Hell——"Beans
anyone?" I hear myself saying as *thump!* I'm awake again! Elliott
has thumped his foot just at that moment on the porch!——I
look over there!——He's doing it on purpose, he knows everything that's going on!——What on earth have I brought these
people for and why just this particular night of that moon that
moon that moon?

I'm up again and pacing up and down and drinking water at
the creek, Dave and Romana's lump figures in the moonlight
dont move, like hypocrites, "Bastard has my only sleeping
spot"——I clutch my head, I'm so alone in all this——I go fear-
fully casting about for control back inside the cabin by the
lighted lamp, a smoke, trying to squeeze the last red drop out of
the rancid port bottle, no go——Now that Billie's asleep and so
still and peaceful I wonder if I can sleep just by lying beside her
and holding her——I do just this, crawling in with all my
clothes which I've put on because I'm afraid of going mad naked
or of not being able to suddenly run away from everything, in
my shoes, she moans a little in her sleep and resumes sleeping as
I hold her with those rigid staring eyes——Her blonde flesh in
the moonlight, the poor blonde hair so carefully washed and
combed, the ladylike little body also a burden to carry around
like my own but so frail, thinnish, I just stare at her shoulders
with tears——I'd wake her up and confess everything but I'll
only scare her——I've done irreparable harm ("Garradarable
narm!" yells the creek)——All my self sayings suddenly blurt-
ing babbles so the meaning cant even stay a minute I mean a
moment to satisfy my rational endeavors to hold control, every
thought I have is smashed to a million pieces by millionpieced
mental explosions that I remember I thought were so wonderful

when I'd first seen them on Peotl and Mescaline, I'd said then (when still innocently playing with words) "Ah, the manifestation of multiplicity, you can actually see it, it aint just words" but now it's "Ah the keselamaroyot you rot"——Till when dawn finally comes my mind is just a series of explosions that get louder and more "multiply" broken in pieces some of them big orchestral and then rainbow explosions of sound and sight mixed.

At dawn also I've almost dimmed into sleep three times but I swear (and this is something I remember that makes me realize I dont understand what happened at Big Sur even now) the little boy somehow thumped his foot just at the moment of drowse, to instantly wake me up, wide awake, back to my horror which when all is said and done is the horror of all the worlds the showing of it to me being damn well what I deserve anyway with my previous blithe yakkings about the sufferings of others in books.

Books, shmooks, this sickness has got me wishing if I can ever get out of this I'll gladly become a millworker and shut my big mouth.

38

Dawn is most horrible of all with the owls suddenly calling back and forth in the misty moon haunt——And even worse than dawn is morning, the bright sun only GLARING in on my pain, making it all brighter, hotter, more maddening, more nervewracking——I even go roaming up and down the valley in the bright Sunday morning sunshine with bag uner arm looking hopelessly for some spot to sleep in——As soon as I find a spot of grass by the path I realize I cant lie down there because the tourists might walk by and see me——As soon as I find a glade near the creek I realize it's too sinister there, like Hemingway's darker part of the swamp where "the fishing would be more tragic" somehow——All the haunts and glades having certain special evil forces concentrated there and driving me away——So haunted I go wandering up and down the canyon crying with that bag under my arm: "What on earth's happened to me? and how can earth be like that?"

Am I not a human being and have done my best as well as anybody else? never really trying to hurt anybody or half-hearted cursing Heaven?——The words I'd studied all my life have suddenly gotten to me in all their serious and definite deathliness, never more I be a "happy poet" "Singing" "about death" and allied romantic matters, "Go thou crumb of dust you with your silt of a billion years, here's a billion pieces of silt for you, shake that out of your shaker"——And all the green nature of the canyon now waving in the morning sun looking like a cruel idiot convocation.

Coming back to the sleepers and staring at them wild eyed like my brother'd once stared at me in the dark over my crib, staring at them not only enviously but lonely inhuman isolation from their simple sleeping minds——"But they all look dead!" I'm carking in my canyon, "Sleep is death, everything is death!"

The horrible climax coming when the others finally get up and pook about making a troubled breakfast, and I've told Dave I cant possibly stay here another minute, he must drive us all back to town, "Okay but I sure wish we could stay a week like Romana wants to do,"——"Well you drive me and come back"——"Well I dunno if Monsanta would like that we've already dirtied up the place aplenty, in fact we've got to dig a garbage pit and get rid of the junk"——Billie offers to dig the garbage pit but does so by digging a neat tiny coffinshaped grave instead of just a garbage hole——Even Dave Wain blinks to see it—It's exactly the size fit for putting a little dead Elliott in it, Dave is thinking the same thing I am I can tell by a glance he gives me——We've all read Freud sufficiently to understand something there——Besides little Elliott's been crying all morning and has had two beatings both of them ending up crying and Billie saying she cant stand it any more she's going to kill herself——

And Romana too notices it, the perfect 4 foot by 3 foot neatly sided grave like you're ready to sink a little box in it—— Horrifying me so much I take the shovel and go down to dump junk into it and mess up the neat pattern somehow but little Elliott starts screaming and grabs the shovel and refuses I go near the hole——So Billie herself goes and starts filling the garbage in but then looks at me significantly (I'm sure some-times she really did aspire to make me crazy) "Do you want to finish the job yourself?"——"What do you mean?"——"Cover the earth on, do the honors?"——"What do you mean do the honors!"——"Well I said I'd dig the garbage pit and I've done that, aint you supposed to do the rest?"——Dave Wain is watch-ing fascinated, there's something screwy he sees there too, something cold and frightening——"Well okay" I say, "I'll dump the earth over it and tamp it down" but I go down to do this Elliott is screaming "NO no no no!" ("My God, the fishes' bones are in that grave" I realize too)——"What's the matter he wont let me go near that hole! why did you make it look like a grave?" I finally yell——But Billie is only smiling quietly and steadily at me, over the grave, shovel in hand, the kid weeping tugging the shovel, rushing up to block my way, trying to shove me back with his little hands——I cant understand any of it——He's screaming as I grab the shovel as tho I'm about to bury Billie in there or something or himself maybe——"What's the matter with this kid is he a cretin?" I yell.

With the same quiet steady smile Billie says "Oh you're so fucking neurotic!"

I simply get mad and dump earth over the garbage and tromp it all down and say "The hell with all this madness!"

I get mad and stomp up on the porch and throw myself in the canvas chair and close my eyes——Dave Wain says he's going down the road to investigate the canyon a bit and when he comes back the girls will have finished packing and we'll all leave—— Dave goes off, the girls clean up and sweep, the little kid is sleeping and suddenly hopelessly and completely finished I sit there in the hot sun and close my eyes: and there's the golden swarming peace of Heaven in my eyelids——It comes with a sure hand a soft blessing as big as it is beneficent, i.e., endless——I've fallen asleep.

I've fallen asleep in a strange way, with my hands clasped behind my head thinking I'm just going to sit there and think, but I'm sleeping like that, and when I wake up just one short minute later I realize the two girls are both sitting behind me in absolute silence——When I'd sat down they were sweeping, but now they were squatting behind my back, facing each other, not a word——I turn and see them there——Blessed relief has come to me from just that minute——Everything has washed away——I'm perfectly normal again——Dave Wain is down the road looking at fields and flowers——I'm sitting smiling in the sun, the birds sing again, all's well again.

I still cant understand it.

Most of all I cant understand the miraculousness of the silence of the girls and the sleeping boy and the silence of Dave Wain in the fields——Just a golden wash of goodness has spread over all and over all my body and mind——All the dark torture is a memory——I know now I can get out of there, we'll drive back to the City, I'll take Billie home, I'll say goodbye to her properly, she wont commit no suicide or do anything wrong, she'll forget me, her life'll go on, Romana's life will go on, old Dave will manage somehow, I'll forgive them and explain everything (as I'm doing now)——And Cody, and George Baso, and ravened McLear and perfect starry Fagan, they'll all pass through one way or the other——I'll stay with Monsanto at his home a few days and he'll smile and show me how to be happy awhile, we'll drink dry wine instead of sweet and have quiet evenings in his home——Arthur Ma will come to quietly draw pictures at my side——Monsanto will say "That's all there is to it, take it easy, everything's okay, dont take things too serious, it's bad enough as it is without you going the deep end over imaginary conceptions just like you always said yourself"—— I'll get my ticket and say goodbye on a flower day and leave all San Francisco behind and go back home across autumn America and it'll all be like it was in the beginning——Simple golden eternity blessing all——Nothing ever happened——Not even this——St.Carolyn by the Sea will go on being golden one way or the other——The little boy will grow up and be a great man——There'll be farewells and smiles——My mother'll be waiting for me glad——The corner of the yard where Tyke is buried will be a new and fragrant shrine making my home more homelike somehow——On soft Spring nights I'll stand in the yard under the stars——Something good will come out of all things yet——And it will be golden and eternal just like that——There's no need to say another word.

"SEA"

Sounds of the Pacific Ocean
at Big Sur

"SEA"

Cherson!
 Cherson!
  You aint just whistlin
    Dixie, Sea——
  Cherson! Cherson!
   We calcimine fathers
    here below!
  Kitchen lights on——
   Sea Engines from Russia
    seabirding here below——
When rocks outsea froth
  I'll know Hawaii
  cracked up & scramble
  up my doublelegged cliff
  to the silt of
   a million years——

Shoo——Shaw——Shirsh——
Go on die salt light
 You billion yeared
  rock knocker
Gavroom
Seabird
Gabroobird
Sad as wife & hill
Loved as mother & fog
Oh! Oh! Oh!
 Sea! Osh!
Where's yr little Neppytune
   tonight?

These gentle tree pulp pages
which've nothing to do
with yr crash roar,
　　liar sea, ah,
were made for rock
tumble seabird digdown
　　footstep hollow weed
　　move bedarvaling
　　crash? Ah again?
Wine is salt here?
　Tidal wave kitchen?
Engines of Russia
　　in yr soft talk——

Les poissons de la mer
　　parle Breton——
Mon nom es Lebris
　　de Keroack——
　Parle, Poissons, Loti,
　　parle——
Parlning Ocean sanding
　　crash the billion rocks——

　Ker plotsch——
　　Shore——shoe——
god——brash——
The headland looks like
a longnosed Collie sleeping
with his light on his
　　nose, as the ocean,
　obeying its accommodations
of mind, crashes in
　rhythm which could
& will intrude, in thy
　rhythm of sand

          thought——
          ——Big frigging shoulders
on *that* sonofabitch

Parle, O, parle, mer, parle,
  Sea speak to me, speak
    to me, your silver you light
    Where hole opened up in Alaska
       Gray——shh——wind in
         The canyon wind in the rain
         Wind in the rolling rash
         Moving and t wedel
            Sea

              sea

              Diving sea
O bird——la vengeance
   De la roche
      Cossez
         Ah

Rare, he rammed the gate
rare over by Cherson, Cherson,
we calcify fathers here below
——a watery cross, with weeds
entwined——This grins restoredly,
  low sleep——Wave——Oh, no,
shush——Shirk——Boom plop
Neptune now his arms extends
  while one millions of souls
  sit lit in caves of darkness
——What old bark? The dog
mountain? Down by the Sea
  Engines? God rush——Shore——
Shaw——Shoo——Oh soft sigh
  we wait hair twined like

larks——Pissit——Rest not
——Plottit, bisp tesh, cashes,
re tav, plo, aravow,
shirsh,——Who's whispering over
there——the silly earthen creek!
The fog thunders——We put
silver light on face——We
took the heroes in——A billion
years aint nothing——

O the cities here below!
The men with a thousand
arms! the stanchions of
their upward gaze! the
coral of their poetry! the
sea dragons tenderized, meat
for fleshy fish——
Navark, navark, the fishes
of the Sea speak Breton——
wash as soft as people's
dreams——We got peoples
in & out the shore, they call
it shore, sea call it
pish rip plosh——The
5 billion years since
earth we saw substantial
chan——Chinese are
the waves——the woods
are dreaming

No human words bespeak
the token sorrow older
than old this wave
becrashing smarts the
sand with plosh

of twirléd sandy
thought——Ah change
the world? Ah set
the fee? Are rope the
angels in all the sea?
Ah ropey otter
barnacle'd be——
Ah cave, Ah crosh!
A feathery sea

Too much short——Where
Miss Nop tonight?
Wroten Kerarc'h
in the labidalian
aristotelian park
with slime a middle
——And Ranti forner
who pulled pearls by
rope to throne
the King by
the roll in the
forest of everseas?
Not everseas, *be* seas
——Creep
Crash
The woman with her body
in the sea——The frog who
never moves & thunders, sharsh
——The snake with his body
under the sand——The dog
with the light on his nose,
supine, with shoulders so
enormous they reach back to
rain crack——The leaves hasten
to the sea——We let them

hasten to be wetted & give
em that old salt change, a
nuder think will make you see
   they originate from the We Sea
      anyway——No dooming booms
   on Sunday afternoons——We
run thru the core of cliffs,
   blam up caves, disengage no
      jelly or jellied pendant
         thinkers——

               Our armies of
         anchored seaweed in the
         coves give of the smell
of jellied salt——
   Reach, reach, some leaves
havent hastened near
enuf——Roll, roll, purl
the sand shark floor
a greeny pali andarva
——Ah back——Ah forth——
Ah shish——Boom, away,
doom, a day——Vein we
firm——The sea is We——
Parle, parle, boom the
   earth——Arree——Shaw,
   Sho, Shoosh, flut,
   ravad, tapavada pow,
coof, loof, roof,——
      No,no,no,no,no,no——
      Oh ya, ya, ya, yo, yair——
      Shhh——

      Which one? the one? Which
one? The one ploshed——

The ploshed one? the same,
    ah boom——Who's that ant
that giant golden saltchange
ant magnifying my mountain
of feet? 'Tis Finder, finding
    the change in thought to join
    the boomer hangers in the
    cave a light——And built a
    house above it? Never fear,
        naver foir, les bretons qui
parlent la langue de la Mar
sont español comme le cul
    du Kurd qui dit le maha
    prajna paramita du Sud?
    Ah oui! Ke Vlum!
        Glum sea, silent me——

    They aint about to try
it them ants who wear
    out tunnels in a week
    the tunnel a million years
    won——no——Down around
    the headland slobs for weed,
    the chicken of the sea
        go yak! they sleep——
    Aroar, aroar, arah, aroo——
Otter me otter me daughter me sea
    ——me last blue lagoon inside of
me, the sea——Divine is the
substance all over the Sea—
        Of space we speak &
        hasten——Let no mouth
        swallow the sea——Gavril——
        Gavro——the Cherson Chinese
            & Old Fingernail sea——Is

ringin yr ear? Dier, dee?
Is Virgin you trying to
fathom me

Tiresome old sea, aint you sick
& tired of all of this merde?
this incessant boom boom
& sand walk——you people
hoary rockies here to Fuegie
& never get sad? Or despair
like a German phoney?
Just gloom booboom & green
on foggy nights——the fog is part
of us——
I know, but tired
as I can be listening to all
this silly majesty——
Bashô!
Lao!
Pop!
Who is this fish
sitting unsunk? Run up
a Hawaii typhoon smash him
against his rock——We'll jelly you,
jellied man, show you essential
jello of the sea——King
of the Sea.

No Monarc'h ever Irish be?
Ju see the Irish sea?
Green winds on tamarack vines——
Joyce——James——Shhish——
Sea———Sssssss——see
———Varash

————mnavash la vache
    écriture————the sea dont say
muc'h actually————

   Gosh, she,
huzzy, tow, led men
  on, Ulysses and all them
   fair headed moin————
   Terplash, & what difference
   make! One little white
    spark of light!
  Hair woven hands
   Penelope seaboat
   smeller————Courtiers in
    Telemachus 'sguise
    dropedary dropedary
    creep————Or————
    Franc gold rippled
   that undersea creek
where fish fish for
   fisher men————Salteen
   breen the wet Souwesters
    of old Portugee Prayers
     Tsall tangled, changed,
salt & drop the sand
  & weed & water brains
   entangled————Rats
   of old Venetian yellers
   Ariel Calibanned
    to Roma Port————
Pow————spell————
   Speak you parler,
in this my mother's
  parlor, wash your

undershoes when you
    come in, say thanks
    to foggy moon

Go brash, Topahta
offat,——we'll gray
    ye rose——Morning
    primord creeper sees
    the bird of paravision
    dying tweet the yellow
mouthroof! How sweet
    the earth, yells sand!
        Xcept when tumble
boom!
        O we wait too
for Heaven——all
in One——
        All is there
in fair & sight

I'm going to wash now
    old Pavia down,
    & pack my salt
        to Either Town——
        Cliffs of Antique
        aint got no rose,
        the morning's seen
        the ledder pose——
        Boom de boom dey
        the sea is me——
        We are the sea——
        It aint all snow

We wash Fujiyama down
    soon, & sand
crookbird back——

We hie bash
rock————ak——
  Long   short——
  Low and easy——
  Wind & many freezing
bottoms on luckrock——
  Rappaport——
Endymion thou tangled
dreamer love my thigh
——Rose, Of Shelley,
  Rose, O Urns!
    Ogled urns in fish eye

    Cinco sea   the Chico sea
   the Magellan headland sea
——What hype sidereal did he put down
  bending beatnik sea goatee
  over old goat manuscripts
  to find the other side of Flat?
    See round, see the end of me?
  Rounden huge bedoom?
    Awp hole cave & shwrul——
   sand & salt & hair eyes
——Strong enuf to make
  coffee grow in your hair——
  Whose plantation Neptune got?
   That of Atlas still down there,
   Hesperid's his feet, Sur his sleet,
    Irish Sea fingertip
    & Cornwall aye his soul
     bedoom

Shurning——Shurning——plop
  be dosh——This sigh old learning's
  high beside me——Rough

old hands have played out
pedigree, we've sunk more boats
than dreamer'll ever ever see
——Burning——Burning——The world
is burning & needs waaater
——I'll have a daughter,
oughter, wait & seee——
Churning, Churning, Me——
Panties——Panties——
these ancient fancies are
so girling——You've not seen
mermaids in my actual sea
——You've not seen sexless babies
with breasts of Majesty——
My wife——My wife——
Her name is Oh so really
high life

The low life Kingdom where
we part out tea, is sea
side Me——
Josh——coof——patra——
Aye ee mo powsh——
Ssst——Cum here read me——
Dirty postcard——Urchin sea——
Karash your name——?
Wanta swim, sink or swim?
Ears ringing again?
Sea vibrate rhythm
crash sets off cave
hanger blowers whistling
dog ear back——to sea——
Arree——
Gerudge Napoleon nada——
Nada

Pluto eats the sea——
Room——
Hands folded by the sea——
"On est toutes cachez, mange
le silence," dit les poissons de la
mer——Ah Mar——Gott——
Thalatta——Merde——Marde
de mer——Mu mer——Mak a vash——
The ocean is the mother——
Je ne suis pas mauvaise quand j'sui
tranquil——dans les tempêtes
j'cril! Come une folle!
j'mange, j'arrache toutes!
Clock——Clack——Milk——
Mai! mai! mai! ma!
says the wind blowing sand——
Pluto eats the sea——
Ami go——da——che pop
Go——Come——Cark——
Care——Kee ter da vo
Kataketa pow! Kek kek kek!
Kwakiutl! Kik!
Some of theserather taratasters
trapped hyra tchere thaped
the anadondak ram ma lat
round by Krul to Pat the lat
rat the anaakakalked
romon t o t t e k
Kara VOOOM
frup——
Feet cold? wade——Mind sore?
sim——sin——Horny?——lay the sea?
Corny? try me——
Ussens here hang no more
here we go, ka va ra ta

plowsh, shhh,
  and more, again, ke vlook
  ke bloom & here comes
      big Mister Trosh
          ——more waves coming,
  every syllable windy

  Back wash palaver
paralarle——paralleling
parle pe Saviour

A troublesome spirit
hanging here cant make it
  in the void——The sea'll
only drown me——These words
  are affectations
of sick mortality——
  We try to make our way
in self reliance, aid
  not ever comes too quick
  from wherever & whatever
  heaven dear may have
  suggested to promise us——

But these waves scare me——
I am going to die
  in full despair——
  Wake up where?
      On second breath in life
    the atmosphere is dearer
    maybe closer to Heaven
      ——O Paradise——
Is the sea really so bad?
  Have you sent men
here for this cold clown

    & monstrous eater at the
      world? whose sound
        I mock?

God I've got to believe in you
    or live in death!
    Will you save us——all?
      Soon or now?
    Send illumination
     to our drowning brains
  ——We're pitiful, Lord,
  we need yr help!
    Save us, Dear——
  (Save yourself, God man,
     ha ha!)
  If you were God man
you'd command these waves
  to very well Tennyson stop
    & even Tennyson
      is dear
        now dead
Leave it to the light
  Concern yourself with supper,
   & an eye

    somebody's eye——a wife,
  a girl, a friend, an animal
 ——a blood let drop——
  he for his sea,
   he for his fire,
    thee for thy desire

"The sea drove me away
  & yelled 'Go to your desire!'
 ——As I hurried up the valley

It added one last yell:-
  'And laugh!' "

Even the sea cant stop me from
  writing something to read in my old age
——This is the chart of brief forms,
  this sea the briefest——Shish yourself——
After scaring me like that, Mar,
I'll excoriate yr slum——yr
 iodine weeds & slime hoops,
 even yr dried hollow seaweed
    stinks——you stink all over——
    Boom——Try that, creep——
  The little Monterey fishingboat
  glides downward home 15 miles to go,
  be home to fried fish & beer b'five——
  It guides the sea its bird routes——
——Silver loss forever outward
——From blue sky of human bridges
 to the massive mawkcloud sea center
  heap——to the gray——
    Some boys call it gunboat blue,
    or gray, but I call it
    the Civil War of Rocks
——Rocks 'come air, rocks 'come water,
    & rock rocks——
Kara tavira, mnash grand bash
——poosh l'abas——croosh
 L'a haut——Plash au pied——
  Peeeee——Rolle test boulles——
  Manche d'la rache——
    The handsome King prevails
    over boom sing bird head——
    "Crache tes idées," spit yr ideas,
    says the sea, to me, quite

appro priate ly——
Pss! pss! pss!
Ps! girl inside!
Red shoes scum, eyes of old
sorcerers, toenails hanging down
in the barrel of old firkin cheese
the Dutchman forgot t'eat that
tempest
nineteen O
sixteen——
When torpedoed by gunboat
Pedro in the Valley
of a Million Fees?

When Magellan crosseyed
ate the Amazonian feet——
And, Ah, when Colombo cross't!
When Drake sir francised the waves
with feeding of the blue jay
dark——pounded his aleward
tank before the boom,
housed up all thoughts of Erik
the Red the Greenland caperer
& builder of rockdungs in New
Port——*New*——yet——
Oldport Indian Fishhead——
Oldport Tattoo Kwakiutl Headpost
taboo potash Coyotl potlatch?
Old Primitive Columbia.——
Named for Colom *bus*?
Name for Aruggio Vesmarica——
Ar!——Or!——Da!
What about Verrazano?
he sailed!——
He Verrazano zailed & we

statened his Island in on deep
in on dashun——
     Rotted the Wallower?
Sinners liars goodmen all
sink waterswim drink Neptune's
nectar the zal sotat——
    Zal sotate name for crota?
  Crota ta crotte, you aint
  'bout to find (Jesus Christian!)
any dry turds here below——
     Why fo no?
      Go crash yonder rock
    of bleak with yr filet mignon teeth
    & see——For you, the hearth,
    the heart, the lock of hair——
     For me, for us, the Sea,
     the murdering of time by eating
     lusty cracks of lip feed wave
    at aeons of sandy artistry
     till nothing's left but old age
        newmorning primordial pain
    of sitters by
     the unborn
      bird
     of roses yet undone——

  With weeds your roses,
sand crabs your hummers?
With buzzers in the sea!
 With runners in the deep!
This Sceptred Osh, this wide leg
 spanning rock U.S. to rock
  Ja Pan, this onstable
  roller roaming all,
  this ploosher at yr gory

dry dung door, this mouth
of silverwhite arring to hold thee,
this purger of conscience
arra for thee——
No mouse in here but's got
a little glee——and
aft, or oft, the osprey
in his glee's agley——
Oh purty purty ocean
me——
Sop! bring the Scepter down!
Again you've accepted me!

Breathe our iodine, filthy yr drink,
faint at feet wet, drop
yr profile move it in the sea,
float weeded watery Adonais
longs for thee——& Shelley three,
that's three——burn in salt
with slow most change——
We've had no crack at eternity
in a billion years of trying——
one grain of sand possesses
3 thousand worlds of glee——
not to mention me——
Ah sea

Ah si——Ah so——
shoot——shiver——mix——
ha roll——tara——ta ta——
curlurck——Kayash——Kee——
Pearls pearls in the yellow West
——Yellow sky to China——
Pacific we named here
water as always meeting

water——Pacific Pacific
    Pacific tapfic——geroom——
gedowsh——gaka——gaya——
    Tatha——gata——mana——
     What sails used old bhikkus?
     Dhikkus? Dhikkus!
What raft mailed Mose
to the hoven dovepost?
    What saved Blackswirl
     from the Kidd plank?
What Go-Bug here?
   Seet! Seeeeeeeeeee
   eeeeeee——kara——
    Pounders out yar——

Big Sur they call this sand
   these rocks this creek?
   Raton Canyon by name pours
   Coyote leaves & old Pomo bones
& old dust of Tomahawks
    into your angler'd maw——
    My salt maw shall salvage
    Taylors——sewing in the room
             below——
Sewing weed shrat for hikers
   in the milky silt——
   Sewing crosswards
    for certainty——Sartan
are we of Price Victory
in this salt War with thee
& thine thee jellied yink!
    Look O the sea here called
     Pacific Sea!
        T a k i !

My golden empty soul'll
outlast yr salty sill
——the Windows of my jelly eye
& fish head muck look out on thee,
slit, with cigar-a-mouth,
some contempt——
Yet I hie me to see you
——you hie thee to eat
me——Fair in sight
and worn, aright——
Arra! Aroo!
Ger der va——
Silly silent cities in the sea
have children playing cardboard
mush with eignyard old Englander
beeplates slickered oer with scum
of histories below——
No tempest as still & awful
as the tempest within——
Sorcerer hip! Buddhalands
& Buddhaseas!
What sails Maudgalyayana used
he only knows to tell
but got kilt by yellers
sreaming down the cliff
"Let's go home!
Now!"
——leave marge smashed djamas
Maudgalyayana was murdered by the sea——
But the sea dont tell——
The sea dont murder——
The seadrang scholars
oughter know that
or
go back to School

Hear over there the ocean motor?
Feel the splawrsh of it?
  Six silly centepedes here, Machree——
        Ah Ratatatatatat——
the machinegun sea, rhythmic
  balls of you pouring in
  with smooth eglantinee
  in yr pedigreed milkpup
    tenor——
  Tinder marsh aright arrooo——
    arrac'h——arrache——
  Kamac'h——monarc'h——
    Kerarc'h Jevac'h——
  Tamana————gavow——
    Va——Voovla——Via——
      Mia——mine——
            sea
            poo

  Farewell, Sur——

  Didja ever tell him
  about water meeting water——?
O go back to otter——
  Term——Term——Klerm
  Kerm——Kurn——Cow——Kow——
  Cash——Cac'h————Cluck——
    Clock——Gomeat sea need
      be deep I see you
          Enoc'h
        soon anarf
      in Old Brittany

21 August 1960
Pacific Ocean at Big Sur
California

AVAILABLE FROM PENGUIN

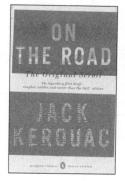

BY JACK KEROUAC

COMING FROM PENGUIN IN JULY 2011:

Jack Kerouac and Allen Ginsberg: The Letters

PENGUIN
BOOKS